Corporate Strategy

A Resource-Based Approach

Corporate Strategy

A Resource-Based Approach   **Second Edition**

David J. Collis

Senior Lecturer
Graduate School of Business
Administration
Harvard University

Cynthia A.
Montgomery

Timken Professor of Business
Administration
Graduate School of Business
Administration
Harvard University

McGraw-Hill
Irwin

Boston   Burr Ridge, IL   Dubuque, IA   Madison, WI   New York   San Francisco   St. Louis
Bangkok   Bogotá   Caracas   Kuala Lumpur   Lisbon   London   Madrid   Mexico City
Milan   Montreal   New Delhi   Santiago   Seoul   Singapore   Sydney   Taipei   Toronto

McGraw-Hill
Irwin

Corporate Strategy: A Resource-Based Approach
Published by McGraw-Hill/Irwin, a business unit of The McGraw-Hill Companies, Inc.,
1221 Avenue of the Americas, New York, NY, 10020. Copyright © 2005, 1998 by The
McGraw-Hill Companies, Inc. All rights reserved. No part of this publication may be
reproduced or distributed in any form or by any means, or stored in a database or retrieval
system, without the prior written consent of The McGraw-Hill Companies, Inc., including,
but not limited to, in any network or other electronic storage or transmission, or broadcast
for distance learning.

Some ancillaries, including electronic and print components, may not be available to
customers outside the United States.

This book is printed on acid-free paper.

2 3 4 5 6 7 8 9 0 DOC/DOC 0 9 8 7 6

ISBN-13: 978-0-07-231286-7
ISBN-10: 0-07-231286-6

Editorial director: *John E. Biernat*
Sponsoring editor: *Ryan Blankenship*
Editorial assistant: *Allison J. Clelland*
Executive marketing manager: *Ellen Cleary*
Lead producer, Media technology: *Victoria Bryant*
Project manager: *Kristin Puscas*
Senior production supervisor: *Sesha Bolisetty*
Designer: *Kami Carter*
Lead media project manager: *Cathy L. Tepper*
Developer, Media technology: *Brian Nacik*
Typeface: *10/12 Palatino*
Compositor: *GTS—New Delhi, India Campus*
Printer: *R. R. Donnelley*

Library of Congress Cataloging-in-Publication Data

Collis, David J.
    Corporate strategy: a resource-based approach / David J. Collis, Cynthia A.
Montgomery.—2nd ed.
      p. cm.
    Includes index.
    ISBN 0-07-231286-6 (alk. paper)
    1. Organizational effectiveness. 2. Strategic planning. I. Montgomery, Cynthia A.,
1952- II. Title.
HD58.9.C644 2005
658.4′012—dc22

                                              2004059727

www.mhhe.com

For Jill, William, Emma, and Charlotte
and For Bjørn and Nils

Preface

Historically, the strategy field has been broken into two discrete fields of study: business-level strategy, focusing on competitive advantage within an industry, and corporate-level strategy, focusing on the overall plan for managing a diversified firm. Pedagogically and intellectually, this book is an attempt to bridge the schism between these two levels of analysis and present a unified treatment of the sources of superior economic performance.

As its subtitle suggests, the book analyzes strategy in terms of a "research-based approach." At the heart of this view is the idea that *corporate* as well as competitive advantage is based on the unique resources of a firm, and the way those resources are deployed in particular competitive settings. The choice of firm boundaries, and the organizational mechanisms that bring strategy to fruition are also essential, and are examined in similar depth.

The view of strategy presented here is dynamic. The presentation traces the growth and development of firms, beginning with single-line businesses and gradually reaching to large diversified and vertically integrated firms. This progression reinforces the inextricable link between corporate and business strategy, thus deepening the traditional understanding of both. It also demonstrates that corporate advantage is usually realized at the business level, through the enhanced performance of individual business units.

The book is founded upon established research traditions. In particular, a number of insights are drawn from two distinct bodies of research: the resource-based view of the firm, which has gained prominence in the field of strategic management; and organizational economics, in particular transactions cost analysis and agency theory. Both of these theoretical traditions have made a substantial contribution to the arguments advanced here.

Also included in the book is a substantial amount of material that is not available elsewhere. Most important, it introduces a unique approach to corporate strategy that the authors have developed over many years of research, teaching, and consulting on the topic. Ideas such as the "Zone of Value Creation," linking industry and competitive analysis with the resource-based view of the firm, and the "Corporate Strategy Triangle," a unique framework for the assessment of corporate advantage, are new intellectual developments that are deeply woven into the central thesis of the text.

This book is an outgrowth of a corporate strategy course we developed and have taught at the Harvard Business School for a number of years. The course has attracted a wide range of students, including those who intend to be consultants, investment bankers, or stock analysts, as well as those who will run family businesses, or look to long-term careers as general managers in major industrial or consumer goods firms. This diversity testifies to the fundamental nature of the ideas and to the range of companies and settings to which they apply. In addition, in executive programs, the ideas have also been well received by seasoned managers whose primary objectives are to acquire useful, pragmatic management tools.

THE TEXT

The book contains nine chapters of text, and three supplemental appendices on related topics. One chapter is entirely new to this edition and one other chapter has been heavily revised. All chapters have been substantially updated with recent references and examples. Each chapter is designed to be a discrete intellectual module and is divided into two sections—Principles and Practice. The Principles sections introduce each topic by describing the relevant theory and supporting empirical research. In the Practice sections, these insights are then incorporated into pragmatic frameworks and tools that can be applied to case studies and strategic analyses.

Chapter 1 begins with a brief introduction to corporate strategy and introduces the "Corporate Strategy Triangle," as the basic organizing framework. The subsequent chapters then address each element of the framework in depth. As the text proceeds, the material cumulates to an overall picture of how to design and implement an effective corporate strategy.

Chapter 2 provides the essential theory about resources and how assets and capabilities earn economic rents. The argument is made that superior performance at the business *and* corporate level is ultimately due to the skillful deployment of competitively superior and scarce resources. The critical step of matching a firm's resources with its competitive environment is illustrated in the "Zone of Value Creation."

Chapter 3 addresses a firm's optimal scope in a given industry and how its pattern of resource deployment can shift over time. The chapter examines forces inside and outside the firm that can cause it to broaden or narrow its scope in order to compete successfully within its industry. Economies of scale and scope are examined in detail, and evaluated against the activities in a firm's value chain.

Chapter 4 addresses the deployment of resources across industries, and the economic rationale for diversified firms. While highly diversified firms have long been considered a class unto themselves, this discussion shows that they, in fact, share much in common with other firms. Most notably, the laws governing performance in diversified firms are not unique, but part of a much more general phenomenon relating to the value of a firm's resources and the attractiveness of the markets in which it competes.

Up to this point, the book has proceeded as if a firm's boundaries are wholly determined by its environmental opportunities and available resources. Chapter 5 complicates this picture by asking not *whether* a particular activity should be performed, but *where* it should be performed—inside the corporate hierarchy or through some form of market exchange. Arguments from agency theory and transaction cost analysis introduce fundamental questions that challenge the primacy of the organizational hierarchy and demonstrate the need to consider a range of alternatives before committing to this choice. Here the issues are primarily illustrated in the context of vertically integrated firms.

Chapter 6 addresses the implementation of strategy, and the structures, systems, and processes that allow a hierarchy to function and a strategy to be fully realized. Many failures of corporate strategy are due not to bad ideas, but to poor implementation. This chapter addresses this predicament by linking the organizational design of a firm to the critical elements of its strategy. Special emphasis is given to the role of the corporate office in controlling the activities of divisions, and sharing resources and coordinating the activities across businesses.

Chapter 7 shifts from a focus on individual elements to a broader examination of how the Corporate Strategy Triangle works as a complete and integrated system. Key points from earlier chapters are synthesized, and criteria and methods for the overall evaluation of a corporate strategy are introduced.

Management texts often assume that senior managers are both able and willing to craft corporate strategies that increase the value of a firm. However, recent upheavals in corporate governance reveal that this is not always the case. Chapter 8 discusses the evidence of this phenomenon, and presents several theories that explain why corporate managers do not always act in the interests of shareholders. The chapter concludes with a discussion of the responsibilities that accompany the privilege of formulating and implementing corporate strategy, and the structural forces that have emerged to discipline errant corporate behavior.

Chapter 9 addresses an entirely new topic for this edition of the text. Until now, the framework of the book has described the requirement for static fit and consistency among the main elements of corporate strategy. This chapter recognizes that many companies face the challenge not of optimizing an existing strategy, but of seeking to transform the entire corporate strategy. It, therefore, addresses the dynamics of creating corporate strategy by explaining how firms can change all elements of the strategy in pursuit of a new corporate vision.

Acknowledgments

This book is the result of a ten-year intellectual odyssey for the authors. As such, we must acknowledge all the assistance received along the way: colleagues at the Harvard Business School, including the research directors who supported and funded our work; other faculty in the Strategy area, our research associates over the years, and our support staff.

Outside the school, we have learned from those who actively work in the field, and we have benefited greatly from those, too numerous to mention, who have taught and commented on the material.

Elizabeth Wynne Johnson deserves a special mention for her role in researching, and above all, writing the book. She went way beyond and above the duty of a research associate in helping us complete the manuscript. We are enormously grateful that we found someone who so willingly dedicated herself to our project, and contributed so much.

Finally we each want to thank our families in our own way. Birger Wernerfelt, Cynthia's husband, not only was one of the original contributors to the resource-based view, but he has personally given us the benefit of his insights throughout the development of this book. David could not have written this book without the loving support of his wife, Jill. She took care of the family's life so that he could concentrate on writing without distraction. And William, Emma, and Charlotte, who accepted an absentee father for so long, can now have the time and attention they deserve.

About the Authors

David Collis

For the past 18 years David J. Collis has been a professor at the Harvard Business School, where he continues to teach and chair executive education programs, the Yale University School of Management, and Columbia Business School. He is currently the MBA Class of 1958 Senior Lecturer in the Strategy group at the Harvard Business School, having previously completed five years as the Frederick Frank adjunct Professor of International Business Administration at the Yale School of Management. He is an expert on corporate strategy and global competition, and is the author of the recent book *Corporate Headquarters* (with Michael Goold and David Young). His work has been frequently published in the *Harvard Business Review, Academy of Management Journal, Strategic Management Journal, European Management Journal,* and in many books including *Managing the Multibusiness Company, International Competitiveness,* and *Beyond Free Trade.* The more than 50 cases he has authored have sold over 400,000 copies worldwide.

David Collis received an MA (1976) with a Double First from Cambridge University where he was the Wrenbury Scholar of the University. He graduated as a Baker Scholar from Harvard Business School, MBA (1978), and received a Ph.D. (1986) in Business Economics at Harvard University where he was a Dean's Doctoral Fellow. From 1978 to 1982 he worked for the Boston Consulting Group in London. He is currently a consultant to several major U.S. corporations, and on the board of trustees of the Hult International Business School, and the Advisory Boards of WebCT, Vivaldi Partners, Folderwave, and formerly of Ocean Spray. He is also the cofounder of the elearning.

Cynthia Montgomery

Cynthia A. Montgomery received her Ph.D. in Industrial Administration from Purdue University. Her dissertation research on corporate diversification received the General Electric Award for Outstanding Research in Strategic Management. Professor Montgomery's first faculty position was at the Graduate School of Business at the University of Michigan. She moved to the Kellogg School of Management at Northwestern where she was recognized with its Outstanding Teacher of the Year Award in 1988. In 1989 she joined the faculty at the Harvard Business School.

Professor Montgomery's research interests center on corporate governance and corporate strategy. Of particular interest are issues relating to boards of directors, mergers and acquisitions, and the creation of value across multiple lines of business.

Professor Montgomery is the editor of *Resource-Based and Evolutionary Theories of the Firm*, and *Strategy: Seeking and Securing Competitive Advantage* (with Michael E. Porter). Montgomery has published in *The Strategic Management Journal*, *The Academy of Management Journal*, *Management Science*, *The Journal of Business*, *The Journal of Economic Perspectives*, *The American Economic Review*, *The Rand Journal of Economics*, *Harvard Business Review*, and others. She is on the board of directors of Newell Rubbermaid Inc. and several Merrill Lynch mutual funds.

Brief Contents

Contents

Corporate Strategy

A Resource-Based Approach

RESOURCES

BUSINESSES

• VISION

• GOALS & OBJECTIVES

ORGANIZATION

1

AN INTRODUCTION TO CORPORATE STRATEGY

▲ The Need for Corporate Strategy

Consider the following list of companies: Aetna, BankOne, Campbell Soup, Coca-Cola, Mattel, Xerox. What do they have in common, besides that they are all well known, all compete in multiple markets, and, in the past, all have enjoyed profits well above the norm for their industries?

More recently, each of them has suffered a reversal of fortune. Between 1995 and 2000 while the index of the S&P 500 nearly tripled, these firms barely maintained their value. One, Mattel, even *destroyed* value during this period (Table 1.1).

Another thing these companies have in common is involuntary CEO turnover. The CEO of each of these firms was replaced in the early 1990s, not necessarily due to poor management skills, but because of the failure of their corporate strategies. Each was unable to develop a strategy that effectively addressed the changing competitive environment or capitalized on the potential benefits of owning a wide set of businesses.

The problems these business leaders wrestled with and failed to remedy were, however, not necessarily of their own making. Corporations, like battleships, have enormous inertia; by the time the adverse consequences of poor strategies appear, things are often badly wrong and the company far off course. This insidiousness does not diminish the importance of formulating and implementing an effective corporate strategy; it increases it. Because the impact of corporate strategy is so pervasive and long lasting, it has more important consequences than most other managerial decisions. Setting corporate strategy, therefore, is a critical task and responsibility of the CEO. Indeed, the recent resurgence of some of these companies under leadership prepared to make fundamental strategic changes only illustrates the primacy of this role.

TABLE 1.1

Changes in Market
Value at Selected
U.S. Corporations

	1995	2000	Annual Change (%)
Aetna	$8.1 billion	$8.7 billion	1.4
BankOne	29.2	35.1	3.7
Campbell Soup	8.6	11.9	6.7
Coca-Cola	69.2	123.8	12.3
Mattel	8.0	5.4	(7.6)
Xerox	12.0	17.3	7.6
S&P 500	**530.0**	**1,407.0**	**21.6**

And getting it right matters; 60 percent of assets in the United States are controlled by multibusiness companies.[1] In Europe, the percentage is about the same,[2] and in developing nations, "groups" account for a substantial fraction of the economy.[3] The efficient working of the modern global economy, therefore, depends on the effectiveness of corporate strategies, and any executive is likely, at some point in his or her career, to work for, work with, or compete against a diversified corporation.

Farcus   by David Waisglass
                  Gordon Coulthart

"I think it's time to review our corporate strategy."

The Pressure to Change

Recent corporate governance scandals have focused attention on the responsibility of corporate executives to truly create shareholder value. Yet this attention only represents the logical conclusion to a set of forces that have been building since an earlier bout of corporate growth and diversification in the sixties. Coming out of that go-go era, which created many sprawling conglomerates whose diversification defied rational economic explanation, there was initially limited pressure to change.

A business environment defined by weak rivals, passive shareholders, and ineffective corporate boards did little to discipline the errant corporate expansion (see "Pressure for Shareholder Value").

The pendulum only began to swing the other way in the 1980s, when a new set of players in the **market for corporate control**—financial capitalists—took aim at the most pathological corporate portfolios. Previously, poor

[1] Belen Villalonga, "Does Diversification Cause the 'Diversification Discount'?" Harvard Business School working paper, 2003.

[2] Torben Pedersen and Steen Thomsen, "European Patterns of Corporate Ownership: A Twelve-Country Study," *Journal of International Business Studies,* Vol. 28, No. 4 (4th Qtr, 1997), pp. 759–78.

[3] Tarun Khanna and K. Palepu, "Is Group Affiliation Profitable in Emerging Markets? An Analysis of Diversified Indian Business Groups," *Journal of Finance,* Vol. 55 (2), April 2000, pp. 867–91.

Pressure for Shareholder Value

1970S: LITTLE

- Growth at any cost

- Weak rivals

- Fragmented, passive shareholders

- Ineffective boards

1980S: INCREASING

- Restructuring pathological portfolios

- Takeover premiums increase

1990S: INTENSE

- Active shareholders

- Active boards

- Global product markets

- Global capital markets

2000S: RETHINKING

- Accounting scandals

- Corporate governance (Sarbanes-Oxley Act)

- Global markets retreat

performance or executive indifference to corporate strategy might have been met with only limited repercussions—at worst, the firing of the CEO. In the eighties a more extreme remedy—the corporate takeover—became a pervasive threat. Between 1980 and 1987, 20 percent of all U.S. manufacturing assets changed hands in some form of financial transaction.[4]

The emergence of the leveraged buyout (LBO) as a restructuring tool during this period epitomized the assertion of shareholder value as the corporation's raison d'être. Beyond being just a tool, the LBO quickly gained prominence as a **new form of corporate organization.** By the end of the eighties it was estimated that LBO groups were responsible for 7 percent of U.S. corporate output.[5] While their prominence later declined, LBOs showed a dramatic resurgence after the stock market bubble burst in the late nineties,[6] demonstrating, at the very least, that buyouts remain a significant factor shaping the corporate landscape.

Other **new organizational forms** also gained prominence during this period. These included employee ownership (see "Avis"); the so-called virtual corporation, in which the command and control hierarchy was

[4] Michael G. Rukstad, "RJR Nabisco and Leveraged Buyouts," Harvard Business School Case No. 9-390-077, 1990. Note, however, that a significant part of the capital market activity during this period involved the same asset moving from one owner to another.
[5] Ibid.
[6] Emily Thornton and S.A. Forest, "Embracing Barbarians at the Gate," *Business Week,* November 18, 2002, pp. 120–21.

Avis

Warren E. Avis founded his car-rental company in 1946. Since that time, the agency has changed hands a total of 11 times. In one 10-year stretch, during the frenzied takeover period of the 1980s, Avis had six different owners. In 1983, then-parent company Norton Simon Inc. was acquired by Esmark, which in turn was acquired by Beatrice Companies in 1984. Beatrice was subsequently taken private in a leveraged buyout orchestrated by Kohlberg Kravis Roberts (KKR). KKR then sold Avis to Wesray Capital Corp. and senior Avis management in 1986.

At Wesray, it was determined that the greatest profit potential would come from an employee stock ownership plan (ESOP) sale. Embraced by workers, the ESOP ended Avis' roller-coaster existence and brought stability to the company.

Throughout its history of merry-go-round ownership, costs had escalated and operations lagged. Avis chairman Joseph Vittoria explained: "Every time we'd get a new owner, I'd have to educate them and become adjusted to them." Within a year and a half after being bought by its employees, Avis saw its earnings soar and operating costs decline. As a consequence, the company performed well and achieved growth despite an industry slump. Avis' management credited their employees with improvements that led to superior quality and service management and a 40 percent drop in the number of customer complaints.

After doing time in a variety of hands, Avis achieved its finest performance on its own. More recently Simmons Bedding, the famous mattress maker founded in 1870, has had a similar experience. Between 1986 and 2003, Simmons had six different owners, including Wesray Capital, its own employees, Merrill Lynch Capital Partners, Investcorp, and Thomas H. Lee. Over that period, its value has fluctuated between a low of $53 million in 1991 and its most recent sale price of $1.1 billion.*

* *Wall Street Journal,* September 9, 2004, p. B1.

replaced by a network of flexible market-based linkages between independent entities;[7] and the explosion in joint ventures and other collaborative arrangements. Another visible change was the rapid growth of franchising, which reached more than $800 billion in sales by 2002.[8]

All of this suggests that in the recent past the performance of many traditional corporations has left a lot to be desired. Indeed, the crisis of faith America suffered about its international competitiveness in the eighties reflected a concern for the fundamental viability of its corporate giants.[9]

In response, many firms in America (and around the world) embarked on major shake-ups to transform their corporate strategies and cultures. Attempts to "restructure, refocus, rationalize, and reengineer" were initiated

[7] William E. Halal, A. Geranmayeh, and J. Pourdehnad, *Internal Markets* (New York: John Wiley & Sons, 1993).

[8] G. Matusky, "The Competitive Edge: How Franchisees Are Teaching the Corporate Elephants to Dance," *Success,* September 1990, pp. 58–65.

[9] Robert E. Hoskisson and M.A. Hitt, *Downscoping: How to Tame the Diversified Firm* (Oxford: Oxford University Press, 1994).

by aggressive CEOs with the goal of rejuvenating and revitalizing their corporations. The notions of *core competence* and *rightsizing* took root as the solution to fundamental corporate problems (see Appendix A, "Past Approaches to Corporate Strategy"). In practice, however, these approaches often led to only partial solutions. Kodak, for example, restructured three times in five years around a competency in imaging before CEO Kay Whitmore was replaced. As the new millenium approached, freshly energized investors and boards began putting more emphasis on shareholder value and showing more concern for corporate strategy. As a consequence, CEO dismissals rose.[10]

The Story Today: "No There, There"

Despite these pressures and all this frenetic activity, the practice of corporate strategy today leaves much to be desired. Empirical research shows that, on average, the stock of diversified corporations trades at a 20 percent discount to the value of their separate businesses.[11] That same research shows that even if 40 percent of diversified companies do create shareholder value, 60 percent actually destroy value. It is clear that we really do not do corporate strategy well today.

In an attempt to assess and understand the state of corporate strategy among the world's leading companies, we initiated a research project that led to extensive conversations with executives in scores of organizations.

A harsh truth emerged from this research: In more than half of the companies we studied, corporate management could not effectively articulate how their firms added value to the businesses in their corporate portfolios. To borrow from Gertrude Stein, when we went in search of corporate strategy, we often found that "there was no there, there."

When asked if he had analyzed the break-up value of his firm, one chief financial officer replied: "Yes. We look at that very carefully, about once a quarter. I honestly do not believe that the pieces would be worth more separately than they are together." Despite the fact that this was a highly visible related-diversified company, none of its senior managers advanced the case that the firm enhanced the competitiveness of its units to such a degree that they were definitely worth more together than apart.

A corporate officer in a well-known consumer products company gave this historic perspective: "[Our firm] has traditionally placed a heavy emphasis on growing the top line. So long as we have been able to do this,

---

[10] Anthony Bianco and L. Lavelle, "The CEO Trap: Looking for Superheroes to Deliver Sky-High Growth Ensures Disappointment," *Business Week*, December 11, 2000, pp. 86–92.
[11] L. Lang and R. Stultz, "Tobin's *q*, Corporate Diversification, and Firm Performance," *Journal of Political Economy*, Vol. 102, December 1994, pp. 1248–80. The extensive research in financial economics, covered in more detail in Chapter 4, is contested and subject to criticism, particularly with regard to the direction of the relationship between poor performance and diversification. Nevertheless, the existence of the diversification discount as an empirical observation is accepted wisdom in the finance field.

and do it profitably, we have not spent a lot of effort on rationalizing the firm as a whole." In his view, the firm was operating with a deadweight of inefficiency that one day, perhaps soon, would need to be addressed. Until then, the mandate was simply "grow."

As these remarks illustrate, despite the radical shifts of the 1980s and 1990s, corporate leadership still often does not provide the kind of strategic direction that welds a company together or creates substantial value over the long run. To do so, management needs a clear idea of what corporate strategy involves and, in particular, what characterizes an effective corporate strategy. Developing and describing a rigorous framework to fill this need is the challenge we undertake in this book.

Principles

▲ What Is Corporate Strategy?

There are many definitions of corporate strategy. Originally the term was used to describe the pattern of decisions that determined a company's goals, produced the principal policies for achieving these goals, and defined the range of businesses the company was to pursue.[12] Taken literally, this would mean that corporate strategy addressed any and every strategic issue facing a company, from Sony's entry into the PC market, to the decision by a restaurant owner to introduce an "all you can eat" buffet.

Over time a distinction came to be made between **business-level strategy**—the issue of how to build a sustainable competitive advantage in a discrete and identifiable market—and **corporate-level strategy**—"the overall plan for a diversified company."[13] This distinction led to the development of a number of valuable analytical frameworks and techniques that were applicable to each level of strategy (see Appendixes A and B). The bifurcation between business- and corporate-level issues, however, downplayed the many important areas of overlap between the two, and impeded their integration. This book introduces a more inclusive definition of corporate strategy:

> *Corporate strategy is the way a company creates value through the configuration and coordination of its multimarket activities.*

This definition has three important aspects. The first is the emphasis on **value creation** as the ultimate purpose of corporate strategy. (See "Value Creation.") The second is the focus on the multimarket scope of the

---

[12] Kenneth R. Andrews, *The Concept of Corporate Strategy* (Burr Ridge, IL.: Dow-Jones–Irwin, 1971).
[13] Michael E. Porter, "From Competitive Advantage to Corporate Strategy," *Harvard Business Review*, May–June 1987, pp. 43–59.

Value Creation

We start from the premise that the purpose of corporate strategy is value creation. Whether that value is completely appropriated by stockholders or whether it is shared with other stakeholders is the decision of those who control the corporation (see also Chapter 8). For example, Hershey Foods Corporation, the leading manufacturer of chocolate confectionery in the United States, is controlled by the Milton Hershey School Trust. The Milton Hershey School was established in 1909 to provide housing, services, and education for youth who are in financial and social need in the Pennsylvania dairy country. When Hershey Foods' managers took steps to sell the company in 2002, the Milton Hershey School Trust blocked the sale, seeking in part to preserve the company's local philanthropic role, even if at the expense of corporate gain from the proposed sale. We will not debate how the value created by a corporate strategy should be distributed, but we will observe that if no value is created, there is nothing to distribute to stockholders, let alone share with other stakeholders.

corporation (**configuration**), including its product, geographic, and vertical boundaries. The third is the emphasis on how the firm manages the activities and businesses that lie within the corporate hierarchy (**coordination**). This point recognizes the importance of both the implementation and the formulation of corporate strategy.

It is important to underscore that this definition, in contrast to past treatments, does not restrict the relevance of corporate strategy solely to large diversified firms (see "Do Universities Need Corporate Strategies?"). Implicitly or explicitly, organizations of every size make choices about the range of markets in which they will compete and how they will manage those activities. Corporate strategy issues, therefore, are as pertinent and important to a small manufacturing firm debating whether to employ its own salespeople or use third-party distributors, as they are to IBM . . . trying to decide whether it should acquire Price Waterhouse Cooper's consulting business.

Moreover, the definition recognizes that corporate strategy involves far more than the operation of corporate headquarters. Regardless of the type of strategy a firm is pursuing, most of its value will ultimately be realized in the business units, through their enhanced ability to produce and deliver goods and services to customers.[14] Thus, for a corporation to create value—to justify its existence as a multibusiness entity—it must be able, in some way, to contribute to the competitive advantage of its businesses. Corporate strategy, therefore, draws on an understanding of business strategy, just as it, in turn, informs that analysis. Its focus is on the

[14] Ibid.

Do Universities Need Corporate Strategies?

There is a tendency to perceive many organizations as single business entities when in fact they are often much more complex. Nearly all the organizations you can think of harbor a myriad of intriguing corporate strategy issues. Consider, for example, universities.

Although they may be thought of simply as institutions of higher learning, universities house a number of distinct units. There may be a business school or a medical school; perhaps a university publisher; perhaps a football or basketball team. Each of these has its own staff and customers, and its own external reference group—each, implicitly or not, has its own way of competing. However, each is also affected by its membership in the broader university: the individual units share a campus, the university's reputation, a central budgeting system, and so forth. The resulting interrelationships affect the

operation of the individual units in many ways, large and small. Anyone who doubts this should consider whether any of the units would be better off as independent entities outside the university.

Although these linkages usually remain in the background, they can quickly come to the fore, and often do over issues of resource allocation. Heated debates, for example, can erupt over questions of cross-subsidization—whether the wealthier units should support the poorer ones, or whether endowments should be held at the school or university level. Questions of standards also generate vigorous debate. One might ask, for example, whether a world-class university should close down a weak academic department or, conversely, invest to bring it up to an appropriate standard. At their core, questions such as these are ones of corporate strategy.

relationship between the whole and the parts of the firm, in particular on whether individual business units are made better or worse by their presence in the corporation.

Practice

▲ A Framework for Corporate Strategy

Our framework starts from the empirical observation that there is **no one right corporate strategy.** There is not even a taxonomy of a limited number of generic corporate strategies that can be identified as leading to success. Instead, an effective corporate strategy is a consistent set of five elements that together as a system lead to a corporate advantage that creates economic value—what we call the Corporate Strategy Triangle (Figure 1.1).

The three sides of the triangle—**resources; businesses;** and **organization**—are the foundations of corporate strategy. When aligned in pursuit of a **vision,** and motivated by appropriate **goals and objectives,** the system can produce a **corporate advantage,** which justifies the firm's existence as a multibusiness entity.

FIGURE 1.1
Corporate Strategy Triangle

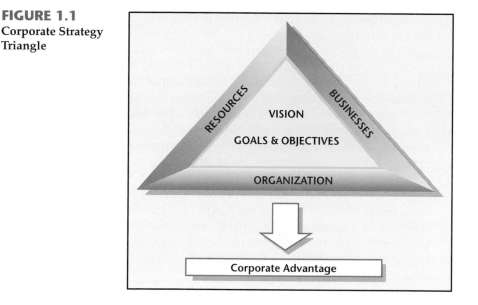

Vision

It has been said that "if you don't know where you are going, any road can take you there." To eliminate such disorientation and provide direction, the discussion of corporate strategy necessarily begins with vision. Its positioning in the center of the Triangle reflects its central role in the formulation and implementation of corporate strategy.

One of the strongest findings of our research was that successful corporations were those that had a vision and were committed to fulfill it over an extended period of time. Indeed, the ability to articulate a coherent vision is a valuable indication that a firm, in fact, *has* a corporate strategy.

A powerful vision should continually stretch the corporation's capabilities. For many companies, therefore, the overarching vision is captured in an **ambitious aspiration,** the time frame of which may be ill-defined and distant.[15] In the 1920s, Ford wanted to put "a car in every home"; in the 1980s, Apple looked toward the future and saw "a computer in every home." By the 1990s, Bill Gates had gone further yet: "a computer on every desk, and in every home, running on Microsoft software." (By the end of that decade, this vision had grown to include the Internet.) Each of these simple expressions offers a compelling statement that challenges and motivates employees by providing meaning and fulfillment to their work. Each also defines the broad domain in which the firm will operate.

[15] C.K. Prahalad and G. Hamel, "Strategic Intent," *Harvard Business Review,* May–June 1989, pp. 63–77.

Importantly, defining the **domain** is primarily concerned with setting the boundaries of the firm—with describing what businesses the corporation will *not* go into—more than with identifying exactly which businesses it *will* compete in.[16] Within those broad bounds, managers will have the autonomy to operate without the distraction of looking outside the domain or the interference of being told precisely where to compete. Thus, a corporate vision should describe, in fairly loose and qualitative terms, the boundary beyond which it will not operate. Nokia's "portable communications" vision describes a sense of what businesses the company will operate in without, for example, being specific as to whether or not liquid crystal displays are part of that domain.

Often, visions also describe the **ethical values** a corporation will adhere to in the conduct of its business. Called the *mission* in some companies, this part of a vision usually reflects the code of behavior by which employees are governed.[17] While important, such statements complement, rather than substitute for, articulations about how the company intends to create economic value.

Goals and Objectives

If the vision describes what the corporation wishes to become in many years' time, an effective corporate strategy must also have a set of shorter-term goals and objectives. These will serve as milestones on the path to the fulfillment of the vision. Goals and objectives will more immediately motivate employees because they are closer at hand and so can be seen to be achievable.

Objectives refer to specific **short- and medium-term quantitative targets,** such as "sustain a 40 percent debt/equity ratio" or "achieve sigma six quality within four years." Goals, on the other hand, refer to **qualitative intentions** in the same time frame, such as "improve new product development capabilities" or "become a global organization."

By providing an immediate challenge to employees, goals and objectives can become powerful incentives that support a formal reward structure. Indeed, many companies use some version of an annual corporate challenge, such as "improve productivity by 7 percent," to supplement the normal incentive scheme and focus attention on particular activities or targets.

While the vision itself may evolve through time, and always appear on the horizon, goals and objectives are important strategic hurdles. Repeated failures to meet goals and objectives imply a threat both to the feasibility of the corporate strategy and to the motivation of employees. On

---

[16] R. Simons, *Levers of Control* (Boston, Harvard Business School Press, 1995).
[17] Andrew Campbell, M. Devine, and D. Young, *A Sense of Mission* (London: The Economist Books Limited, 1990).

the route to "encircling Caterpillar," Komatsu, among other things, had to build a presence outside Japan and license state-of-the-art technology. Had it not met these goals, Komatsu not only might have failed to "encircle Caterpillar," it might not have survived. Thus, goals and objectives should always be in line with the vision, but should be less of a stretch than the vision itself.

Resources

This book articulates a concept of corporate strategy that rests on the resources—the **assets, skills, and capabilities**—of the firm.

Resources are the critical building blocks of strategy because they determine not what a firm *wants to do,* but what it *can do.* They are the durable stocks that determine competitive advantage at the business unit level, and can distinguish one firm from another. If all firms had identical resources, all could pursue the same strategy, and the basis for competitive advantage would disappear.[18] It is only when there are important resource differences among firms that each can develop a distinctive strategy.

Moreover, resources determine the range of market opportunities that are appropriate for a firm to pursue and so have a major impact on corporate strategy. Many valuable resources enable a firm to compete successfully in more than one market. For example, in the early years of the PC industry, IBM was able to build on its reputation and customer list in the computer mainframe business to gain dominance in the market for desktop machines, even though it was a late entrant and did not have the best technology. Similarly, Emerson Electric's efficient production processes and skills in assembling small electric motors supported its success in a number of different markets.

Resources are the ultimate source of value creation both within and across businesses. Therefore, identifying, building, and deploying valuable resources are critical aspects of both corporate and competitive strategy.

Businesses

The "businesses" side of the Triangle refers to the industries in which a firm operates, as well as to the competitive strategy it adopts in each.

Industry choice is critical to the long-term success of a corporate strategy. It has repeatedly been demonstrated that the best predictor of firm performance is the profitability of the industries in which it competes.[19] This is true not only for single business firms, but for firms that operate

---

[18] Jay Barney made this point in "Firm Resources and Sustained Competitive Advantage," *Journal of Management,* 1991, pp. 99–120.

[19] Richard P. Rumelt, "How Much Does Industry Matter?" *Strategic Management Journal,* March 1991, pp. 167–85; Cynthia A. Montgomery and Birger Wernerfelt, "Diversification, Ricardian Rents, and Tobin's q," *Rand Journal of Economics,* Winter 1988, pp. 623–32; and R. Schmalensee, "Do Markets Differ Much?" *American Economic Review,* 1985, pp. 341–51.

in multiple businesses. The underlying economics of the industries in which a firm competes, therefore, will play an instrumental role in its performance.

The set of industries in which a firm operates also influences the extent to which it will be able to share resources across its businesses. The notion of portfolio relatedness, for example, which has underpinned corporate strategic thinking for 30 years, has been used to assess a firm's ability to create synergy among its businesses. Thus, it would be expected that an ice-cream manufacturer like Ben & Jerry's could compete successfully in frozen yogurt. In contrast, a firm that competes in both aerospace and insurance would be expected to have few opportunities to exploit scope economies. (Although that did not deter either General Motors or ITT from trying to do so!)

The particular **competitive strategy** a firm pursues within each industry also affects corporate performance. Only effective strategies that create competitive advantages produce superior returns in the long run. Moreover, the range of competitive strategies a firm pursues may be constrained by their competing requirements. For example, following a low-cost strategy in personal computers and a differentiation strategy in mainframes may well be futile: The key success factors for each strategy are so different that a firm striving to do both is unlikely to succeed.

Thus, an analysis of a firm's businesses should include the attractiveness of their industries, the competitive strategy the firm will adopt in each, as well as the constraints on, and opportunities that exist for, cross-fertilization.

Structure, Systems, and Processes

In a complex firm, corporate managers rarely can, or should, make all the critical business-unit decisions. Instead, they influence delegated decision making through the careful design of the context in which business-unit managers operate. Even the most decentralized corporations, therefore, impose some organizational requirements on their businesses, whether it be financial reporting, capital expenditure budgeting, or human resource management. In turn, these policies have important direct and indirect influences on the decisions made in the businesses, as managers follow the rules and respond to the incentives set by the corporate office.[20]

In establishing a firm's infrastructure, corporate managers have a wide array of organizational mechanisms at their disposal, from the formal boxes in an organization chart to the more subtle elements of corporate culture and style. It is these structure, systems, and processes that determine how the company controls and coordinates the activities of its various business units and corporate staff functions. **Structure** refers to

[20] Joseph H. Bower, *Managing the Resource Allocation Process* (Cambridge, MA: Harvard University Press, 1970).

the way the corporation is divided into discrete units. It describes the formal organization chart that delineates the allocation of authority inside the corporate hierarchy. **Systems** are the set of formal policies and routines that govern organizational behavior. They are the set of rules that define how tasks, from strategic planning to personnel evaluations, are to be fulfilled. **Processes** describe the informal elements of an organization's activities. The network of personal relationships that accompany the flow of work inside a company, for example, can be just as influential on behavior as any formal procedures.

Because every corporate strategy is different, there is not one optimal set of structures, systems, and processes for all firms. Rather, as Alfred Chandler long ago noted, *structure follows strategy*.[21] In other words, a firm's internal design should flow from its strategy and be customized to fit the resources and businesses of the particular firm. In fact, an inappropriate design often causes the failure of otherwise well-constructed corporate strategies.

Corporate Advantage

An effective corporate strategy results from a harmonious combination of the previously discussed five elements. The elements work together as a **system to create value through multimarket activity;** that is, to yield a corporate advantage. Although some value may be created at the corporate level itself—through a lower cost of capital, for example—most corporate advantages are realized at the business-unit level, where individual businesses use the benefits of corporate affiliation to outperform their rivals in a particular industry.

Michael Goold and colleagues suggested three questions a firm should ask to test whether or not it possesses a corporate advantage.[22] A modified version of those questions is presented here, in order of increasing difficulty, and can be applied to every business a company owns or is considering acquiring:

- Does ownership of the business create benefit somewhere in the corporation?

- Are those benefits greater than the cost of corporate overhead?

- Does the corporation create more value with the business than any other possible corporate parent or alternative governance structure?

The first of these questions simply asks whether benefits are created anywhere in the corporation through the firm's ownership of the business. Generally, these would occur within the business itself, through the transfer

[21] Alfred D. Chandler, *Strategy and Structure* (Cambridge, MA: MIT Press, 1962).
[22] M. C. Goold, A. Campbell, and M. Alexander, *Corporate-Level Strategy* (New York: John Wiley & Sons, 1994).

of resources from other business units or from the corporate level. In some circumstances, the benefits appear elsewhere in the corporation. The ownership of Medco, a leading drug distributor, by the pharmaceutical giant Merck may have been such an example. Even if Merck did not improve the distributor's performance (in fact, Merck's ownership may even have harmed the distributor because other pharmaceutical companies preferred to supply competitors), it may, nevertheless, have benefited from the guaranteed market for its drugs and improved information about customers' pharmaceutical usage.

The second question recognizes that enhancing the competitiveness of a business unit is not sufficient justification for corporate ownership. Whatever they are, the benefits of corporate ownership do not come costlessly. No matter how small the corporate office, or how little intervention there is in the daily affairs of the divisions, the extra layer of management incurs costs and delays and dampens incentives. To justify ownership these costs must be less than the benefits generated.

The third question is a very strenuous test to pass. It implies that the corporation must be the optimum owner for a business. Many firms add value to their businesses and so appear to justify their corporate ownership. However, if other companies could add more value to the businesses, and would be willing to pay a correspondingly high price to do so, keeping those businesses in the corporate portfolio would be inconsistent with value maximization. Moreover, the firm might be able to realize much of the value of its resources through market contracts with independent entities. Justifying ownership of a business, therefore, requires that the value created be greater than that which could be achieved if the business were operated outside the corporate hierarchy. The retailer JC Penney must have understood this when it decided to outsource the running of its catalog business. Although there was value created by JC Penney offering a catalog, managing it within the corporate infrastructure created less value than operating it as a separate unit.

Managers often find this third test hard to accept. In particular, they often resist selling profitable businesses to which they demonstrably add some value. Nonetheless, a strict interpretation of corporate advantage and the maximization of firm value implies that they should do so.

The Road Ahead

We stated that there is no one right strategy to create corporate advantage. The variety of resources that can generate competitive advantages across multiple businesses, the breadth of industries available to operate in, and the numerous organizational design parameters that shape decisions inside the corporation all make single prescriptions impossible. However, there is an **enduring logic** that all great corporate strategies have in common. This relates to the quality of the individual items of the triangle; the way those elements work together as a system; and the fit of the whole with the evolving external environment.

Having introduced the Corporate Strategy Triangle as the overall framework for the book, we will devote Chapters 2–6 to examining the individual elements in detail. Following this, in Chapter 7, we return to the whole, and evaluate how the Triangle operates as a system. As we integrate the pieces, we identify patterns that typify successful corporate strategies and outline the logic underpinning such strategies. Until this point we have been concerned with the need for static fit and consistency in the corporate strategy system. Chapter 8 introduces dynamics to this analysis by explaining how to transform a company and move to a new corporate strategy. Rather than being concerned with the alignment of the individual parts, Chapter 8 demonstrates how to change the whole.

The final chapter of the book returns to the pressing need for effective corporate strategies, and the governance mechanisms that are in place to monitor and evaluate progress toward this goal. At issue here is the question of who bears responsibility for corporate strategy, and how the competing interests of various stakeholders should be reconciled.

This development of ideas mirrors the growth of many firms, progressing from straightforward single businesses, to firms that are grappling with intriguing questions of scope within an industry, to very large organizations that face complex diversification or vertical integration issues.

Wherever they are located along this path, many companies have developed powerful corporate strategies. This book contains examples of several such companies that have started with very little and yet turned it into something quite remarkable. Their accomplishments, in many respects, offer the purest examples of what superior corporate strategy is all about.

This book is designed to provide a framework, approach, and perspective to improve the practice of corporate strategy around the world in the 21st century.

Recommended Readings

Andrews, K.R. *The Concept of Corporate Strategy.* Burr Ridge, IL: Dow Jones–Irwin, 1971.

Ansoff, H.I. *Corporate Strategy: An Analytic Approach to Business Policy for Growth and Expansion.* New York: McGraw-Hill, 1965.

Berger, P., and E. Ofek. "Diversification's Effect on Firm Value." *Journal of Financial Economics,* Vol. 37, 1995, pp. 39–65.

Boston Consulting Group. *The Product Portfolio Concept. Perspective 66.* Boston: Boston Consulting Group, Inc., 1970.

Campbell, A., M. Devine, and D. Young. *A Sense of Mission.* London: The Economist Books Limited, 1990.

Collis, D.J., and C.A. Montgomery. "Creating Corporate Advantage." *Harvard Business Review,* May–June 1998, pp. 71–83.

Copeland, T., T. Koller, and J. Murrin. *Valuation: Measuring and Managing the Value of Companies.* New York: John Wiley & Sons, 1990.

Goold, M.C., and A. Campbell. *Strategies and Styles.* Oxford: Blackwell, 1987.

Goold, M.C., A. Campbell, and M. Alexander. *Corporate-Level Strategy.* New York: John Wiley & Sons, 1994.

Haspeslagh, P. "Portfolio Planning: Uses and Limits." *Harvard Business Review,* May–June 1982, pp. 58–73.

Hoskisson, R.E., and M.A. Hitt. *Downscoping: How to Tame the Diversified Firm.* Oxford: Oxford University Press, 1994.

Lang, L., and R. Stultz. "Tobin's *q*, Corporate Diversification, and Firm Performance." *Journal of Political Economy,* Vol. 102, December 1994, pp. 1248–80.

McTaggart, J.M., P.W. Kontes, and M.C. Mankins. *The Value Imperative.* New York: Free Press, 1994.

Mintzberg, H. *The Rise and Fall of Strategic Planning.* New York: Free Press, 1994.

Montgomery, C.A. "Corporate Diversification." *Journal of Economic Perspectives,* Vol. 8, No. 3, Summer 1994, pp. 163–78.

Porter, M.E. "From Competitive Advantage to Corporate Strategy." *Harvard Business Review,* May–June 1987, pp. 43–59.

Prahalad, C.K., and G. Hamel. "The Core Competence of the Corporation." *Harvard Business Review,* May–June 1990, pp. 79–91.

Villalonga, B. "Does Diversification Cause the 'Diversification Discount'?" Harvard Business School working paper, 2003.

Appendix **A**

Past Approaches to Corporate Strategy

The analysis of corporate strategy described in this book builds on previous approaches to the subject (see Figure A.1). Much of this work deserves study, not only because it is still used in companies today, but also because it provides the conceptual foundation for a number of useful tools and techniques. There is not enough space here to provide an exhaustive account of each of these contributions, but we highlight several that have had a lasting impact.[1]

The Concept of Corporate Strategy

Among the most important of the early contributions to corporate strategy was a body of work produced in the 1960s and 1970s by Kenneth Andrews, C. Roland Christensen, and their colleagues in Harvard Business School's business policy group.[2] At a time when management thinking was oriented

[1] The early part of this appendix draws heavily on the Introduction (pp. xi–xii) from *Strategy: Seeking and Securing Competitive Advantage,* edited by Cynthia A. Montgomery and Michael E. Porter (Boston, MA: Harvard Business Review Book, 1991.)

[2] This critical groundwork was laid in E. P. Learned, C. Roland Christensen, and Kenneth Andrews, *Business Policy: Text and Cases* (Burr Ridge, IL: Irwin, 1965). See also, Kenneth R. Andrews, *The Concept of Corporate Strategy* (Burr Ridge, IL: Dow Jones-Irwin, 1971).

FIGURE A.1   **Historic Perspectives on Corporate Strategy**

Perspective	Concept of Corporate Strategy	Organization Structure	Diversification	Portfolio Planning	Value-Based Strategy	Generic Corporate Strategies	Resource-Based View	Financial Economics
Representative author(s)	Ansoff 1965 Andrews 1971	Chandler 1962 Bower 1970 Vancil 1978	Wrigley 1970 Rumelt 1974 Montgomery 1985 Hill 1988	BCG 1968 Haspeslagh 1982	Jensen 1985 Schmalensee 1985 Rumelt 1991	Porter 1987 Goold & Campbell 1987 McKinsey 1989	Wernerfelt 1984 Dierickx and Cool 1989 Barney 1991 Collis & Montgomery 1998	Berger & Ofek 1995 Lang & Stultz 1994 Villalonga 2003
Concern	General management role	Organization structure	Extent and mode of diversification	Resource allocation	Corporate contribution to SBU performance	Source of corporate advantage	Firm idiosyncracy and growth	Shareholder value
Contribution	Early statement of corporate and competitive strategy	Structure follows strategy, "fit," decentralization	Set of businesses as strategic variable, "synergy"	Portfolio management	Limited evidence of corporate value; market for corporate control	Typology of corporate advantage	Tangible and intangible assets and capabilities	Empirical evidence of diversification discount
Output	Corporate vision, distinctive competence, SWOT analysis	M-form multidivisional structure	Measure of relatedness, analysis of performance	Growth/share matrix	Free cash flow, value-based strategy	Corporate role	Characteristics of valuable resources	Value of corporate membership

toward individual functions such as marketing, production, and finance, these scholars articulated the concept of strategy as a holistic way of thinking about a firm.

With respect to strategy in multibusiness firms, Andrew et al. identified corporate strategy as defining the businesses in which a company will compete, "preferably in a way that focuses resources to convert distinctive competence into competitive advantage."

Although enormously valuable as a conceptual framework, this treatment did not lay out an explicit methodology for demonstrating how distinctive competence could be translated into competitive advantage at the business unit level. In particular, because the approach was conceptual rather than analytical, it could not address the underlying economics of corporate advantage, and what specifically made the whole more than the sum of the parts.

Nonetheless, the work of Andrews and Christensen, along with that of others such as Igor Ansoff, and Peter F. Drucker,[3] propelled the notion of strategy into the forefront of management practice. Since then, there have been many advances and refinements in both the practice and theory of strategy. It is a tribute to the soundness of this original work, however, that it can encompass, and indeed has led to, many of these developments.

Organization Structure and Diversification

At the same time that Andrews and his colleagues were developing their ideas on strategy formulation, Alfred D. Chandler was studying the corporation's organizational structure.[4] His seminal work demonstrated that the multidivisional (M-form) structure allowed corporations to control an extensive array of different businesses. As many U.S. and European corporations diversified widely during the 1960s and 1970s, they adopted M-form structures by creating discrete strategic business units (SBUs).

[3] For an extended history of strategic planning in general, see H. Mintzberg, *The Rise and Fall of Strategic Planning* (New York: Free Press, 1994).
[4] Alfred D. Chandler, *Strategy and Structure* (Cambridge, MA: MIT Press, 1962).

The increasing scope of many corporations, along with the emergence of conglomerates in the 1960s, also stimulated research on the performance implications of diversification. (See Chapter 4.) This research attempted to discover the optimal type and extent of diversification. Its main contribution was the introduction of archetypes of diversification patterns and their linkage to particular organization structures.

Portfolio Planning

In the seventies, the major source of ideas about corporate strategy shifted from the academic world to management consulting firms. Specialist firms, such as the Boston Consulting Group (BCG), emerged to challenge the strategy practices of the traditional management consulting firms. Indeed, BCG was responsible for the first analytic breakthrough in corporate strategy. Their so-called **growth/share matrix,** best known for its cow and dog metaphors (see Figure A.2), became, for a while, the primary tool for resource allocation in diversified companies.

FIGURE A.2
Growth Share Matrix Was Used to Map Businesses

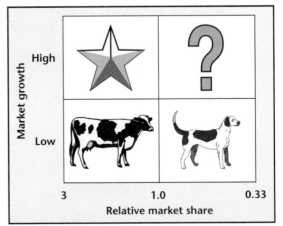

Source: The Boston Consulting Group, Inc. "The Product Portfolio," *Perspectives* (Boston, MA: Boston Consulting Group, Inc., 1970). Used by permission.

The two dimensions of the matrix were industry growth rate, which attempted to capture the potential cash usage of a business, and relative market share, which was a surrogate for overall competitive strength and hence the cash generation potential of a business. Mapping the location of a company's businesses in this matrix and sizing each according to its asset or revenue base gave a picture of the flow of financial resources in the corporation (see the General Foods example in Figure A.3).

A fast-growing business with low relative market share would require a lot of cash to grow; because of uncertainty about their future performance, businesses in this quadrant were called *question marks*. Conversely, a business with high relative market share in a slow-growing industry would be very profitable and would require little reinvestment. Since this implied it would throw off a lot of cash, businesses in this quadrant of the matrix were called *cash cows. Dogs* were to be found in the lower-right quadrant, at a competitive disadvantage and with little hope of changing that position because of the slow industry growth. In principle, the best strategy for this last category of business was divestment or harvesting. The top-left quadrant contained the *stars*—businesses that were users of cash today because of their rapid growth, but whose dominant market position warranted investing in for the time when industry growth slowed and the business became the next corporate cash cow.

FIGURE A.3
Classic Growth Share Matrix (General Foods Corporation, 1980–1982)

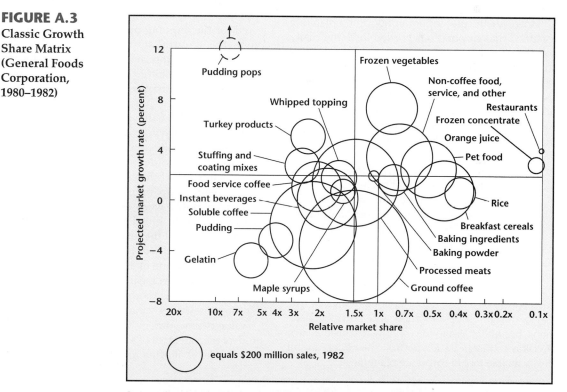

The first prescription of the matrix concerned resource allocation. Dogs would receive no investment unless they could demonstrate a very rapid payback. In contrast, stars would receive funding even though their current profitability might be low or negative. The second prescription was for the CEO to balance the portfolio of business among the quadrants so that the corporation would grow faster than GNP and be neither a net user nor generator of cash.

Such prescriptions allowed corporate executives to regain control of the strategic planning and capital budgeting processes. A CEO could deal with capital requests from the divisions with a particular bias in mind—to harvest the dogs, milk the cash cows, invest in the stars, or give the question marks a chance to become stars before the industry growth rate slowed. He or she could also trade businesses in and out of the portfolio to achieve the desired balance. As a result, portfolio planning had been adopted by over half of the largest companies surveyed in the early eighties.[5]

However, the prescriptions of portfolio planning assumed that corporations needed to be internally self-financing. In practice, there is no rationale for such a policy when the capital markets are efficient. Moreover, portfolio planning largely ignored the relatedness of the businesses in the matrix and did not address the question of whether and how the corporation added value to completely unrelated businesses. The growth-share matrix, for example, would suggest that a high-growth semiconductor business could, in principle, be acquired to balance a company's cash cow steelmill business.

As a consequence of these limitations, portfolio planning went out of fashion. What remains of portfolio planning is the notion of treating businesses differently according to their position in the portfolio. A market leader in a slow-growth business should perform differently than a follower in a high-growth business, and to expect the same performance of each would be a mistake. Used not as a mechanistic device for resource allocation and portfolio decisions, but rather as a guide for how to consider each division's strategic issues, portfolio planning can still be a valuable tool in corporate planning.

Value-Based Strategy

During the 1980s, developments in the capital markets, and opportunities to profit from revitalizing underperforming corporations, gave rise to the corporate raiders and leveraged buyout firms. Their activities highlighted the vulnerability of many large diversified corporations, and led to several sensational takeovers such as RJR Nabisco. As a result of this pressure, corporate executives increasingly focused their attention on the stock-market valuation of their firms.

To help them, a number of consulting firms developed approaches to value-based management. These adopted the objective of **maximizing shareholder value.** In a diversified company, this involved imputing a stock market price for each business unit. Most commonly, this was done by applying the industry average price/earnings ratio to the business's reported earnings. These estimates were then compared to the value projected for the ongoing operation of the business. When the imputed capital market value was higher than the internal valuation, the recommendation was to either improve the operational efficiency of the business, or to sell the unit.[6] (see Figure A.4.)

More generally, value-based strategy advocated a holistic approach to managing for shareholder value. Arguing that free cash flow was the correct measure of shareholder value, it emphasized careful measurement of the cash flow consequences of any strategic or operating decision. Importantly, those cash flows were to be discounted at the *business-specific* weighted average cost of capital. It was recommended that the resulting calculation of **economic value added** (EVA) be incorporated into the incentive scheme of all corporate and business unit executives as a means to discipline managers by directly linking the consequences of their actions to shareholder value.

Value-based strategy focused attention on the prudent management of a firm's capital. At the business unit level, it often resulted in the cancellation

[5] Philippe Haspeslagh, "Portfolio Planning: Uses and Limits," *Harvard Business Review,* May–June 1982, pp. 58–73.

[6] T. Copeland, T. Koller, and J. Murrin, *Valuation: Measuring and Managing the Value of Companies* (New York: John Wiley & Sons, 1990).

FIGURE A.4
Framework for
Assessing
Restructuring
Opportunities

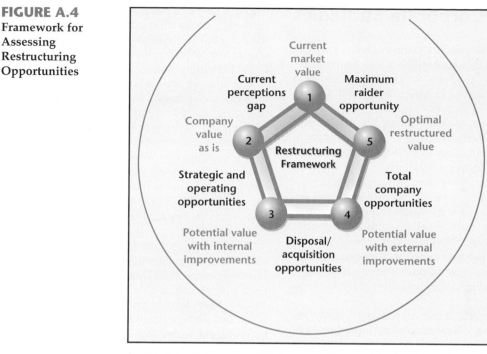

Source: From T. Copeland, T. Koller, and J. Murrin. *Valuation: Measuring and Managing the Value of Companies* (New York: John Wiley & Sons, 1990). Reprinted with permission of John Wiley & Sons, Inc.

of investment projects and the rationalization of product lines that generated negative EVA. At the corporate level, it led to the sale of many underperforming business units and the restriction on investment in other marginal businesses, and was consistent with the need to continually improve a company's stock price. As a consequence, value-based planning had much appeal and its ideas were adopted by a number of innovative companies, including Marriott, PepsiCo, and Walt Disney.[7]

Despite these advantages, value-based planning was not a panacea. First, the approach required the accurate projection of cash flows from each business. However, these projections were only as good as the ability of managers to accu-

rately measure the financial consequences of competitive position. Incorrect estimates of future returns from a business or investment easily invalidated the whole approach. Second, the implicit assumption of value-based strategy was that all business units and all investment proposals were self-contained. It was usually expected that divesting a business or curtailing an investment project would have no financial repercussions elsewhere in the corporation. This assumption of independence ignored the many linkages and interrelationships that often existed across businesses and among investments. Third, strict financial measurement of many long-term investments, particularly in intangible assets, was impossible. Indeed, value-based strategy is best at improving the efficient utilization of existing assets rather than developing creative long-term strategic initiatives.

[7] J.M. MacTaggart, P.W. Kontes, and M.C. Mankins, *The Value Imperative* (New York: Free Press, 1994).

Generic Corporate Strategies

The 1980s highlighted the failure of many very visible diversification strategies, such as Exxon entering the office products market and Coca-Cola acquiring Columbia Pictures. As a result, the notion that "sticking to the knitting"[8] might be the most desirable corporate strategy was widely promulgated. Indeed, by the late 1980s, many managers were struggling to justify the existence of their multibusiness corporations.

Into this void came the development of generic strategies that classified corporate strategies according to the ways in which value was created. Following the success of his notion of generic strategies at the business unit level, Michael Porter identified four types of corporate strategy. These lay along a continuum of increasing corporate involvement in the operation of the business units.[9]

Two of Porter's archetype corporate strategies, **portfolio management** and **restructuring,** could be applied in corporations whose businesses were essentially unrelated. A firm following a portfolio management strategy added little real value to its units because they were run autonomously with minimal corporate involvement. Its logic, therefore, depended on the firm's ability to identify and acquire companies that were undervalued, and on its willingness to sell any unit for an opportunistically high price. In contrast, the restructuring strategy required the corporate office to act as more than just a banker and reviewer of individual business units. Restructurers fundamentally changed underperforming companies and so created value by altering strategy, replacing management, improving efficiency, and so forth.

The remaining two strategies, **transferring skills** and **sharing activities,** could only be used in companies where the businesses were related to some degree. Transferring skills involved disseminating a particular capability, such as consumer marketing, across multiple business units. This had the potential to create significant value when the transferred skills improved the competitive positions of the units.

The strategy that involved the most intervention, sharing activities, literally required that business units shared an important function, such as research and development, a distribution channel, or a component manufacturing facility. Ideally, the scale economies that were generated in the shared activities contributed to the competitive advantage of each business unit. By necessity, however, the configuration of the function, and the allocation of its use, required some level of coordinated decision making.

The consulting firm McKinsey and Company also addressed corporate strategy from the headquarters perspective. They identified nine roles for the corporate office that could potentially create value. These, for example, included the roles of *coach* and *orchestrator* whereby the abilities and accumulated experience of corporate executives could be used to train, motivate, and coordinate the behavior of divisional managers.[10]

These ideas had barely gained currency when the focus of research and managerial practice shifted from the corporate office itself to the resources and capabilities of the firm as a whole.

Resource-Based View

Reminiscent of the original work by Andrews on distinctive competence, in 1990, C.K. Prahalad and Gary Hamel introduced the enormously influential notion of **core competence** to the managerial audience.[11] As described by Prahalad and Hamel, core competence was a capability or skill that provided the thread running through a firm's businesses, weaving them together into a coherent whole.

[8] T.J. Peters and R.H. Waterman, Jr., *In Search of Excellence* (New York: Warner Books, 1982).
[9] Michael E. Porter, "From Competitive Advantage to Corporate Strategy," *Harvard Business Review,* May–June 1987, pp. 43–59.
[10] McKinsey and Company, Inc., "What Is the Right Role for a Corporate Parent?" *McKinsey Quarterly,* 1989.
[11] C.K. Prahalad and G. Hamel, "The Core Competence of the Corporation," *Harvard Business Review,* May–June 1990, pp. 79–91.

The idea that a core competence uniquely defined a firm and was the source of value creation was intuitively appealing. Consequently, managers in multibusiness firms began to conceive of their firms as portfolios of competencies, not just as portfolios of businesses. Their role became to nurture these competencies and deploy them into the businesses. This perspective suggested a new, viable, and important role for CEOs that resonated with executives, particularly after the pressures they had felt in the 1980s.

However, the initial discussion left out much of the detail regarding how to develop a corporate strategy based on core competence. Thus, meaningful application of the core competence notion was difficult because of the generality of its level of analysis and the absence of specific prescriptions.

As a result, advances in corporate strategy in the nineties shifted back to the academic arena with the articulation of the **resource-based view of the firm.** This more broadly and accurately defines the assets that can function as core competences and lays out the conditions under which they can be sources of value in multiple businesses. The resource-based theory underpins the treatment of corporate strategy in this book.

Financial Economics

In the nineties, the performance implications of diversification were revisited, this time by the finance discipline. Scholars, like Lang and Stulz,[12] applied a capital market test to the value of diversification and discovered a substantial, approximately 20 percent, **"diversification discount."** Their "chop shop" approach compared the actual stock market capitalization of a multibusiness corporation with the sum of the imputed value of its business segments, assuming each segment was valued at the market price at which stand-alone single business entities in that segment traded. The

resulting discount, it was argued, implied that diversified firms destroyed shareholder value. Later research also found diversification discounts, although of differing magnitudes, over different time periods and in other countries.[13] Finance research also demonstrated that corporate restructurings, such as spinoffs, that focused the corporate portfolio increased stock market value and showed that at least part of the discount was due to multibusiness corporations allocating resources to underperforming business units[14]—a subsidy impossible in the single business firm.

The diversification discount is now considered an act of faith in the finance field, but is vigorously disputed by many strategy scholars. Part of their argument is methodological—segment measures are inadequate, or that comparisons with publicly quoted single businesses involve a substantial survivor bias. Part of their argument concerns the direction of causation—is the problem that poor performers diversify, rather than diversification leads to poor performance? At this points in time we would have to say the verdict is still out on the normative implications of this research, even if the descriptive facts appear to be agreed.

However, and more importantly, the diversification discount only refers to a phenomenon that is true on average—on average, diversified firms trade at a 20 percent discount to the stand-alone value of their business units. What is not true is that all diversified firms trade at a discount. In fact, even the original research by Lang and Stulz recognized that 40% of diversified firms actually traded at a premium to the stand-alone value of their businesses! If anything, this most recent research, therefore, supports the basic thesis of this book that corporate strategy can (indeed should) create shareholder value by making the whole worth more than the sum of the parts, but that its effective practice is still uncommon.

[12] Larry H.P. Lang and Rene M. Stulz, "Tobin's *q*, Corporate Diversification, and Firm Performance," *The Journal of Political Economy,* Vol. 102, No. 6 (December 1994), pp. 1248–80.

[13] K. Lins and H. Servaes, "International Evidence on the Value of Corporate Diversification," *Journal of Finance,* 54 no. 6 (1999), pp. 2215–39.

[14] J. M. Campa and S. Kedia, "Exploring the Diversification Discount," *Journal of Finance,* 57 (2002), pp. 1731–62.

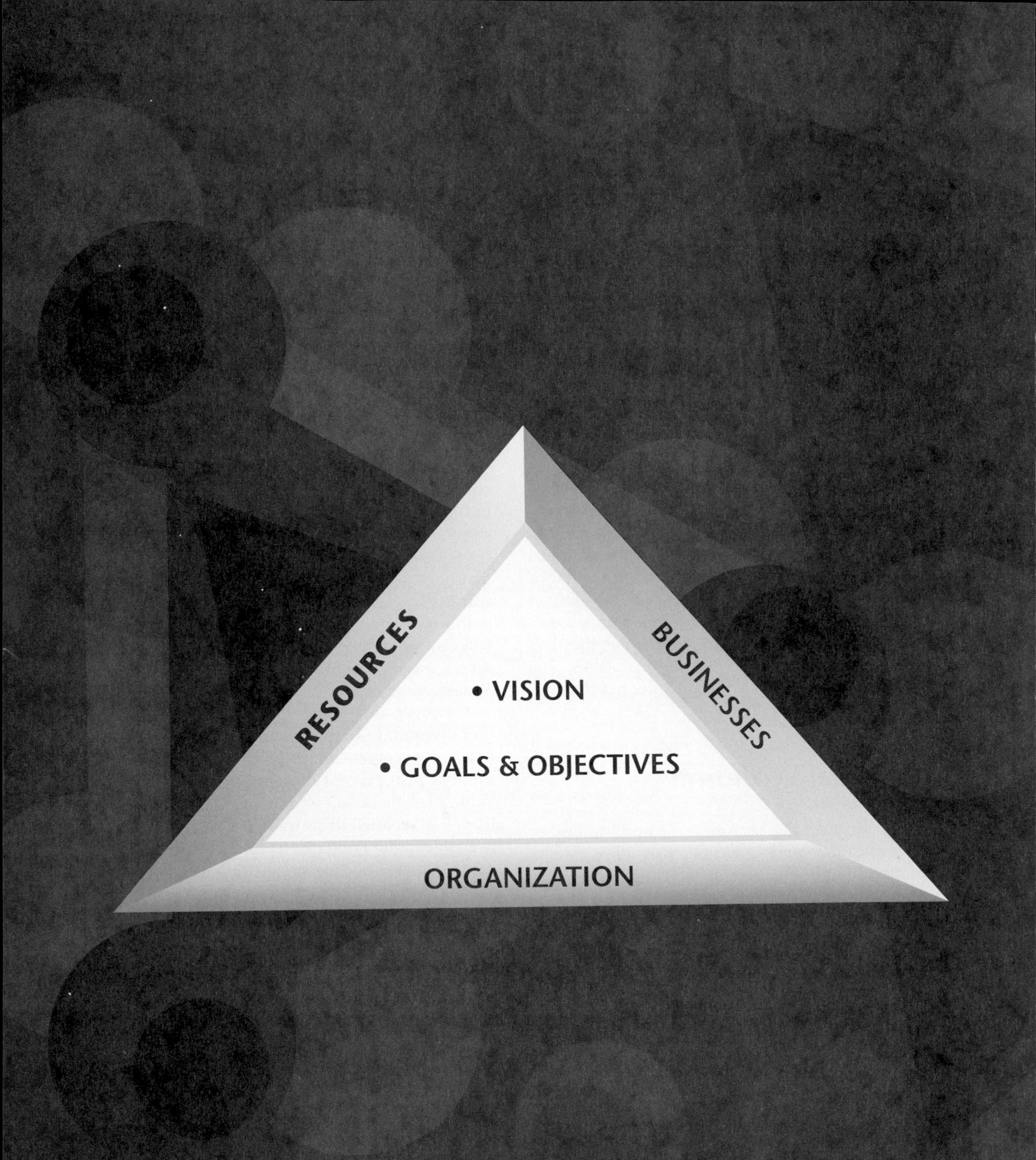
RESOURCES
BUSINESSES
• VISION
• GOALS & OBJECTIVES
ORGANIZATION

RESOURCES AND RENTS

2

▲ Introduction

This chapter draws on a theory called the resource-based view of the firm (RBV).[1] Though relatively new to the field of strategic management, it addresses some of the most fundamental questions of business-unit strategy: Why is one firm different from another? Why is one firm more profitable than another? What makes a competitive advantage sustainable? It also provides a powerful explanation of firm scope, and diversified expansion in particular.

One of the great strengths of the resource-based approach is that it explains why a firm possesses both a competitive advantage in a single business and a corporate advantage that extends across many businesses. The approach unifies the treatment of corporate- and business-level strategy, and facilitates strategic analysis at both levels.

The chapter begins with a brief review of industry analysis and competitive positioning. In this context, the resource-based view is introduced and applied to business-unit strategy. Proceeding in this way establishes a rigorous foundation for the analysis of resources that is later extended to more complex settings. It also assists in the development of a dynamic view of the firm, starting with small, focused companies and progressing to very large, complex organizations.

---

[1] Portions of this chapter draw heavily from David J. Collis and Cynthia A. Montgomery, "Competing on Resources: Strategy in the 1990s," *Harvard Business Review,* July–August 1995, pp. 118–28. See also, "Resources: The Essence of Corporate Advantage," Harvard Business School Note No. 792-064, 1992.

Principles

▲ Business-Unit Strategy

In a world of perfect competition, products are homogeneous. There are countless buyers and sellers, all of whom have access to complete and timely information, and none of whom can influence the price of the goods they buy or sell. In such a world, there is no need for strategy, nor any benefit from having one.

Most markets, however, are not perfectly competitive; they have a number of imperfections or asymmetries. Either the number of sellers or buyers is limited, the products are heterogeneous, the information flows are flawed, or a firm is advantaged by possessing an input that is nonreproducible or in limited supply. A carefully crafted strategy can help a firm exploit the market inefficiencies that exist in these imperfectly competitive settings and, therefore, can play an essential role in maximizing its profits.

In such situations, strategy fulfills two vital purposes.[2] One is the **external positioning** of a firm relative to its competitors in a given industry. By adroitly matching a firm's strengths and weaknesses to market threats and opportunities, an effective strategy can create a competitive advantage that allows the firm to earn superior profits. An essential part of formulating any strategy, therefore, requires an understanding of the environment in which the firm competes.

The second purpose of strategy is the **internal alignment** of all a firm's activities and investments.[3] Once a firm's product market position has been identified, all the firm's activities from R&D to marketing can be aligned with that position and made consistent with each other. Similarly, investments can be chosen that reinforce one another and cumulate over time in the creation of new and better competitive advantages.

Industry and Competitive Positioning

With its strategy in place, every business unit's profitability can be disaggregated into two components: the industry average level of profitability, and the divergence from that average that is attributable to the competitive advantage (or disadvantage) that the firm's strategy produces within the industry. Estimates of the relative importance of so-called industry effects and firm effects differ across studies, but a wealth of research suggests that

---

[2] This critical groundwork was laid by E.P. Learned, C. Roland Christensen, and Kenneth Andrews, *Business Policy: Text and Cases* (Burr Ridge, IL: Irwin, 1965).
[3] Strategy implies *choice* of product market position, not the efficiency with which that choice is implemented. Michael E. Porter, "What Is Strategy?" *Harvard Business Review*, November–December 1996, pp. 61–78.

both are very important.[4] A widely used approach to analyzing industry profitability and competitive advantage was developed by Michael Porter.[5] His framework for **industry analysis** is a systematic methodology for examining the impact of industry structure on a firm's performance. Drawing on industrial organization economics, Porter argued that the long-run average profitability of industries differs as a function of five forces: the threat of new entrants, the power of buyers, the power of suppliers, the intensity of rivalry within the industry, and the threat of substitute products or services.[6] Porter also showed that the structure of an industry "has a strong influence in determining the competitive rules of the game as well as the strategies potentially available to the firm."

Porter went on to describe a set of **generic strategies** a firm could use to overcome or exploit industry forces and achieve a competitive advantage vis-à-vis its rivals through low cost or differentiation. The effective implementation of either of these strategies with a broad or narrow scope requires a set of organizational arrangements that support the key success factors behind the strategy. Across generic strategies, the pattern of these arrangements differs in predictable ways so that their pursuit is mutually exclusive (for more detail see Appendix B: "Business Strategy and Industry Analysis").

At both the industry and the firm level some market imperfection must exist for abnormal returns to endure. High industry-level profits, for example, are often sustained by **entry barriers** that make it difficult for new competitors to enter an industry. Similarly, profitable strategic groups within an industry are protected by **mobility barriers** that make it difficult for firms pursuing one source of competitive advantage to move to another.[7] Within an industry or strategic group, the superior performance of any one firm must be similarly protected by factors that make it difficult for rivals to duplicate its advantage; otherwise its success will be fleeting. Richard Rumelt called such impediments to the imitation of what a firm has, or does, **isolating mechanisms**—the Great Wall around a *sustainable* competitive advantage.[8] Studying these phenomena gave rise to a new area of inquiry: the resource-based view of the firm.[9]

---

[4] See, for example, Anita M. McGahan and Michael E. Porter, "How Much Does Industry Matter, Really?" *Strategic Management Journal,* Vol. 18, 1997, pp. 15–30.

[5] Michael E. Porter, *Competitive Strategy* (New York: Free Press, 1980).

[6] An alternative perspective on industry structure—the value net—introduced the notion of a sixth force: complements that increase the value or demand for a product or service. A. Brandenburger and B. Nalebuff, *Coopetition* (New York: Doubleday, 1998).

[7] Richard E. Caves and M.E. Porter, "From Entry Barriers to Mobility Barriers: Conjectural Decisions and Contrived Deterrence to New Competition," *Quarterly Journal of Economics,* May 1977, pp. 241–61.

[8] Richard P. Rumelt, "Theory, Strategy, and Entrepreneurship," in *The Competitive Challenge,* ed. D.J. Teece (Cambridge, MA: Ballinger, 1987), pp. 137–58.

[9] This term was first introduced in 1984 by Birger Wernerfelt, "A Resource-Based View of the Firm," *Strategic Management Journal,* 1984, pp. 171–80.

▲ Resources

The premise of the resource-based view is that firms differ in fundamental ways because each firm possesses a unique bundle of resources. Because many of these resources cannot be accumulated instantaneously, a firm's choice of strategy is constrained by its current resource stock and the speed at which it can acquire or accumulate new resources. Without asymmetries in resource stocks, and constraints on the rate of change, any firm could elect to follow any strategy it wished. As a result, successful strategies would be very quickly imitated and profits rapidly driven to zero. Resource asymmetries, therefore, are the substance of strategy, the very essence of sustainable competitive advantage.

What Are Resources?

Resources come in many forms, from common factor inputs that are widely available and easily purchased in arms-length transactions, to highly differentiated resources, like brand names, that are developed over many years and are very difficult to replicate.

Resources can be classified into three broad categories: tangible assets, intangible assets, and organizational capabilities.

Tangible assets are the easiest to value and often are the only resources that appear on a firm's balance sheet. They include real estate, production facilities, and raw materials, among others. Although tangible resources may be essential to a firm's strategy, because of their standard nature they are only occasionally a source of competitive advantage. There are, of course, notable exceptions. The mundane, twisted copper telephone and coaxial cable wires that link homes to the outside world increased in value as they became the on-ramp to the information superhighway. Real estate locations adjacent to popular tourist sites are also one-of-a-kind resources that may support unusual profits.

Intangible assets include such things as company reputations, brand names, cultures, technological knowledge, patents and trademarks, and accumulated learning and experience. These assets often play important roles in competitive advantage (or disadvantage) and firm value (see "Gerber Products Co."). Intangible assets also have the important property of not being consumed in usage. Indeed, if applied judiciously, some intangible assets can grow with use, rather than shrink. For this reason, they can provide a valuable base for diversified expansion.

Organizational capabilities are not factor inputs like tangible and intangible assets; they are complex combinations of assets, people, and processes that organizations use to transform inputs into outputs. Applied to the firm's physical production technology, these organizational routines govern the efficiency of the firm's activities. Finely honed capabilities can be a source of competitive advantage. They enable a firm to take the same

Gerber Products Co.

Few firms can boast the kind of brand recognition and loyalty enjoyed by one company in particular, one that made its name as a purveyor of much-sought-after foods like strained peas and pureed squash. When it comes time to feed their own children, generations of American parents, themselves raised on Gerber baby food, wouldn't buy anything else.

When Gerber was acquired by Sandoz Ltd., a Swiss pharmaceutical firm, in 1994, its tangible net worth, including its plants and inventory, was less than $300 million. One might wonder why Sandoz was willing to pay $3.7 billion for the firm—almost 33 times Gerber's annual profits.

The answer lies in Gerber's intangible assets: its brand name, reputation, and considerable expanse of supermarket shelf space. These are the assets Gerber's competitors vied to imitate for decades, with little success. When Sandoz acquired it, Gerber commanded more than 70 percent of the U.S. baby food market.

factor inputs as rivals and convert them into products and services, either with greater efficiency in the process or greater quality in the output.

The list of organizational capabilities includes a set of abilities describing efficiency and effectiveness—faster, more responsive, higher quality, and so forth—that can be found in any one of the firm's activities, from product development, to marketing, to manufacturing. Over the last several decades, some Japanese automobile companies, for example, have developed a number of outstanding organizational capabilities.[10] The first was in low cost, "lean" manufacturing, next in high-quality production, and most recently in fast product development. These organizational capabilities generated important efficiency advantages, particularly against foreign rivals, and played major roles in the competitiveness of these firms.

Some authors have identified higher-order **dynamic capabilities** as a different and better type of resource.[11] They argue that dynamic routines that are "directed at establishing new competences" are superior to static routines or capabilities which merely "replicate previously performed tasks" because they allow firms to adapt to changing strategic demands. While intuitively appealing, and suggestive that the ultimate source of advantage is knowledge—a perspective that has spawned its own literature[12]—such capabilities are neither intellectually different from the above definition of organizational capabilities, nor definitively more valuable than simpler organizational capabilities (or indeed better than higher-order

---

[10] Carliss Y. Baldwin and Kim B. Clark, "Capabilities, Time Horizons and Investment: New Perspectives on Capital Budgeting," Harvard Business School mimeograph, 1990.

[11] D.J. Teece, G. Pisano, and A. Shuen, "Dynamic Capabilities and Strategic Management," *Strategic Management Journal,* Vol. 18, No. 7, August 1997, pp. 509–33.

[12] See, for example, R.M. Grant, "Toward a Knowledge-Based Theory of the Firm," *Strategic Management Journal,* Winter Special Issue, Vol. 17, 1996, pp. 109–22.

FIGURE 2.1
Resource Stocks
and Flows

Source: Copyright © Cynthia
A. Montgomery

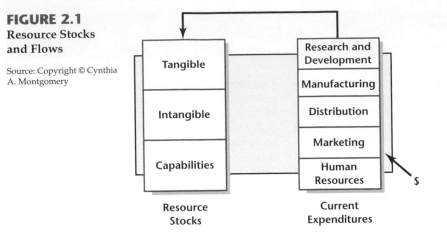

capabilities of the "learning to learn to learn" variety).[13] Every capability incurs costs to create, and produces some competitive advantages in a product market. The strategic question when evaluating any capability remains the same—does the benefit outweigh the cost?[14] Unless dynamic capabilities are systematically cheaper to build than static capabilities—an assumption violated by the complexity and current lack of understanding of change management—it is not clear that it is always strategically sensible to focus competition only on dynamic capabilities.

Stocks and Flows

In addressing the roots of sustainable competitive advantage, the resource-based view emphasizes the **stocks** of assets and capabilities (resources) a firm possesses. By doing so, it offers a different, more dynamic, perspective on competitive advantage than an analysis of current **flows** of revenues and expenses might suggest. While flows are transitory and can be adjusted instantaneously, stock levels carry over from period to period and only accumulate slowly over time (see "The Bathtub Metaphor"). As an explanation for *enduring* advantage, therefore, stocks are more important than current flows.

To understand the difference between stocks and flows, consider a firm that has a well-established brand name. A flow analysis of competitive advantage would show that it did indeed earn higher profits by spending less on advertising and charging higher prices than competitors. But the reason a new competitor cannot successfully replicate this strategy—spending little on advertising and charging a high price—is that it does not have a

[13] D.J. Collis, "How Valuable Are Organizational Capabilities?" *Strategic Management Journal,* Special Issue, Winter 1994, pp. 143–52.
[14] S. Winter, "Understanding Dynamic Capabilities," *Strategic Management Journal,* Vol. 24, October 2003, pp. 991–96.

The Bathtub Metaphor

The fundamental distinction between stocks and flows may be illustrated by the "bathtub" metaphor: at any moment in time, the stock of water is indicated by the level of water in the tub; it is the cumulative result of flows of water into the tub (through the tap) and out of it (through the drain). In the example of R&D, the amount of water in the tub represents the stock of know-how at a particular point in time, whereas current R&D spending is represented by the water flowing in through the tap; the fact that know-how depreciates over time is represented by the flow of water leaking through the drain. A crucial point illustrated by the bathtub metaphor is that while flows can be adjusted instantaneously, stocks cannot. It takes a consistent pattern of resource flows to accumulate a desired change in strategic asset stocks.

Source: Ingemar Dierickx and K. Cool, "Asset Stock Accumulation and Sustainability of Competitive Advantage," *Management Science,* 1989, pp. 1504–11.

comparable brand reputation. In this example, it is the stock of brand-name recognition that makes firms different and so sustains a leader's competitive advantage.[15] Resource stocks, therefore, underlie a firm's ability to generate profit and sustain durable firm differences (strategic asymmetries).

Flows are nonetheless important in themselves. The activities a firm pursues and the resource investments it makes in the current period are determined by the strategy it is pursuing. Further, many flows accumulate over time into highly valued resource stocks. For example, the continued performance of certain activities, such as launching new products, can result in the development of a unique capability in product development. Thus, while most expenditure flows are expensed on the income statement, many in fact represent long-term investments in the firm's most critical capabilities.

What Makes Resources Valuable?

Although the notion that resources underpin the sustainability of competitive advantage is simple, companies often have a hard time identifying and evaluating their own resources, assessing whether they are strengths or weaknesses, and understanding whether they can be sources of sustainable competitive advantage.

Indeed, as firms evaluate the set of resources they possess, they will find a mixed bag. Some lucky firms will own "crown jewels"—resources that can be the basis for successful strategies. Some will find that their resources are actually liabilities. IBM's mainframe culture of "big iron," for example, which had served it well for nearly 40 years, became a liability by the late

---

[15] Stocks and flows are duals of one another. While the stock of brand recognition determines the flow of advertising expenditures required each period, the expenditures determine how the stock level alters over time.

Resources and Product Market Strategy

It is important to remember that owning a valuable resource does not permit the firm to sit back and clip dividend checks. Valuable resources will only reap the profits they can theoretically generate if they are applied in an effective product market strategy. Traditional strategy formulation—that is, externally positioning the firm to capitalize on its strengths and minimize its weaknesses—remains essential to realizing competitive advantage.

Moreover, the firm still has to deploy its resources in a way that correctly aligns all its activities in pursuit of its chosen source of competitive advantage. If the strategy is ill-conceived or unsustainable, the value of the firm will suffer, as will the value of most of its resources.

The connection between the competitive strategy of a firm and the resource strategy that supports it is on going and reciprocal: valuable resources help build strong strategies; strong strategies help build valuable resources.

Kodak, for example, recently added to its century-old photographic resources a world-class capability in digital imaging. Unfortunately, the company has been much less successful at bringing that research and knowledge to market in an effective strategy. Kodak has had four CEOs and at least as many digital imaging strategies since the late 1980s, and yet is still struggling to compete in the new environment. Indeed, it has had exceptional write-offs for each of the last 11 years!

eighties. Yet other firms might discover that some of their resources are not markedly better than those of competitors or are not particularly highly valued by consumers. The challenge for managers is to understand what distinguishes valuable from pedestrian resources and to use that knowledge to craft strategies that generate an enduring competitive advantage.

Historically, attempts to evaluate resources often resembled inward-looking exercises that lacked critical objectivity. The resource-based view added discipline to this subjective process by bringing back into the analysis the external perspective of the industry and competitive dynamics. It is important to stress that resource evaluation can only take place in the context of the firm's competitive environment (see "Resources and Product Market Strategy"). As shown in Figure 2.2, the value of a firm's resources lies in the complex interplay between the firm and its competitive environment along the dimensions of **demand, scarcity,** and **appropriability.** Value is created in the intersection of the three sets: when a resource is demanded by customers, when it cannot be replicated by competitors, and when the profits it generates are captured by the firm.[16]

Some genius invented the Oreo—we're just living off the inheritance.

Ross Johnson, CEO of RJR Nabisco, 1986–1989[17]

[16] For a related view on sustainability, see Pankaj Ghemawat, *Commitment* (New York: Free Press, 1991), Chapter 4.
[17] Bryan Burrough and John Helyar, *Barbarians at the Gate: The Fall of RJR Nabisco* (New York: Harper and Row, 1990).

FIGURE 2.2
The Value Creation Zone

Source: Reprinted by permission of *Harvard Business Review.* From "Competing on Resources: Strategy in the 1990s" by David J. Collis and Cynthia A. Montgomery, July–August 1995. Copyright © 1995 by the Harvard Business School Publishing Corporation; all rights reserved.

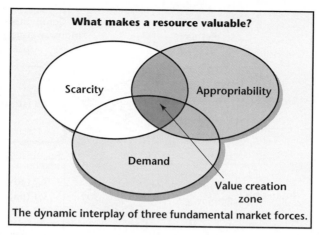

Customer Demand The first determinant of resource value is found in the product market. A valuable resource must contribute to the **fulfillment of a customer's needs,** at a price the customer is willing to pay. At any given time, that price will be determined by customer preferences, available alternatives (including substitute products), and the supply of related or complementary goods.[18] These structural forces change over time as consumer preferences and competitive offerings evolve. Therefore, firms must continually reassess their customers' "willingness to pay" and the degree to which their resources meet current and projected needs.

For example, recognizing that generic cigarettes caused a shift in customers' willingness to pay for branded tobacco products, Philip Morris cut the price of its Marlboro cigarettes by nearly 25 percent in April 1993. The move demonstrated the firm's recognition of the change in consumer demand for one of its primary resources, the Marlboro brand name. (Indeed, one study indicated that over a period of three years, all the world's leading tobacco brands declined sharply in value: Marlboro dropped 27 percent to $33 billion; Camel, 70 percent to $1.6 billion; and Winston, 73 percent to $2.3 billion.[19])

In addressing customer demand, it is important to keep in mind that resources are only valuable if they meet customers' needs better than those of their competitors. For this reason, the term *distinctive competence*, rather than core competence, is more appropriate. Even though a resource may be necessary to the implementation of a strategy, if it does not distinguish the firm's product offerings or ways of doing business, it will not be a source of a competitive advantage. It is only when resources contribute to

[18] Adam M. Brandenburger and H.W. Stuart, "Value-Based Business Strategy," *Journal of Economics and Management Strategy,* Vol. 5, No. 1, Spring 1996, pp. 5–24.
[19] Alexandra Ourosoff, "When the Smoke Clears," *Financial World,* June 21, 1994, pp. 38–42.

FIGURE 2.3
Wal-Mart's
Resource-Based
Advantage in
Discount Retailing

Source: Reprinted from
"Wal-Mart Stores' Discount
Operations," by Pankaj
Ghemawat, HBS case
number 9-387-018. Used by
permission of Harvard
Business School Publishing
Corporation; all rights
reserved.

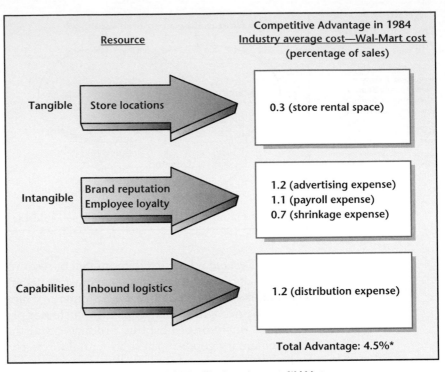

*Each percentage point advantage is worth $500 million in net income to Wal-Mart

competitive superiority in the product market that they will be valuable. Cocoa beans, for example, may be a necessary input for chocolate manufacturers, but they do not lead to important product differences.

An analysis of a firm's resources, therefore, must involve more than just an internal assessment of which activities the firm performs well. In particular, it is necessary to show how a firm's resource stock can be translated into specific measures of competitive advantage. Figure 2.3, for example, shows the resources that give Wal-Mart an edge over its rivals. Noted alongside each resource is the quantitative measure of the product market advantage it supports.

Demand for a particular resource, and hence the value of that resource, is also very sensitive to the possibility of **substitution.** Porter's five forces analysis highlighted the threat substitute products may pose to an industry's profitability—for example, the way facsimile machines reduced the demand for overnight delivery services. However, even when demand for an end product remains high, competitors can substitute alternative resources for the production of a similar offering. Bricks-and-mortar travel agencies learned this lesson the hard way, as the Internet spawned a number of online services for comparing ticket prices, planning trips, and booking reservations.

While substitute resources often accompany a new technology, as when Nucor's minimill steel technology substituted for the huge physical infrastructure that the leading steel manufacturers had built in integrated steel mills, there are many cases where substitution comes from a new way of combining existing resources. Wal-Mart's discount retailing model substituted new resources for the traditional department stores. Southwest Airlines, with its short-haul, point-to-point route structure connecting second-tier airports with one airplane type, was a substitute for the hub-and-spoke route structure and computer reservation systems of the major airlines.[20]

In summary, enduring demand for the good or service a resource generates is a necessary condition for the resource itself to be valuable. However, it is not a sufficient condition. For that, a firm must have an advantage, and a resource, that others do not have and find difficult to replicate.

Resource Scarcity The second essential requirement for a resource to be valuable, therefore, is that it be in short supply. If the resource is plentifully available, any competitor could acquire it and so replicate the firm's advantage.[21] Indeed, by definition, resources that yield a competitive advantage must be uncommon. Further, to be a source of *sustainable* competitive advantage, the rarity of the resource must persist over time.

Inimitability is, therefore, at the heart of value creation because it limits competition. Possessing a resource that competitors can readily copy will only generate temporary value—it cannot be the basis of a long-run strategy.[22] There are four characteristics that make resources difficult to imitate. Resources that play a central role in a firm's strategy should possess at least one of these.

The first category comprises *physically unique* resources that by definition are virtually impossible to copy. A magnificent real estate location, mineral rights, or legally protected drug patents simply cannot be imitated. Although it is tempting to think of most resources as falling into this category, on closer inspection, few do. Even resources that appear to be one of a kind often subsequently prove to be inimitable. Xerox fell into this trap in the seventies when it believed that no one else could ever replicate its reprographic capabilities. Canon proved otherwise, and the seventies

---

[20] Many of these substitutions can be thought of as disruptive technologies, or disruptive business models, a phenomenon identified by Clayton Christensen. C. Christensen, *The Innovator's Dilemma* (Boston: HBS Press, 1997); and C. Christensen and M. Raynor, *The Innovator's Solution* (Boston: HBS Press, 2003).

[21] Jay Barney, "Firm Resources and Sustained Competitive Advantage," *Journal of Management,* 1991, pp. 99–120.

[22] Richard Rumelt (1987 op. cit) made this point in "Theory, Strategy, and Entrepreneurship." The characteristics of inimitability are the isolating mechanisms referred to earlier—"impediments to the ex-post imitative dissipation of entrepreneurial rents."

turned into the "Lost Decade" for Xerox as its market leadership in photocopiers fell to Canon.

Many more resources are difficult to imitate because of what economists call *path dependency* in their accumulation.[23] These are resources that cannot be instantaneously acquired, but rather must be built over time in ways that are difficult to accelerate. Coca-Cola's brand-name recognition, for example, was not built, and cannot be replicated, just by spending hundreds of millions of dollars on advertising. Rather, it comes from the experiences consumers associate with drinking Coke over the years; to match it would take the passage of time and the accumulation of another set of experiences drinking the new cola. Similarly, crash R&D programs, where many scientists work in parallel, often cannot replicate the results of programs whose problems have been solved sequentially. This need to re-create the path that predecessors took protects the first mover by delaying imitation.

The third source of inimitability is *causal ambiguity.* This implies that potential replicators either cannot disentangle what the truly valuable resource is, or cannot identify the precise recipe for duplicating it. For example, what is the resource that enables a mutual fund to outperform the market? Is it just skilled fund managers, or is it the training of those managers? Or a team approach of managers and stock analysts? Or the advocacy method for picking stocks? Or the incentive schemes that the company employs? And if a senior executive left for another company, could he or she take away the knowledge in a set of written blueprints?

Causally ambiguous resources are often organizational capabilities. They are embedded in complex social structures and interactions and may even depend on the personality of a few exceptional individuals. As Delta and United tried to mimic Southwest Air's successful low-cost strategy, for example, the most difficult thing they had to copy was not the planes, the routes, or the fast gate turnaround. These were readily observable and, in principle, easily duplicated. The most difficult thing to copy or surpass was Southwest's culture of fun, family, and frugality, because no one could quite identify what it is or how it arose.

The last source of inimitability is *economic deterrence.* This occurs when a market leader's competitors have the capability to replicate its resources but, because of limited market size, choose not to do so. This is most likely when strategies are built around large capital investments, such as complex continuous process machines, that are scale sensitive and specific to a given market. When such assets cannot be redeployed—that is, they are sunk in a given market—they represent a credible commitment that the firm will stay in the market and fight any competitor that attempts to

---

[23] The discussion of path dependency and causal ambiguity follows Dierickx and Cool, "Asset Stock Accumulation," 1989.

FIGURE 2.4
Resource
Imitability

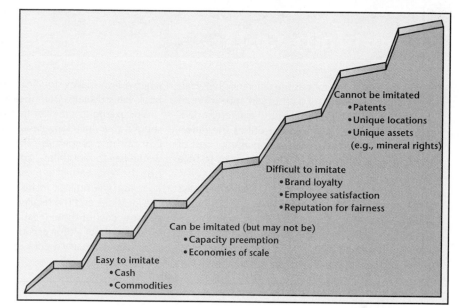

replicate the investment. Faced with such a threat, potential imitators may choose not to duplicate the resource when the market is too small to profitably support two players the size of the incumbent.[24]

Resources may be even more valuable when there are multiple barriers to imitation. For example, a reputation for high-quality, innovative products may involve path dependencies as well as causal ambiguity. Further, imitating a bundle of resources that form an integrated whole can be even more difficult. For this reason, carefully aligned, internally consistent strategies can be particularly difficult to imitate. Would-be followers would be faced not only with the challenges of imitating one resource, but also a set of resources, all carefully entwined.[25] It is also worth noting that the very qualities that make resources difficult to imitate may also make them difficult for the firm itself to reproduce or change.

Although it may be tempting to think of imitability as an either/or condition, more often it is a matter of degree—a question of time and difficulty. The characteristics discussed above often do not prevent imitation; they make it more difficult, or more uncertain. Figure 2.4 captures this by illustrating the range of resource imitability.

[24] For an excellent discussion, see Pankaj Ghemawat, *Commitment* (New York: Free Press, 1991.)

[25] Formally, a bundle of resources is worth more than the sum of individual resources when there are complementarities among them. Jan Rivkin eloquently makes this statement with respect to the benefits of aligning activities in support of a business strategy (J. Rivkin, "Imitation of Complex Strategies," *Management Science,* Vol. 46, 2000, pp. 824–44).

Opportunity Costs

Accountants define profit as the difference between the total revenue and total costs that appear on an income statement. Economists use a different definition. They define **economic profit** as the difference between revenue and the opportunity cost of employing the firm's resources. This proves to be a crucial distinction.

Opportunity costs consider the alternative ways a resource could be employed. When a firm uses a resource in a given application, it incurs an opportunity cost that is equal to the maximum amount the resource could have earned in its next best employment. This distinction is particularly important when a firm makes significant use of assets whose book value deviates from their market value.

For example, a retailer that owns land in highly sought-after locations should recognize the true cost of those properties—the amount anyone else would pay to rent them—and take care not to confuse the rents earned as a landowner with the profits made as a retailer. If the valuable resources are the locations and the retailer does not charge itself the true cost of those locations, the retailing business may show a total accounting profit even if the company is actually a poor retailer, but a fortuitous landowner.

Appropriability Even if a resource is fulfilling a consumer demand and is in short supply, there still remains a question about the **distribution of profit:** Who actually captures the profits created by a resource?

It is a mistake to think that profits automatically flow to a firm's legal owners (the providers of capital). Rather, one must consider who has the property rights to a firm's critical resources; how obvious it is which resources generate profits; and other factors that influence the bargaining power of the relevant stakeholders. (See "Opportunity Costs.")

Generally, if the source of value creation is obvious, and property rights to the critical resources are clearly established, profits will flow to the **owner of the resources,** be it the firm itself, or an external party. For this reason, firms are more likely to appropriate profits from resources they develop themselves, rather than from those they purchase in the market. Warren Buffet, for example, recognized the value of the Walt Disney Company owning the copyright to Mickey Mouse. Commenting in the mid-nineties on why he liked the firm as an investment, Buffet explained, "because the mouse does not have an agent."[26]

In contrast, the explosion in the number of private equity funds in the 1990s illustrates the delicate issues concerning the ownership of resources by a firm or its employees. One critical resource of such firms was the contacts and relationships they held in the investment banking community. Unfortunately, for many firms, this resource was often vested in the

[26] *The Harbus,* March 25, 1996, p. 12.

Employees and Rent Generation

In annual reports and end-of-year speeches, management often proclaims that the firm's employees are its most valuable resource. Without denying the importance of the human contribution, it is important to remember that, in the absence of slavery, people are resources that firms must rent, not own. Unlike the assets on a firm's balance sheet, these resources can quit their jobs or attempt to renegotiate their contracts with the firm.

In a reasonably efficient labor market, employees that bring clearly defined talents and skills to a firm should be able to appropriate the value of those resources in personal wages and bonuses. The compensation of skilled athletes, for example, reflects the value they are expected to create for any team. For employees to be a source of economic rent for the firm itself, something must tie them to the firm, or make their skills more valuable in the firm than they would be elsewhere. For example, a firm may appropriate a portion of the rent if it contributes a valuable resource, such as a distribution system, to a management team, so that it would be difficult for the team to leave the firm as a unit and reestablish itself elsewhere. In such settings, when relationship-specific investments tie the parties together, the firm may earn rents not only on resources it owns, but also as a partner of employees who possess valuable resources.

individuals "doing the deals," not in the firm itself. These people could, and often did, trade their skills by establishing their own funds, or by moving to another firm where they could reap a greater share of the profit their resource (skills) generated.

For many firms, the most difficult situations to assess are those where property rights are not clear, or where resources are employed in combination, making it difficult to identify the individual contribution of each. Such situations give rise to bargaining among a host of parties, which can include customers, distributors, partners, and suppliers, as well as the firm's own employees. (See "Employees and Rent Generation.") Many joint venture partners, for example, have found that difficult questions of appropriation arise when contracts and property rights are not iron-clad.[27]

More generally, whenever a firm owns valuable resources its ability to appropriate profits is always threatened by the pressure to pay them out in the form of abnormal payments for inputs or, equivalently, to dissipate them as slack inside the organization.[28]

---

[27] David Teece refers to these as co-specialized assets. See D.J. Teece, "Profiting from Technological Innovation: Implications for Integration, Collaboration, Licensing, and Public Policy," in *The Competitive Challenge,* ed. D.J. Teece (Cambridge, MA: Ballinger, 1987), pp. 185–220.

[28] Pankaj Ghemawat, *Commitment,* Chapter 4.

How Do You Know If Your Resources Are Valuable?

DEMAND

Does the resource produce something customers desire, and for which they have a high willingness to pay?

Does the resource contribute to competitive advantage in the product market?

Are there alternative products or resources that provide more value for the customer?

SCARCITY

Is the resource rare?

Is the resource hard to copy?

APPROPRIABILITY

Can the firm capture the value created by the resources?

Returning to the zone of value creation shown in Figure 2.2, we can now see how the conditions for valuable resources apply (see "How Do You Know If Your Resources Are Valuable?"). The test of demand demonstrates that the resource produces a good or service that customers want, at a price they are willing to pay. The test of scarcity demonstrates that a resource is in short supply and that competitors will not be able to imitate it. Finally, the test of appropriability demonstrates that the firm itself can capture the profits generated by the competitive advantage the resource provides. Resources that meet these conditions benefit from a substantial zone of value creation; the firm itself is better off when it has an ample supply of such resources, and can apply them across several markets.

It is important to recognize, however, that conditions that affect the value of resources can shift over time, sometimes abruptly. When this happens, the zone of value creation shrinks (or expands). (See "Shrinking the Value Creation Zone.") Recognizing that this occurs underscores the importance of a dynamic evaluation of resources, and the role they play in sustaining a firm's competitive (or corporate) advantage.

Intrinsic Properties of Resources

As the above discussion indicates, most characteristics that affect the value of a resource are determined in the complex interplay within a system of competitors, customers, and suppliers of factor inputs. For this reason, the value of a resource changes as the state of competition and the chosen strategy evolve. Other characteristics of a resource are, however, primarily intrinsic in nature.

Resources differ dramatically in **capacity,** that is, how much a firm has and how long the supply will last. Some resources have fixed levels, while

Shrinking the Value Creation Zone

The Walt Disney Company had a magnificent decade of performance in its first 10 years under Michael Eisner. Unfortunately, since 1994 the company has struggled to maintain that performance, until suffering the indignity of a hostile takeover bid from the cable company Comcast in early 2004. Part of the explanation for Disney's decline was the contraction in the size of the value creation zone around its valuable resource in animated cartoons.

The **competitive superiority** of that capability was initially challenged by Dreamworks which, under former Disney creative head Jeffrey Katzenberg, made great animated cartoons of its own. Moreover, the **scarcity** of the resource declined as many other entertainment giants, like Sony and Warner, realizing the profit that animated cartoons could earn when synergistically marketed across multiple media formats, started their own production companies. The result was a proliferation of cartoons, where previously Disney had the market

to itself. Worse still, animated cartoons were **substituted** by a new technology—computer-generated graphics. This technology allowed for much cheaper and higher-quality graphics with far more realism. Such hits as *Toy Story* and *Finding Nemo,* which generated much higher box office sales than any Disney cartoon, although distributed by Disney, were actually developed by Pixar. Finally, some of the profit that Disney made from cartoons was **appropriated** by the animators themselves. The boom in cartoon production by Disney and its competitors raised demand for skilled animators. They quickly became in short supply because of the years taken to train them as well as the requirement for innate talent. At one time, Disney employed several thousand animators at salaries of close to $1/4 million each.

Unfortunately for Disney, the shrinkage in value of its critical resource created a threat to the continued independent existence of the company itself.

others have a capacity that varies according to how they are used. A stamping machine, for example, has a finite capacity, whereas a brand name or a company's reputation is not bounded in the same way.

It is also important to distinguish between short- and long-term capacity. If a firm's competitive advantage from a resource is to be maintained, the resource itself must not deteriorate and disappear. Only then can resources carry over between periods and so support long-lived strategic asymmetries.

Resources accumulate *and decay* at different rates. Clearly, the slower the rate of depreciation, the more valuable the resource. Although physical resources, like oil reserves, deplete as they are used, calculating their precise decay rates may nonetheless be difficult. The task is even more onerous when dealing with intangible resources. Economists have traditionally assigned annual decay rates of .3 and .1, respectively, to a firm's investments in advertising and R&D. In practice, however, judging the **durability** of intangible resources is extraordinarily difficult because their longevity depends heavily on how they are cultivated and on how market demand evolves. The Disney brand, for example, thrived for decades, often of benign neglect, whereas the value of technological knowledge can depreciate rapidly, as the success of different firms in each new generation of semiconductor memories illustrates.

Resources also differ greatly in **specificity.** Some can be used in a variety of applications, and some in only one. Highly fungible resources, such as cash, multipurpose machinery, and general management skills, can be extended across a wide range of markets. More specialized resources, such as expertise in narrow scientific disciplines and secret product formulas, tend to have only limited applications. Consider, for example, the very successful British extermination company, Rentokil. As the firm expanded into plant and garden care, it found itself suddenly burdened by its highly recognizable brand name (read "Rent-to-Kill") to such an extent that it had to change the corporate name. To be the basis for a diversified firm, resources must be fungible to some degree, but specific enough to provide a meaningful advantage in the settings in which they are applied.

▲ Economic Rent

Ultimately the resource-based view argues that all profits can be attributed to the ownership of a scarce resource. Economists interpret these profits as rents accruing to a factor that is in short supply.[29] However, they make an important distinction between two types of economic rent:[30]

- **Ricardian** or **scarcity rents** are due to valuable factors that are inherently in limited supply. Ricardian rents are due to scarcity.

- **Schumpeterian** or **entrepreneurial rents** are earned by innovators and occur during the period of time between the introduction of an innovation and its successful diffusion. It is expected that innovations, in time, will be imitated, but until that occurs, the innovator will earn Schumpeterian rents.

[29] See, for example, the textbook treatment in H.R. Varian, *Microeconomics Analysis* (New York: Norton, 1978).

[30] Some very insightful articles have been written on strategy, resources, and economic rents. See, for example, K. Conner, "A Historical Comparison of Resource-Based Theory and Five Schools of Thought within Industrial Organization: Do We Have a New Theory of the Firm?" *Journal of Management,* 1991, pp. 333–87; M.A. Peteraf, "The Cornerstones of Competitive Advantage: A Resource-Based View," *Strategic Management Journal,* 1993, pp. 179–91; R. Rumelt, "Theory, Strategy, and Entrepreneurship," and Sidney Winter, "Four Rs of Profitability: Rents, Resources, Routines and Replication," in *Resource-Based and Evolutionary Theories of the Firm: Towards a Synthesis,* ed. C.A. Montgomery (Boston: Kluwer Academic Publishers, 1995), pp. 147–78. These articles also identify "monopoly rents," which accrue to a sole producer that artificially restricts output. While a useful distinction, the question still remains whether the monopoly position is short term or long lived— whether it is due to scarce factors that earn Ricardian or Schumpeterian rents.

The important distinction between the two types is that Ricardian rents are long-lived and Schumpeterian rents are not. Ricardian rents are due to factors that are difficult or impossible to imitate, such as unique geographic locations, complex organizational routines, or long-standing corporate reputations. Schumpeterian rents, on the other hand, are due to innovations that, ultimately, will be imitated.

These issues raise a number of fundamental questions for managers. First, assuming a firm is earning economic rent, to what is it due? Second, are the factors more Ricardian or Schumpeterian in nature? Are they the result of an innovation that, with a certain amount of time, competitors will be able to imitate, or is there something about them that makes them inherently difficult to reproduce? Further, is it likely that competitors will introduce innovations that will reduce the value of the resource? When is that likely to occur?

The Sting of Schumpeterian Competition

When the resource-based view was first introduced, the immediate focus was on Ricardian rents and on the kind of resources that generate vast amounts of value over extended periods of time. Not surprisingly, it was soon recognized that while such resources are of critical importance, they are, in fact, relatively rare. Many more resources, and the competitive advantages they confer, are Schumpeterian in nature and can better be described as matters of time and degree (see "Creative Destruction: Inventors, Innovators, and Imitators").

Geoff Waring dramatically illustrated this point in his study of firm-level deviations from industry average profitability (Figure 2.5). Although industries differed somewhat in their speed of convergence, Waring's large sample analysis revealed a remarkable movement to the mean over a six-year period.

Most firms are engaged in a never-ending struggle for competitive advantage. They cannot merely sit back and collect rents from resources that will effortlessly retain their value. Indeed, most strategies and the resources that support them are under intense competitive pressure from imitators and innovators that will in time erode their value. An excellent example of the dynamic between incumbents and innovators can be found in the hard disk drive industry, where technology changes so rapidly that success in serving an existing customer base can contribute, paradoxically, to failure in the more strategic arena of conceiving and identifying new applications and new markets.[31] Given these threats, managers are well advised to conceive of strategies for confronting the eventual sting of Schumpeterian competition. Their responsibility is to cultivate their firms' current interests while acting today to secure future rent streams.

[31] C. Christensen, *The Innovator's Dilemma* (Boston: HBS Press, 1997).

Creative Destruction: Inventors, Innovators, and Imitators

Joseph A. Schumpeter, an economist working in the first half of the 20th century, believed strongly that economic life had to be seen as a dynamic process. He distinguished among three important economic functions: **invention**, wherein a novel idea, or model for a new product or process, was developed; **innovation,** wherein that product was commercialized; and, **diffusion**, where competitors successfully imitated the innovation.

Of these, Schumpeter believed the innovator, or entrepreneur, played a particularly important role in economic development. As described by Arnold Heertje, "The gifted few, pioneering in the field of new technologies, new products, and new markets, carry out innovations and, joined some time later by many imitators, they are at the heart of the short and long cycles observed in economic life."*

Schumpeter recognized that entrepreneurs, and innovation, could be found in organizations of any size, not just start-up ventures. They were the people who first gathered the resources to bring an invention, whether a widget or an organizational form, to market, not the inventors. They were also the ones who created profits, not the risk-bearers who provided the necessary capital.

Schumpeter used the term *creative destruction* to describe the life cycle of innovations. In this dynamic perspective, new innovations drive out old ones, and in the process sweep away resources, firms, professions, and the profits of the previous entrepreneurs. Thus, profits ebb and flow in a continual cycle, peaking during the period of innovation and declining, first as imitation becomes widespread, and then as a new innovation is pioneered.

* *The New Palgrave: A Dictionary of Economics* (London: Macmillan Press Limited, 1987), p. 264.

FIGURE 2.5
Convergence of Firm-Specific Rents

Source: Geoff Waring, "Industry Differences in the Persistence of Firm-Specific Returns," *American Economic Review,* Vol. 86, No. 5, December 1996, pp. 1253–65. Used by permission.

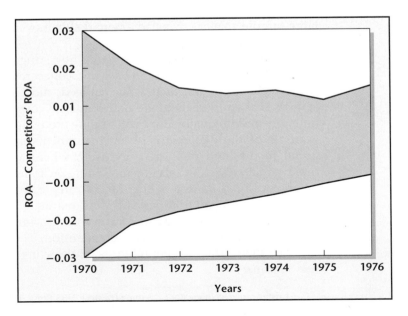

Practice

▲ Resource-Based Strategy

A prime responsibility of management is to formulate a strategy that will develop the resources that underpin performance at both the business unit and the corporate level. This involves identifying, investing in, upgrading, and leveraging a set of valuable resources (see Figure 2.6).

Identification of Valuable Resources

To craft a resource-based strategy, a firm must first identify and evaluate its resources to determine those on which it should base its future competitive (and/or corporate) advantage. This process involves defining the set of resources the firm possesses, and then applying the tests laid out in the principles section to determine which of those (if any) are truly valuable.

The first step in this process is to **inventory** the firm's resources. Typically, this can be achieved by inquiring of senior executives what they view as core competences or sources of competitive advantage for the business. The list of ideas generated can then be categorized according to three types of resource identified above, and extended by determining how those categories apply in the business under investigation.

The second step is to **assess the value** of each of those resources according to the three tests of competitive superiority, scarcity, and appropriability. Often answering the first of these tests is the most important and most difficult because the other two tests are typically more obvious or less controversial. The preferred method for determining whether a firm's resource is competitively superior is to directly link the resource to a flow measure of competitive advantage as in the example of Wal-Mart in

FIGURE 2.6   **Current Assessment Resource Value**

	Disadvantaged	Competitively Equal	Valuable
Critical to competitive advantage			
Real estate location	x		
Rapid product development			x
Necessary to compete			
Merchandising displays		o	
Friendly customer service	x		
Required but not competitively important			
IT platform		o	
Supply chain management	o		

x = invest, o = maintain.

Figure 2.3. A valuable resource will generate a demonstrable advantage in the product market, and the challenge is to find that connection. When there is no direct link between a resource and a P&L flow measure, it is still necessary to quantitatively prove superiority. If, for example, the resource is a capability to perform an activity faster or at higher quality, data need to be collected that show the firm does indeed have faster product development times than competitors, or that its objectively assessed quality is higher.

In all of these assessment exercises, the emphasis should be on linking the internal and the external environments. Resource analysis is not the inward-looking "navel contemplating" exercise that too many "core competence" retreats degenerate into. These can always identify some core competences, since by definition every firm does some activities relatively better than all the other activities they perform. Unfortunately, such competences are not valuable resources. Rather the audit should realistically confront a firm's resources against the external competitive environment. The harsh truth of many such exercises is that the firm does not possess any valuable resources. After all, the majority of firms are not market leaders with sustainable competitive advantages.

Once the audit of the firm's current resources has been completed, the process turns to identifying **gaps** in the current complement of resources. This can be achieved by asking what resources will be needed in the future to fulfill the strategic goals set for the organization. The forward-looking exercise works from an analysis of the industry in five to seven years' time, to highlight the capabilities necessary for success in that future scenario. A matrix can then be constructed (Figure 2.6) that maps the current position of the firm against the strategic importance of each resource. Resources where the firm is currently disadvantaged but are critical to success or necessary to compete are then highlighted as requiring investment, along with those valuable resources that must underpin future competitive advantage.

In this process, it is important that the firm finds the appropriate level at which to **disaggregate its resources.** Broad categorizations of competences are typically far less helpful than more disaggregated ones that can be directly related to flow measures of competitive advantage. (Figure 2.7 provides such an example.)

Saying that a consumer packaged goods company has good marketing skills, for example, conveys almost no worthwhile information. But dividing marketing skills into subcategories such as brand management that, in turn, can be divided into product-line extensions and cost-effective couponing allows for **data-driven analysis** of whether the firm truly possesses competitive superiority on these dimensions. Evaluating whether Kraft Foods or Unilever has better consumer marketing skills may be impossible, but analyzing which is more successful at launching product-line extensions is feasible.

FIGURE 2.7
Whitbread
Restaurants'
Resources

Source: Reprinted from
Strategic Synergy, by Andrew
Campbell and Kathleen
Luchs, p. 185, copyright
1992, with permission from
Elsevier.

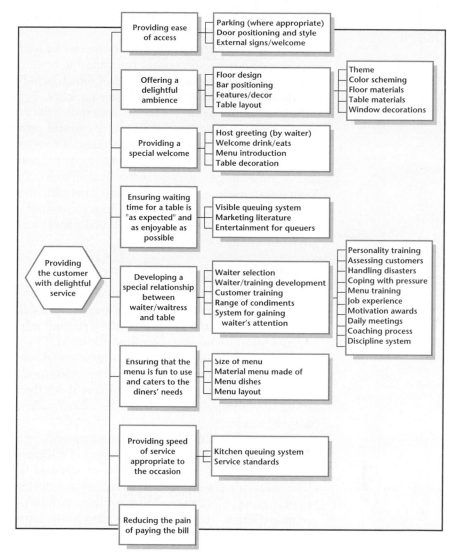

Disaggregation is also necessary when developing implications for action. One manufacturer of medical diagnostics test equipment initially defined its core competence as instrumentation. Unfortunately, this intuitively obvious definition was too broad to act upon. By pushing to deeper levels of disaggregation, the company came to a powerful insight: its strength in instrumentation was mainly attributable to its competitive superiority in designing the human/machine interface. As a result, the firm decided to hire ergonomists to reinforce that valuable capability and to design a product for the faster-growing doctors' office market where the equipment would be operated by medical staff members who were not skilled technicians.

Although disaggregation can be the key to identifying competitively superior resources, sometimes the valuable resource may be a combination of assets and capabilities, none of which is individually superior, but which when combined make a better package. For example, none of the individual components in a Honeywell industrial automation system may be highly distinctive, but the company can still provide a superior overall system. This implies that the firm's competitive superiority lies either in the weighted average (although the company doesn't rank first in any resource, on average it may be better than other competitors) or in the company's systems integration capability. This conclusion may be correct, but it should be reached only after careful scrutiny, not instinctively jumped to as a means of short-circuiting a detailed analysis of the individual disaggregated resources.

Investing in Resources

Because all resources depreciate, an effective corporate strategy requires continuous investment to maintain and expand a firm's critical resources. Brand names age unless supported by current advertising expenditures. Technological know-how becomes outdated. Organizational capabilities grow rigid and fail to adapt.[32] These investments should focus on building and maintaining competitively superior resources. However, investments must also be made in resources which will not themselves earn economic rents, but which must nevertheless be at competitive parity to successfully implement a strategy.

Often the investment in key resources will be overseen by corporate management rather than left to divisional managers because it is so critical to the firm's performance. One of Michael Eisner's first actions as CEO of Disney, for example, was to reassert the company's commitment to animation. He invested $50 million in *Roger Rabbit*, making it the company's first animated feature film hit in many years, and quadrupled the output of animated feature films to one a year—generating successive hits like *Beauty and the Beast, Aladdin,* and *The Lion King.* These rebuilt the Disney brand name and reestablished its competitive superiority with new generations of children and parents. In contrast, Edward Brennan of Sears attempted to build a host of new businesses around its core retailing operations, while failing to reinvest to maintain the health of the core itself.

Importantly, the rents a firm expects to accrue to the resources in which it is investing must not be **dissipated** in a competitive struggle to acquire

---

[32] Dorothy Leonard-Barton suggested how core capabilities through time can become core rigidities, "Core Capabilities and Core Rigidities: A Paradox in Managing New Product Development," *Strategic Management Journal,* 1992, pp. 111–25.

them. If many firms see the value in a particular resource, in a reasonably efficient market the price of that resource should reflect its demand. For example, one would not expect any firm bidding for oil reserves to acquire them at below market value unless it was lucky or had private information concerning their value.[33] It may seem that the problem goes away when resources are accumulated internally. However, even when resources such as organizational capabilities are built through internal investments, the profits from them will, in part, depend on the number of competitors that have made similar investments. If many companies develop the same logistics capability, on average none will earn a substantial return on that resource investment.

Investment, then, requires careful analysis of a firm's strategic position, and likely competitor investments.[34] As this suggests, choosing which resources to invest in is not a straightforward exercise. It actually raises two of the most difficult trade-offs firms have to face. These are the choices between continuity and adaptability, and between commitment and flexibility.[35]

Continuity and Adaptability   When a firm's current resources and those required for future competitive success appear to differ, its management faces a dilemma. Does it stick with the historic resources that have served the firm well in the past, but which may be substituted by other resources or other strategies in the future? Or does it elect to alter its strategy and develop different resources? Or does it choose an intermediate path of wait and see, holding back from investing in either set of resources until the uncertainty has been resolved?

Many firms have faced this quandary. For example, should Sotheby's have adopted the online auction format to block eBay's growth? Or was the firm correct not to follow the example of Kodak, which struggled to develop a new set of resources to accommodate what it saw in the 1990s as a shift from film to digital imaging?

Although investing in resources that were valuable historically is easy to justify as the continuation of a successful strategy, the risk is that the investment will lock the firm into an increasingly unfavorable position. Investing in new resources, however, is also risky because it can involve a fundamental change in the organization with no guarantees that the new strategy will be a success; plus, there are the possible costs of cannibalizing existing profitable sales.

For managers, giving up what has worked well in the past for the uncertain possibility of future success from a different strategy can be very

---

[33] Jay Barney made this point in "Strategic Factor Markets: Expectations, Luck and Business Strategy," *Management Science,* 1986, pp. 1231–41.
[34] The asymmetry among firms' existing resources is the primary reason all profits are not dissipated in the struggle to acquire resources, even when their value is common knowledge.
[35] For a thorough treatment of these issues, see Ghemawat, *Commitment.*

difficult. As a consequence, the change is often made too late, when a crisis, brought about by the imminent failure of the original strategy, triggers dramatic action.

Commitment and Flexibility   Many firms solve the dilemma of choosing between stability and change by avoiding commitments to either strategy. Instead of making resource investments that commit them to either strategy, they try to remain sufficiently flexible to be able to choose whichever strategy turns out to be correct at a later date.[36] Although firms should avoid commitments that can economically be deferred, the choice between commitment and flexibility often involves a fundamental trade-off that cannot be avoided and has no general solution.

By committing to a strategy and making irreversible resource investments to support it, a firm is locked into that strategy. This is dangerous if there is uncertainty as to whether or not the strategy is appropriate. But not making the investment is also dangerous because it carries with it the threat of being locked out. By not investing, the firm allows others to preempt it, or, if there are strong path dependencies and the firm fails to make early investments, it may not be able to make later ones. Further, many resources require ongoing investment to stay viable. Once a firm stops a research program, for example, it may be very difficult to restart it later.[37] Similarly, failing to maintain customer relations can make it prohibitively expensive to reenter an industry.

As wrenching as these dilemmas may sound, it is important to recognize the role uncertainty plays in creating opportunities for strategic gain. If all decisions were made with perfect information from the start, strategies would tend to converge and excess returns might not be possible. Although it is popular to fret about strategic uncertainty, doing so must not obscure its powerful role in creating strategic asymmetries and competitive advantage.[38]

Upgrading Resources

When approached with the kind of systematic rigor implied by the tests described above, the resources of many firms will fail to make the grade. The tests of value are strenuous, and few firms that apply them rigorously will be able to demonstrate conclusively that their resources pass with

---

[36] Ibid.

[37] Wesley M. Cohen and D. Levinthal, "Absorptive Capacity: A New Perspective on Learning and Innovation," *Administrative Science Quarterly,* March 1990, pp. 128–52.

[38] Jay Barney, "Strategic Factor Markets," addressed the role of expectations and luck in business strategy. P.J. Schoemaker, "Strategy, Complexity, and Economic Rent," *Management Science,* October 1990, pp. 1178–92; and R. Amit and P.J. Schoemaker, "Strategic Assets and Organizational Rent," *Strategic Management Journal,* 1993, pp. 33–46, also provide compelling accounts of the dilemma.

flying colors. For these firms, doing more of what they are already doing is unlikely to be a sufficient plan for superior performance.

Even those few firms that do possess "crown jewels" have to recognize that the twin threats of Schumpeterian competition—imitation and substitution—make most competitive advantages, and the value of the resources on which they are based, temporary. This challenges firms to struggle ceaselessly to upgrade their resources in a race that has no finish line, or else risk being overwhelmed in the "gale of creative destruction" that Schumpeter described so well.

The quality of a firm's resource base can be upgraded in a number of ways, including: **strengthening existing resources** by increasing their quality; **adding complementary resources** that enhance the firm's position in its existing markets; and **developing new resources** that enable the firm to enter new, more attractive industries.

The Ford Motor Company provides an excellent example of a company that has deliberately moved to strengthen its organizational capabilities in the last decade. Through concerted effort, the firm has made dramatic improvements in quality control and customer service. This was done by reengineering these functions, changing organizational routines, and resetting measurement yardsticks. Intel, on the other hand, added a further resource, brand identity, to its corporate arsenal: "Intel Inside" was intended to complement the firm's technological base and provide an added degree of protection now that competitors, such as AMD and Cyrix, imitated its technology, and others, such as Motorola, used substitute technology.

Upgrading resources is often best done internally. Attempting to acquire the desired resources in a market transaction would generally involve purchasing an entire business, parts of which the firm may have no interest in. Moreover, in an aggressive market for corporate control, unless the company can bring something unique to an acquisition, it is difficult to avoid dissipating the profits it would hope to eventually earn from those resources.

In contrast, if an incremental strategy to upgrade resources takes on a single challenge each time, while otherwise drawing on existing corporate resources, it can become a remorseless and relatively low risk process of improvement. Nucor, a successful U.S. steel company, provides an instructive example of a firm that has done this (see Figure 2.8).[39] In the 1960s, Nucor was a small manufacturer of steel joints. Intent on diversifying out of a very competitive industry, it decided to invest in the new steel minimill technology. Continually improving its manufacturing capabilities as it accumulated experience and opened additional minimills, Nucor was a major player in bar steel by the mid-1980s. As that market became

[39] Pankaj Ghemawat and Henricus J. Standler, III, "Nucor at a Crossroads," Howard Business School case number 9-793-039.

FIGURE 2.8
Nucor Steel

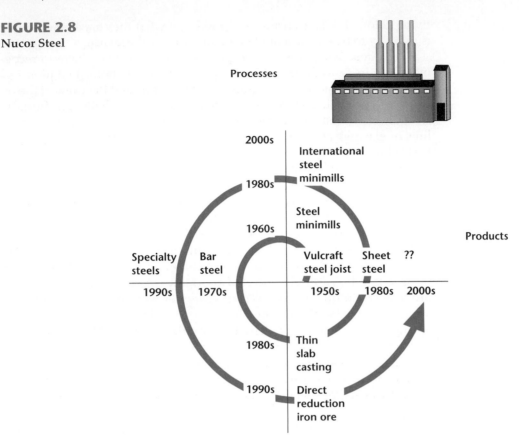

saturated, Nucor decided to apply its new-found continuous process skills to commercialize a new technology: continuous thin slab casting. Success with this technology enabled Nucor to enter the sheet steel market. Its next challenge was to diversify geographically, which it accomplished by opening a joint venture minimill in Southeast Asia. It then took its skill in international management and invested in a Jamaican plant for the direct reduction of iron ore. At each stage, Nucor leveraged its existing capabilities into a new product or process. This required it to master a new skill, which it could in turn deploy in a new product market, until it became a global leader in the steel industry.

Leveraging Resources

When a firm is not fully employing its valuable resources in its existing markets, the last step in a resource-based strategy is to leverage those underutilized resources into other segments or industries where they may create value. Failure to do so may well mean that firm value is not being maximized. In many analysts' view, this was the situation at the Walt

Disney Company in the years following Walt's death. Not surprisingly, the company was made a takeover target by investors who recognized its unrealized potential.

The leveraging of resources into new markets changes the scope of the firm and represents a transition from business-level to corporate strategy. This critical step is the focus of the next two chapters.

Recommended Readings

Amit, R., and P.J. Schoemaker. "Strategic Assets and Organizational Rent." *Strategic Management Journal,* 1993, pp. 33–46.

Barney, J.B. "Organizational Culture: Can It Be a Source of Sustained Competitive Advantage?" *Academy of Management Review,* 1986, pp. 656–65.

Barney, J.B. "Strategic Factor Markets: Expectations, Luck, and Business Strategy." *Management Science,* 1986, pp. 1231–41.

Barney, J.B. "Firm Resources and Sustained Competitive Advantage." *Journal of Management,* 1991, pp. 99–120.

Brandenburger, A., and B. Nalebuff. *Coopetition.* New York: Doubleday, 1998.

Brandenburger, A., and G. Stuart. "Value Based Strategy." *Journal of Economics and Management Strategy,* Vol. 5, No. 1, Spring 1996, pp. 5–24.

Christensen, C. *The Innovator's Dilemma.* Boston: Harvard Business School Press, 1997.

Collis, D.J. "How Valuable Are Organizational Capabilities?" *Strategic Management Journal,* 1994, pp. 143–52.

Collis, D.J., and Cynthia A. Montgomery. "Competing on Resources: Strategy in the 1990s." *Harvard Business Review,* 1995, pp. 118–28.

Conner, K. "A Historical Comparison of Resource-Based Theory and Five Schools of Thought within Industrial Organization: Do We Have a New Theory of the Firm?" *Journal of Management,* 1991, pp. 333–87.

Dierickx, I., and K. Cool. "Asset Stock Accumulation and Sustainability of Competitive Advantage." *Management Science,* 1989, pp. 1504–11.

Ghemawat, P. *Commitment.* New York: Free Press, 1991.

Leonard-Barton, D. "Core Capabilities and Core Rigidities: A Paradox in Managing New Product Development." *Strategic Management Journal,* 1992, pp. 111–25.

Lippman, S.A., and R.P. Rumelt. "The Payments Perspective: Micro Foundations of Reserve Analysis." *Strategic Management Journal,* Vol. 24, October 2003, pp. 903–28.

Lippman, S.A., and R.P. Rumelt. "A Bargaining Perspective on Resource Advantage." *Strategic Management Journal,* Vol. 24, November 2003, pp. 1069–86.

Peteraf, M.A. "The Cornerstones of Competitive Advantage: A Resource-Based View." *Strategic Management Journal,* 1993, pp. 179–91.

Porter, M.E. *Competitive Advantage*. New York: Free Press, 1985.

Prahalad, C.K., and G. Hamel. "The Core Competence of the Corporation." *Harvard Business Review*, 1990, pp. 79–91.

Rumelt, R.P. "Theory, Strategy, and Entrepreneurship." In *The Competitive Challenge*, ed. D.J. Teece. Cambridge, MA: Ballinger, 1987, pp. 137–58.

Schoemaker, P.J. "Strategy, Complexity, and Economic Rent." *Management Science*, October 1990, pp. 1178–92.

Schumpeter, J.A. *The Theory of Economic Development*. Cambridge, MA: Harvard University Press, 1934.

Teece, D.J., G. Pisano, and A. Shuen. "Dynamic Capabilities and Strategic Management." *Strategic Management Journal*, Vol. 18, No. 7, August 1997, pp. 509–33.

Wernerfelt, B. "A Resource-Based View of the Firm." *Strategic Management Journal*, 1984, pp. 171–80.

Winter, S.G. "Four Rs of Profitability: Rents, Resources, Routines and Replication." In *Resource-Based and Evolutionary Theories of the Firm: Towards a Synthesis*, ed. C.A. Montgomery. Boston: Kluwer Academic Publishers, 1995, pp. 147–78.

Winter, S.G., "Understanding Dynamic Capabilities." *Strategic Management Journal*, Vol. 24, October 2003, pp. 991–96.

Appendix B

Business Strategy and Industry Analysis

Strategy Identification

The concept of business-level strategy was first articulated in the 1960s and 1970s by a number of business policy scholars.[1] Central to their ideas was the notion that firms needed to adopt a unified approach to their activities and resource allocation decisions. Rather than haphazardly allowing each function to pursue its own objectives, a strategy could align all of a firm's functional policies and plans in a coherent pattern, directed toward the fulfillment of the firm's overarching objectives. The value of the strategy, then, would come from eliminating inconsistencies in behavior and making the firm's activities mutually reinforcing.

This notion was depicted in what came to be called the **strategy wheel.** The hub of the wheel was the vision for the firm and the competitive advantage that it sought to achieve. The spokes of the wheel represented the policies and plans of the separate functions. As in a wheel, these emanated from, and were aligned by, the hub. (See Figure B.1).

For a business, defining what is at the hub of its strategy wheel is clearly the most critical part of strategy formulation. To do this—to identify the vision and competitive advantage the firm will pursue, it is necessary to carefully match the

[1] For example, see E.P. Learned, C. Roland Christensen, and Kenneth Andrews, *Business Policy: Text and Cases* (Burr Ridge, IL: Irwin, 1965); H. Igor Ansoff, *Corporate Strategy: An Analytical Approach to Business Policy for Growth and Expansion* (New York: McGraw-Hill, 1965).

FIGURE B.1
The Strategy Wheel

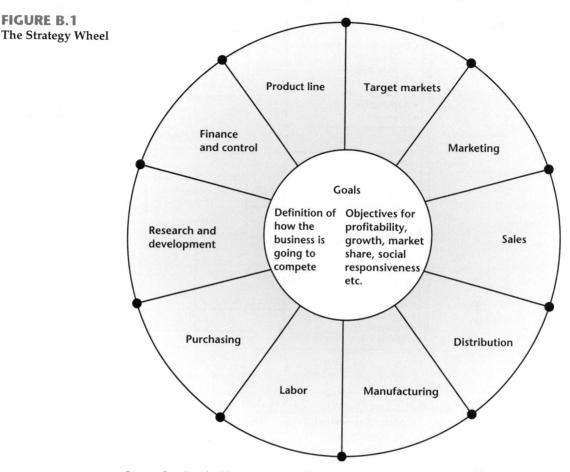

Source: Reprinted with permission of The Free Press, a Division of Simon & Schuster Adult Publishing Group, from Competitive Strategy: Techniques for Analyzing Industries and Competitors by Michael E. Porter. Copyright © 1980, 1988 by The Free Press. All rights reserved.

company's (**S**)trengths and (**W**)eaknesses to the (**O**)pportunities and (**T**)hreats presented by its environment (see Figure B.2). This approach, called **SWOT**, still underlies many contemporary approaches to strategic planning.

The central concept here is the notion of *fit* between the unique capabilities of a company and the competitive requirements of an industry. The challenge for management is to choose or create a market position where the company's distinctive competence and resources could produce a competitive advantage.

Industry Analysis

When an industry with a reputation for difficult economics meets a manager with a reputation for excellence, it is usually the industry that keeps its reputation intact.

Warren Buffet

A rigorous examination of a firm's external environment was systematized in the methodology of

FIGURE B.2
SWOT Analysis

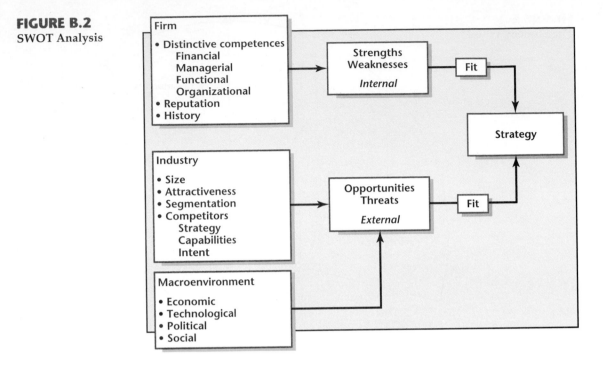

industry analysis.[2] Careful industry analysis can help establish whether a particular industry is likely to prove attractive to the average competitor; it can also shed light on profit differences among the competitors in that industry. More broadly, industry analysis illuminates the competitive landscape in a way that aids the formulation of effective strategies.

The methodology is most often used to assess the prospects for long-run average industry profitability. As Figure B.3 shows, this can vary widely across industries. A substantial amount of research indicates that the profit potential of an industry is bounded by basic conditions that are largely exogenous, such as the price elasticity of demand and the production technology. The extent to which such profit potential is actually realized by the in-

dustry then depends on its internal structure, such as its concentration level, and on the strategies adopted by competitors.

By far the most popular application of these ideas is Michael Porter's "five forces" framework for assessing average industry profitability (see Figure B.4).

THE DEGREE OF RIVALRY

The intensity of rivalry is the most obvious of the five forces in an industry, and the one that strategists have focused on historically. The structural determinants of the degree of rivalry in an industry are numerous. One set of conditions concerns the number and relative size of competitors. The more concentrated the industry, for example, the more likely it is that competitors will recognize their mutual interdependence and so restrain their rivalry. The presence of a dominant competitor rather than a set of equally balanced competitors also tends to lessen rivalry because the dominant player can set industry prices and discipline

[2] Substantial portions of this appendix draw on D. Collis and P. Ghemawat, "Industry Analysis: Understanding Industry Structure and Dynamics," in *The Portable MBA in Strategy,* ed. L. Fahey and R.M. Randall (New York: Wiley & Sons, 1994), pp. 171–94.

FIGURE B.3
Profitability by
Manufacturing
Subsector,
1971–1990.

	Return on Equity	Return on Assets	Return on Sales
Drugs	21.4 %	11.8%	13.1%
Printing and publishing	15.5	7.1	5.5
Food and kindred products	15.2	6.6	3.9
Chemicals and allied products	15.1	7.5	7.2
Petroleum and allied products	13.1	6.5	6.5
Instruments and related products	12.9	7.2	6.9
Industrial chemicals and synthetics	12.9	6.2	6.1
Paper and allied products	12.5	6.0	5.1
Aircraft, guided missiles, and parts	12.4	4.1	3.7
Fabricated metal products	12.3	5.7	3.7
Motor vehicles and equipment	11.6	5.6	3.7
Rubber and misc. plastic products	11.6	5.1	3.4
Electric and electronic equipment	11.5	5.4	4.4
Machinery, except electrical	11.1	5.8	3.4
Stone, clay, and glass products	10.4	4.8	4.0
Textile mill products	9.3	4.3	2.5
Nonferrous metals	8.3	3.9	3.6
Iron and steel	3.9	1.5	1.3

Source: Reprinted from "Selected Profitability Data on US Industries and Companies," by Anita McGahan, HBS case number 9-792-066. Used by permission of Harvard Business School Publishing Corporation; all rights reserved.

defectors. In contrast, equally sized players often compete vigorously to outdo each other and gain advantage.

A second set of attributes that influence rivalry is related to the industry's basic conditions. In capital-intensive industries, for example, low levels of capacity utilization encourage firms to engage in price competition to fill their plants. More generally, high fixed costs, excess capacity, slow growth, and lack of product differentiation all increase the degree of rivalry.

The degree of rivalry also has behavioral determinants. If competitors have diverse objectives or attach high strategic stakes to their positions in an industry, they are likely to compete aggressively. For example, Cummins Engine, a firm with strong family roots that specializes in diesel engines for trucks, unilaterally cut prices almost in half in the early 1980s to stop Japanese competitors from getting market share, even though this condemned the industry to negative average profitability for nearly a decade.

THE THREAT OF ENTRY

The key concept in analyzing the threat of entry is entry barriers, which act to prevent an influx of firms into an industry whenever profits, adjusted for the cost of capital, rise above zero. In the restaurant industry, for example, if a new format such as mesquite grilling becomes popular, the limited height of entry barriers allows almost any interested party to open a mesquite grill restaurant, eroding the format's profitability. In contrast, entry barriers exist whenever it is difficult or uneconomic for an outsider to replicate the position of the incumbents.

Figure B.4 illustrates that entry barriers can take many different forms. Some barriers reflect intrinsic physical or legal obstacles to entry. It would probably be hard to discover a diamond mine rich enough to justify entry into the diamond industry. Similarly, the existence and efficacy of patents on aspartame (Nutrasweet) and other artificial sweeteners impeded entry into that industry until these patents expired.

FIGURE B.4
Elements of
Industry Structure

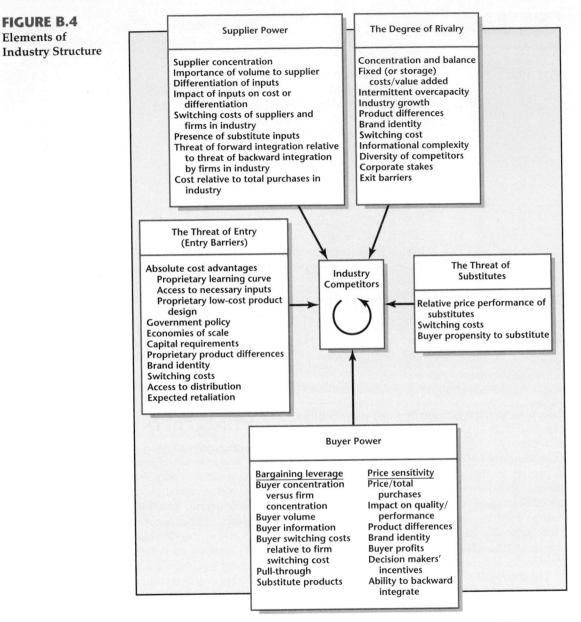

Supplier Power

Supplier concentration
Importance of volume to supplier
Differentiation of inputs
Impact of inputs on cost or
  differentiation
Switching costs of suppliers and
  firms in industry
Presence of substitute inputs
Threat of forward integration relative
  to threat of backward integration
  by firms in industry
Cost relative to total purchases in
  industry

The Degree of Rivalry

Concentration and balance
Fixed (or storage)
  costs/value added
Intermittent overcapacity
Industry growth
Product differences
Brand identity
Switching cost
Informational complexity
Diversity of competitors
Corporate stakes
Exit barriers

**The Threat of Entry
(Entry Barriers)**

Absolute cost advantages
  Proprietary learning curve
  Access to necessary inputs
  Proprietary low-cost product
    design
Government policy
Economies of scale
Capital requirements
Proprietary product differences
Brand identity
Switching costs
Access to distribution
Expected retaliation

**Industry
Competitors**

**The Threat of
Substitutes**

Relative price performance of
  substitutes
Switching costs
Buyer propensity to substitute

Buyer Power

Bargaining leverage	Price sensitivity
Buyer concentration versus firm concentration	Price/total purchases
Buyer volume	Impact on quality/performance
Buyer information	Product differences
Buyer switching costs relative to firm switching cost	Brand identity
Pull-through	Buyer profits
Substitute products	Decision makers' incentives
	Ability to backward integrate

The most common entry barriers, however, involve the scale and the investment required to enter an industry as an efficient competitor. For example, no one is likely to enter the aluminum industry on an integrated basis, because an efficient integrated facility would cost several billion dollars and account for 5 percent or more of worldwide demand. Similarly, when incumbent firms have well-established brand names and clearly differentiated products, it may be prohibitively expensive for a potential entrant to undertake the marketing campaign necessary for effective introduction of a competing product.

THE THREAT OF SUBSTITUTES

The existence of substitutes that perform the same functions as the products or services of the industry being analyzed caps the amount of value an industry can create. When high-fructose corn syrup (HFCS) was replacing sugar as the sweetener in soft drinks, Pepsi and Coca-Cola were willing to switch when the cost of the HFCS needed to sweeten a can of cola fell below the cost of sugar. The availability of HFCS as a substitute therefore constrained the market price of sugar.

The analysis of the threat of demand-side substitution must focus on the customer function performed, not just on physically similar products. Overnight delivery services, which provide rapid document delivery, must consider facsimile machines to be an important substitute, even though the two use entirely different means to achieve the same end.

BUYER POWER

Buyer power allows customers to squeeze industry margins by pressing competitors to reduce prices or to increase the level of service offered without recompense.

Probably the most important determinant of buyer power is the size and concentration of the customers. In its heyday, for example, General Motors (GM) enjoyed enormous bargaining power because it dominated the automobile industry; it regularly threatened its component suppliers with loss of its business. Those suppliers, desperate to avoid losing such a large fraction of their business, often agreed to price or nonprice concessions. GM's bargaining power was also enhanced by other factors, including the extent to which it was informed about suppliers' costs, the credibility of its threat to integrate backward into suppliers' businesses, and the relatively low costs it would incur if it switched suppliers.

It is often useful to distinguish buyer power from the willingness or incentive to use that power. The U.S. government is one of the most powerful buyers in the market by virtue of its size; yet, unfortunately for U.S. taxpayers, it has not historically been one of the most price-sensitive purchasers.

It is necessary to look at a set of behavioral conditions to understand why some firms have the incentive to use their inherent purchasing power. Prime among these conditions is the share of the buyer's cost that is accounted for by the products in question. Purchasing decisions naturally focus on larger-cost items first. Suppliers of incidental products can, therefore, often escape the keenest attention of purchasing agents.

Of almost equal importance is the risk of failure associated with the use of a product. Purchase decisions for items critical to a whole system's operation, such as oil-rig blowout prevention equipment, are usually influenced by such risks of failure, which substantially reduce the buyer's price-sensitivity.

SUPPLIER POWER

Supplier power is the mirror image of buyer power. It varies with the size and concentration of suppliers relative to their customers, and with the degree of differentiation in the inputs supplied. The most profitable players involved in the personal computer (PC) industry, for example, are not the manufacturers, but the suppliers of microprocessors and operating systems, which have virtual monopolies on the supply of critical components for IBM-compatible PCs.

The acid test of supplier power is whether suppliers are able to set prices that reflect the value of their inputs to the industry and not just their own production costs. Suppliers of many commodity chemicals and other raw materials, for example, manage to pass along cost increases without necessarily possessing supplier power. Their margins may already be very low, and a price increase simply serves to keep them in business at low rates of return. What must be tested instead is whether suppliers are able to extract a substantial portion of the value created in the industries that they serve.

COMPLEMENTS

Modern analysis of industry structure considers a sixth force—complements. Complementors[3] are the opposite of substitutes in that they increase demand or customer willingness to pay for a good or service. Examples include the complementarity of the Windows operating system and Intel microprocessors, or roads and cars. A road does not buy or supply cars, or compete with cars, and yet without roads the demand for cars would be substantially lower. In many high-tech industries where standards are important and software and hardware must complement each other, strategy toward complements has become vital. Intel, for example, invests billions of dollars in entrepreneurial companies that produce high-end graphics applications that require the latest and fastest Intel chip. If these software applications were not introduced, consumers would never upgrade their PCs, since for most of us, even a 286 chip is sufficient to meet our needs for word processing, presentations, and data analysis. Complements, therefore, are key determinants of industry structure and attractiveness, and focal points for contemporary strategy.

SUMMARY

The inherent attractiveness of an industry—measured by its expected average profitability—is not determined by just one factor. Rather, it reflects the interaction of the competitive forces described above. Using the factors in Figure B.4 as a checklist to determine the strength of each of those competitive forces is, therefore, a critical part of a thorough industry analysis.

[3] The concept was introduced by Adam Brandenburger and Barry Nalebuff in A. Brandenburger and B. Nalebuff, *Coopetition* (New York: Doubleday, 1998).

Generic Strategies

To understand how to achieve a competitive advantage and how to generalize about the relative position of individual firms within an industry, Porter developed the concept of generic strategies, categories of strategy that follow particular patterns. At the business level, Porter identified two basic types of competitive advantage: **low cost and differentiation.**

For Porter, a firm with a successful low cost strategy has the ability to "design, produce, and market a comparable product more efficiently than its competitors."[4] For prices at or near those of competitors, the resulting lower cost translates into superior returns. In the 1970s, for example, Du Pont built a dominant position in the titanium dioxide market by exploiting superior technology, scale economies, and accumulated experience to achieve the low-cost position. Du Pont then nearly doubled its market share, to 60 percent, using aggressive pricing to squeeze out smaller, less efficient competitors.[5]

Differentiation is the "ability to provide unique and superior value to the buyer in terms of product quality, special features, or after-sale service."[6] Differentiation allows a firm to command a premium price, which leads to superior profitability, provided that costs are comparable to those of competitors. Gillette, for example, competes with a differentiation strategy in disposable razors by exploiting its superior technology, reputation, and broad distribution.

Although the key success factors of these strategies differ, Porter warns that "any successful strategy must pay close attention to *both* types of advantage while maintaining a clear commitment to superiority on one. A low-cost producer must offer acceptable quality and service to avoid nullifying its cost advantage through the necessity to discount prices, while a differentiator's cost position must not be so far above that of competitors as to offset its price premium."[7]

[4] M. Porter, *The Competitive Advantage of Nations* (New York: Free Press, 1990).
[5] Ghemawat, *Commitment* (New York: Free Press, 1991).
[6] M. Porter, *The Competitive Advantage of Nations.*
[7] Ibid.

FIGURE B.5
Generic Strategies

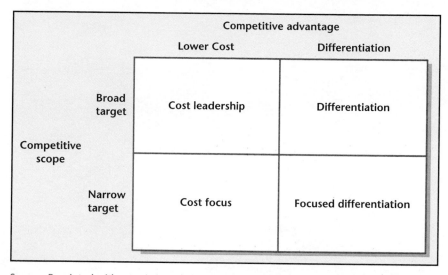

The other important aspect of strategic choice is **competitive scope,** or the breadth of segments the firm targets within its industry. Serving different segments requires different strategies and calls for different capabilities. Thus, the type and the scope of advantage can be combined into the notion of generic strategies (see Figure B.5).

In the consumer electronics industry, for example, Sony is a broad differentiator, with a well-known brand and successful history of product innovation. Bang and Olufsen, the Scandinavian firm, is a focused differentiator serving only those customers who seek modern Scandinavian design. Matsushita (which sells in the United States under the Panasonic brand) pursues a broad, low-cost strategy, aiming to match Sony's innovations within six months at lower cost. And any number

of small Chinese or Malaysian consumer electronics companies use focused, low-cost strategies, producing a limited range of cheaply manufactured items to be sold by mass merchants under private label.

Each of these strategies requires the internal alignment of a set of functional activities in support of the overall objective of the strategy. Across generic strategies, these patterns differ in predictable ways. The idea of generic strategies, therefore, underscores many of the original principles of business strategy. It emphasizes the consistency of a firm's activities and the need to tie each to the firm's overall mission. It also stresses the importance of not getting stuck in the middle—being a little of this and a little of that—and ultimately failing to build a distinctive competence that creates a competitive advantage.

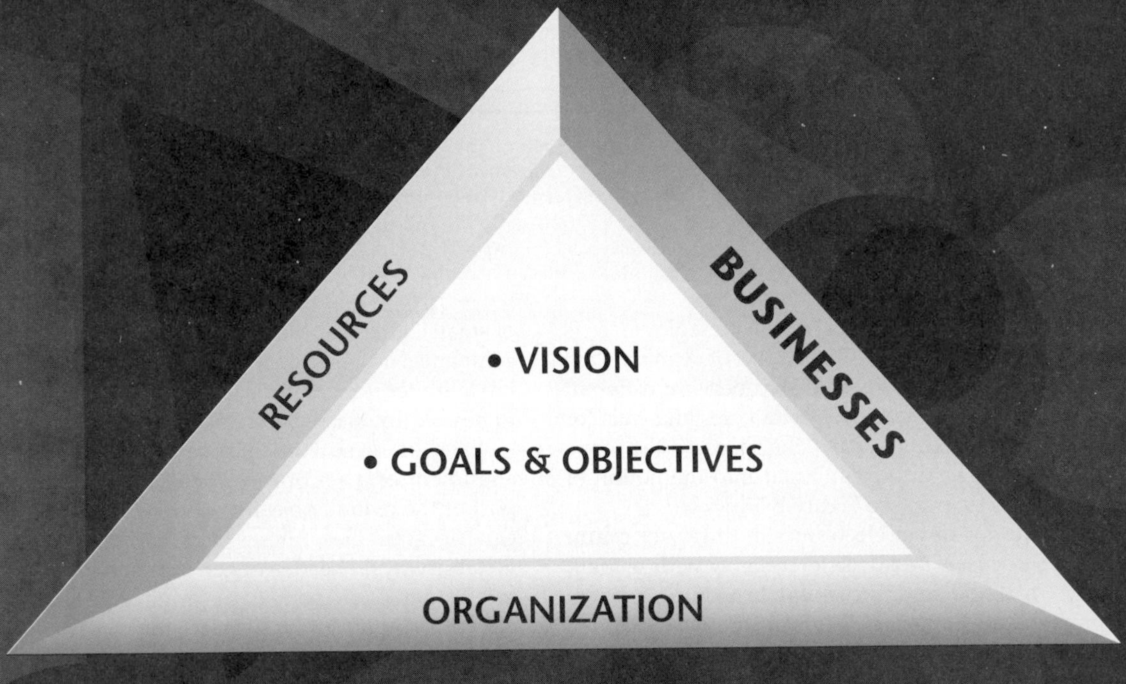
RESOURCES
BUSINESSES
• VISION
• GOALS & OBJECTIVES
ORGANIZATION

SCALE AND SCOPE WITHIN AN INDUSTRY

▲ Introduction

Once a firm has chosen a strategy within an industry and identified the valuable resources that will underpin its competitive advantage, the challenge shifts to implementing that strategy: investing in or internally accumulating the required resources and deploying them appropriately in that product market. This may take a number of years, during which time competitors will be pursuing their own strategies. In due course, as investments and other long-term commitments come to fruition, market leaders will emerge, having adopted what turn out to be the winning strategies for the industry. At this juncture, it may appear that, for the triumphant firms, the hard work is over.

On occasion this is so, and the industry proceeds with few perturbations. In such cases, resource barriers lock in competitive positions, external conditions remain stable, and the market experiences a long-term equilibrium. In most cases, however, the environment is not so placid. As Schumpeter warned, it is rare for markets to experience a long-term equilibrium with few disturbances. Firms at a competitive disadvantage will be striving to dislodge the market leader. Technology and customer tastes may change and radically alter either supply or demand conditions. Such upheavals disturb industry equilibria, create the need for new resources, and provide opportunities for competitors to craft new strategies that are better suited to the altered industry environment.

As we will discuss in this chapter, these transformations often involve the exploitation of *scale* or *scope* economies in an industry. These forces can play an important role in reconfiguring industry structure and shaping new competitive strategies.

Principles

▲ Dimensions of Scope

The principles that underlie expansion within an industry are similar to those that underlie expansion across industries, the subject of the next chapter. To grasp these ideas, it is helpful to think of the resources that support the initial business as a nucleus within a broader competitive space. Expansion, or contraction, begins from this core and proceeds along three dimensions: **geography, product market, and vertical integration** along the value chain. The scope of any firm, at any time, can be represented in these three dimensions, whether or not the firm explicitly selected that configuration (Figure 3.1).

It is important to recognize that firms must actively grapple with scope questions throughout their histories, regardless of their size or success. Microsoft's first breakthrough was as a supplier of the DOS operating system to PC manufacturers. During the eighties, it diversified into the applications software business with the introduction of Excel and Word, deepening its upstream activities in programming and extending its activities downstream by marketing directly to home users. All the while it continued to upgrade its original business, creating Windows to replace DOS and introducing operating systems for networking. In 2003, the company continued to struggle with issues of scope: backward integrating into the ownership of content for multimedia applications and the Internet, aggressively expanding overseas, and striving to add new products, such as the Xbox video game console.

Too often, firms take a narrow view of their own opportunities and fail to see alternative directions that may be available. Many costly mistakes could be avoided if firms recognize that there are three possible dimensions for expansion. Consider the example of Federal Express: instead of pouring hundreds of millions of dollars into a failed diversification for the provision of facsimile services in the early eighties, Federal Express could have

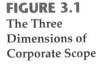
FIGURE 3.1
The Three
Dimensions of
Corporate Scope

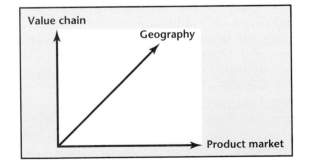

preempted competitors in the international document delivery business. Instead, when it finally did go global, Federal Express had to incur additional losses in the hundreds of millions of dollars as it struggled to catch up with the entrenched leader, DHL. Conversely, Marks & Spencer's failed 30-year attempt at international expansion seemed to blind it to valuable diversification opportunities in other retailing segments in the United Kingdom.

Expansion within an Industry

For most firms, expansion begins within their original industry,[1] by increasing the scale of output, vertically integrating, producing closely related products, or entering new geographies. Firms often pursue such expansions proactively, to increase their size and enhance their competitive positions. In other cases, the same moves are taken reactively, to defend a firm's position as others move to exploit scale and scope advantages.

The underlying scale and scope economies in an industry are often apparent to all competitors. For example, the benefits of size are well understood in oil refining.[2] In other cases, the economies may be inherent in an industry, but either not well recognized, or not exploited, because firms' attention has been elsewhere. In such situations, creative strategic moves can unlock these latent sources of advantage and dramatically alter industry dynamics. Further, new sources of scale and scope economies continually arise as economic and technological conditions change. It is therefore important for firms to continually reassess the existence of, and potential to exploit, such economies.

▲ Economies of Scale

Economies of scale exist when the average cost of producing each unit declines as more units of a good or service are produced. These economies occur in a wide range of industries and may be found in any one of a firm's activities, from research to service.

Single-site economies often occur in physical production processes and are related to the size of the manufacturing unit. When technological scale economies exist, for example, capacity can be increased at a greater rate than the associated cost of plant and equipment. The volume of liquid through a pipe, for example, is squared for each doubling in radius, while the area of material from which it is built increases only linearly. Such an

---

[1] The definition of a discrete market or industry is one of the thorniest issues in strategy (D. Abell, *Defining the Business: The Starting Point of Strategic Planning,* Englewood Cliffs, NJ: Prentice Hall, 1979). There are always some interactive effects (cross-price elasticities) among related industries. Boundaries, therefore, are ultimately defined somewhat arbitrarily, according to similarities among customers, technologies, competitors, and channels of distribution (M.E. Porter, *Competitive Strategy,* New York: Free Press, 1980.)
[2] Alfred D. Chandler, *Scale and Scope* (Cambridge, MA: Harvard University Press, 1990).

Beaten by Scale: Taxman and H&R Block in the Tax-Preparation Industry

A contrast between Taxman, Inc., a small, fledgling tax preparation company, and H&R Block illustrates the strategic significance scale effects can have in a rapidly growing service industry.

In the early 1970s, Taxman and H&R Block were competitors in the low-to-middle end of the individual tax-preparation market. Compared to Taxman's 31 offices, H&R Block had 3,286, and its total costs per return were about half of Taxman's. This discrepancy was due primarily to Block's sizeable scale advantages in office management, advertising, and quality assurance (corporate reputation and a year-round presence to stand behind the work it performed). Significantly, within individual offices and across regions, Block had the scale that was necessary to fully employ its highest paid workers. An area manager could oversee five offices, an office manager could oversee numerous tax preparers, and tax preparers could spend all their time doing tax returns, rather than waiting for business to appear or performing less critical operations such as collating and mailing the returns. (Part-time high school students did these tasks.)

As Block's business grew, these advantages increased. Profits were reinvested in the business and used to support additional growth. In time, Block had established a formidable first-mover advantage, building a scale and cost structure that proved increasingly difficult for competitors to thwart or imitate.

effect is pronounced in cement manufacturing, petroleum refining, iron ore reduction, and a host of other processing industries. Economies may also occur in other functions as fixed costs are spread across higher volumes.[3]

Importantly, scale allows specialization, which may be of considerable benefit to a firm. With higher volume production, individual employees can focus their attention on a narrower range of activities and develop or employ more specialized skills. Moreover, highly skilled and expensive labor may only be fully employed when there is sufficient scale of production.

In most industries, dominant firms operate more than one plant or establishment, suggesting there may also be important **multiple-site economies.** These are more likely to be found in R&D and marketing than in the physical production process. Examples include distribution systems and brand names that can be used to sell and distribute products and services from multiple locations. Multiple-site firms may also benefit from economies of risk-spreading and lower capital costs. Finally, larger organizations may be more successful in attracting and holding highly talented people, the cost of which can be spread across a larger volume of output. (See "Beaten by Scale.")

Scale economies in part determine the maximum number of firms that can compete profitably in an industry. When the **minimum efficient scale**

[3] F.M. Scherer, *Industrial Market Structure and Economic Performance* (Boston, MA: Houghton Mifflin, 1980), pp. 82–83.

TABLE 3.1 **A Historic View of Scale: Minimum Efficient Plant Sizes**

Source: Adapted and reprinted by permission of the publisher from *The Economics of Multi-Plant Operation: An International Comparisons Study* by F.M. Scherer, Alan Beckenstein, Erich Kaufer, R. Dennis Murphy, p. 80, 94, 208, Cambridge, Mass.: Harvard University Press, Copyright © 1975 by the President and Fellows of Harvard College.

Industry	MES Plant Size as Percentage of U.S. Consumption	Percentage Elevation of Unit Costs (at 1/3 MES)	Number of Plants Needed to Have Not More than a "Slight" Overall Handicap	Share of U.S. Market Required in 1967
Beer brewing	3.4%	5.0%	3–4	10–14%
Cigarettes	6.6	2.2	1–2	6–12
Fabric weaving	0.2	7.6	3–6	1
Paints	1.4	4.4	1	1–2
Petroleum Refining	1.9	4.8	2–3	4–6
Shoes	0.2	1.5	3–6	1
Glass bottles	1.5	11.0	3–4	4–6
Cement	1.7	26.0	1	2
Steel	2.6	11.0	1	3
Bearings	1.4	8.0	3–5	4–7
Refrigerators	14.1	6.5	4–8*	14–20
Storage batteries	1.9	4.6	1	2

*including other appliances.

(MES) of production is large in relation to demand, the industry can support relatively few players. Significant multisite economies also increase the market share each competitor must command to remain viable. Table 3.1 shows estimates of single-site and multiple-site economies in a number of industries and the required share of the U.S. market a firm would need to maintain a competitive cost structure.

Experience Curve

Whereas economies of scale refer to cost reductions that accompany increases in total current output, a related concept, the **learning,** or **experience curve,** refers to cost reductions that occur as *cumulative* volume rises. Studies have shown that average unit production costs in many industries decline 10 percent to 30 percent with each doubling of cumulated output. Figure 3.2 illustrates the phenomenon in the context of computer chip production and shows a 70 percent experience curve—costs fall to 70 percent of their previous level whenever cumulative output doubles.

Although the concept of experience curves emerged out of a manufacturing environment, it is important to note that the underlying logic is also

FIGURE 3.2
Experience Curve for Dynamic RAMs

Source: Reprinted by permission of *Harvard Business Review.* From "Building Strategy on the Experience Curve" by Pankaj Ghemawat, March–April 1985. Copyright © 1985 by the Harvard Business School Publishing Corporation; all rights reserved.

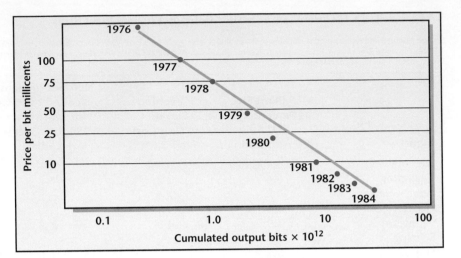

applicable to service firms (see "Saving Lives and Money"). Initially, the effect was attributed to worker learning alone. Later studies identified other factors that contributed to the experience curve, such as ongoing engineering and technical improvements. As a consequence, firms are now more likely to identify broader organizational experience curves for each of their processes.[4]

The important difference between scale and experience effects is that scale, in principle, can be quickly replicated by building a large plant, whereas experience must be built through time.[5] Thus, experience effects are classic examples of path dependency: shortcuts and speeded-up processes often fail. Experience effects also explain why it may be difficult to transfer knowledge across locations even within a firm. To the extent that competence is a function of the firsthand experience of individuals, transfers of knowledge within firms may be as difficult to achieve as those across firms.

Limits to Scale and Experience

Do costs decline indefinitely as scale and experience continue to rise? The answer to this question is no, or most industries with sizable scale or experience effects would be dominated by a single firm. Even within the range in which such effects are possible, many are not smooth functions; they occur in discrete steps, often with considerable plateaus in between. Further, physical properties often limit efficiency gains beyond certain levels. Cement kilns, for example, experience unstable internal aerodynamics

[4] D.D. Pattison and C.J. Teplitz, "Are Learning Curves Still Relevant?" *Management Accounting,* February 1989, pp. 37–40.
[5] Marvin Lieberman has systematically examined many of the issues of scale and experience within the chemical industry. "The Learning Curve and Pricing in the Chemical Processing Industries," *RAND Journal of Economics,* Summer 1984, pp. 213–28.

Saving Lives and Money: Experience and Its Impact on the Cost of Heart Transplants

In the early 1990s, a multiple regression model was used to analyze the cost patterns associated with 71 heart transplants conducted by a single institution. The model included controls for various preoperative risk factors and differences in individual surgeons' levels of experience. The model predicted that the first heart transplant would cost $81,297, but would have cost only $48,431 had it been the 10th. Had it been the 50th, the cost would have been $25,458.

More recent research shows not only that cost is reduced in hospitals that perform a high volume of a particular operation, but also that mortality rates are reduced. In some high-risk surgeries, the mortality rate is reduced by 75 percent.

Arguments had already been made in favor of concentrating certain highly specialized medical procedures in a few facilities. But these findings bolster an argument to do so based on the cost reduction and quality improvement that would result from exploiting the experience curve at a single hospital.

Source: J. Woods, "The Learning Curve and the Cost of Heart Transplants," *Health Services Research,* June 1992, pp. 219–38; and J. Birkmeyer, "Leapfrog Patients Safety Standards," *The Business Roundtable,* November 2000.

above 7 million barrels per year capacity.[6] Indeed, in most processes, **diseconomies of scale** set in at some point, and costs *rise* rather than fall as volume increases. This may be due to logistics bottlenecks, coordination costs, or worker motivation problems.

There are also strategic risks to consider. Exploiting scale economies requires considerable investment, often in specialized assets, that firms expect to recoup through cost savings that will be realized over extended periods of time. If tastes change, input prices alter, or competitive strategies shift, these sunk investments may lock a firm into an unattractive strategy and not be recovered. Henry Ford's effort to automate large-scale production of a standard Model T in the mammoth, vertically integrated River Rouge plant met this unhappy end. When customers flocked to the variety of models General Motors introduced, Ford's highly efficient but rigid production process, which (almost literally) converted iron ore and sand into a finished car, could not manufacture the kind of products customers were demanding. Ford had to shut down the plant for nearly 12 months to retool, and has never regained its leadership position in the U.S. automobile market.

Finally, it is not unusual for the magnitude of scale economies to shift over the life of an industry. As technology evolves and industries mature, scale economies often increase in many activities. However, the reverse can also happen. In the steel industry, for example, minimill technology replaced the traditional vertically integrated mills and substantially

---

[6] This example is taken from F.M. Scherer, *Industrial Market Structure and Economic Performance* (Boston: Houghton Mifflin, 1980), p. 84.

reduced industry minimum efficient scale. Moreover, these changes do not necessarily occur evenly across all the activities of a firm. Rather than leading to straightforward increases or decreases in firm size, changing scale economies may spark the reconfiguration of an industry and the emergence of specialist producers at particular stages in the vertical chain.

> *Network externalities* exist when a consumer's valuation of a product increases as more consumers buy or use the good or service.

> *Economies of scale* exist when average cost declines as a good or service is produced or sold in larger volume.

> *Economies of scope* exist when the cost of producing and selling multiple products together is lower than the cost of producing and selling the same quantity of goods individually.

▲ Economies of Scope

The size and scope of a firm is influenced not only by the scale economies of various activities, but also by the presence of **cost savings *across* functions or units.** Economies of scope exist when "it is less costly to combine two or more product lines *in one firm* than to produce them separately."[7] A classic example of scope economies is a sporting goods chain that sells ski equipment in the winter and tennis equipment in the summer, thus utilizing its physical facilities and its purchasing and sales staffs on a year-round basis.[8]

Economists traditionally believed that, to the extent they existed at all, scope economies would be found primarily in a firm's physical production processes. The notion was that a factory that made television sets might be more efficient if it also made computer monitors. This view, however, has been challenged by recent empirical work. U.S. Census Bureau data for the years 1963–82 reveal an upward trend in firm-level diversification, but a persistent decline in plant-level diversification. Examining this data, Frank Gollop and James Monahan concluded that over time, firms are "shifting toward a more diverse portfolio of increasingly homogeneous plants. Technical economies of scope appear to play little role in explaining the measured increase in [firm-level] diversification."[9]

Even though technical economies of scope are not plentiful, scope economies may be occurring in activities that are not directly related to the physical production process, including research and development,

[7] John C. Panzar and Robert D. Willig, "Economies of Scope," *American Economic Review,* May 1981, p. 268. The relationship is formally expressed as $C(x+y) < C(x) + C(y)$.
[8] Scope economies have to be distinguished from joint production. It is physically impossible to separately produce lamb and wool from sheep, or hydrogen and oxygen from the electrolysis of water. In contrast, Microsoft can choose whether or not to compete in the spreadsheet and the word processing application businesses.
[9] Frank Gollop and J. Monahan, "A Generalized Index of Diversification: Trends in U.S. Manufacturing," *Review of Economics and Statistics,* 1991, pp. 318–30.

FIGURE 3.3
The Advantage of Scope Economies

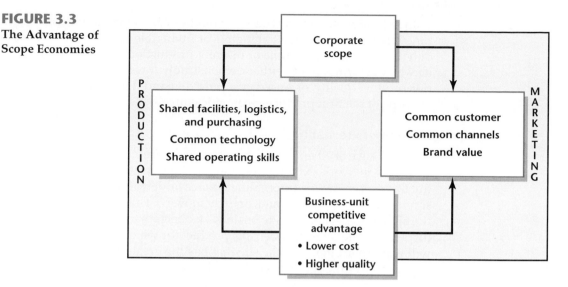

sales and marketing, distribution, transportation, and overhead.[10] When R&D, for example, generates knowledge that is applicable to a range of products, it is subject to economies of scope. (See Figure 3.3.)

The role of intangible resources in scope economies has recently received considerable attention. The value of a firm's reputation, for example, can extend across a range of markets. The individual businesses of a firm like General Electric may well benefit from the corporate reputation for integrity and high-quality management. More specifically, by using the same brand name on multiple products, a practice called *umbrella branding,* firms put at risk the future sales of all products as bonds for the quality of each product marketed under that name. By doing so, they can lower the average cost of assuring quality while delivering a powerful message to the customer—a clear benefit of scope.[11]

More generally, scope economies explain the value of truly distinctive corporate competences.[12] These may be the result of large investments and may include routines that embrace tacit knowledge and many years of trial and error. The costs incurred in building such competences, however, can often be recovered by applying them to a succession of products or markets over time. Thus, the creation of competences can produce sizable scope economies, and so serve as a valuable source of competitive advantage across multiple products.

[10] M.L. Streitweiser, "The Extent and Nature of Establishment-Level Diversification in 16 U.S. Manufacturing Industries," *Journal of Law & Economics,* October 1991, pp. 503–34.
[11] C.A. Montgomery and B. Wernerfelt, "Risk Reduction and Umbrella Branding," *Journal of Business,* 1992, pp. 31–50.
[12] Paul Milgrom and John Roberts, *Economics, Organization, and Management* (Englewood Cliffs, NJ: Prentice Hall, 1992).

In summary, scale and scope economies may conceivably occur in any function, and may be due to tangible or intangible factors. However, it is only when increased volume or the joint production of two or more products by one firm leads to either demonstrably lower average costs, superior product quality, or raised customer demand that expanding the size or scope of the firm produces economic gain.

Network Externalities

A third source of advantage that encourages a firm to expand within an industry is network externalities. Rather than creating advantage by reducing cost, network externalities increase demand for the product or service of the large player and/or early mover.[13] The archetypal example is the eBay Internet auction site business. Collectors wishing to sell their Pez dispensers (the original collectible product for which eBay was designed), will want to list items on the site that has the greatest number of visitors. This increases the set of possible bidders and hopefully raises the selling price of their item. Similarly, purchasers will prefer to visit the site with the greatest number of listings as this maximizes the selection they have to choose from. The result is a **positive feedback** loop, or virtuous cycle in which both vendors and purchasers congregate on the eBay site. The more items that are listed in a category, the more visitors to the site, which induces new vendors to list on the site, which in turn attracts new visitors, and so on.

In the extreme version of network externalities, the **winner-takes-all.** Once a firm, like eBay gets a little bit ahead of its competitors, its advantage will quickly compound. Unfortunate latecomers, or those competitors, like Yahoo's auction site, which did not gain the early lead, fall by the wayside—trapped in a downward spiral of losing listings and visitors— until only one firm is left standing. This phenomenon provided the strategic incentive for many Internet startups to ignore profitability in the desperate attempt to capture "eyeballs." They spent whatever it took, including millions on Super Bowl advertisements, in the hope of gaining the early lead in their business and so "tipping" the market their way.

Many industries and businesses show network externalities, the telephone system and PC operating systems among them. An important difference is whether the system is **open or closed.** An open system, like today's phone system, shows network externalities at the system level but not at the firm level. A customer's value from owning a phone increases as more customers have phones, but it does not favor AT&T over Sprint since the two operate on the same system. In contrast, a closed or proprietary system, such as Microsoft's operating system, does create a firm specific network externality, as Apple has found to its cost. The interesting

---

[13] See, for example, C. Shapiro and H.R. Varian, *Information Rules* (Boston, MA: Harvard Business School Press, 1999).

strategic dilemma this poses is the choice between adhering to a closed system or cooperating to create an industry-wide open system or standard. The trade-off is between the potential to be the winner with a highly profitable proprietary system, and the risk that few customers adopt the closed system or that a competitive system wins out. Sony's Betamax, although offering the best videotape system, lost out to VHS as more companies adopted that standard and exploited network externalities.

These demand-side network externalities sometimes interact with supply-side economies of scale and experience curves. When they do, as in the case of a personal computer's operating system, they create enormously powerful forces that reward the larger firm and so lead to market concentration. It is no wonder then that Microsoft has both been found guilty of monopolizing the business, and is one of the most valuable companies in the world.

▲ Obstacles to Exploiting Scale and Scope

Although the benefits of scale and scope economies can be impressive, they can also be elusive. Simply increasing the volume of a business in no sense guarantees that a firm's cost structure will improve; similarly, combining two related business lines does not mean that product quality will improve or costs will decline.

In some cases, these disappointments are due to poor analysis: some firms simply miscalculate the size of scale or scope benefits that a given strategy may yield. In other cases, however, the disappointments are due to sheer implementation difficulties. Exploiting scale economies can substantially increase the size of an organization, complicating administrative functions and producing bureaucratic inefficiencies. Scope economies often require profound changes in organizational structure and systems because they depend on sharing of resources and some level of coordination across previously separate units. This may place intensive demands on people and their time and introduce inevitable trade-offs and compromises. If the process is mismanaged, net costs may increase rather than decline, and the firm's competitive advantage in each of the products may suffer.[14]

Firms can also fail to exploit scale or scope economies that emerge in an industry because they are locked into a given way of competing. Consider the example of a firm with a leading market position which, over a number of years, developed a set of resources specifically tailored to that strategy. Further, the firm's routines, power structure, and value system were all aligned with that strategy. Such embedded practices make change difficult for two reasons: they interfere with signals that suggest change is necessary

---

[14] In Chapter 6 we will describe how firms can structure and organize themselves to realize the benefits of scale and scope without many of the costs that can result.

The Advantages and Limitations of Successful Generic Strategies I

IOWA BEEF

Iowa Beef, later known as IBP, entered the U.S. beef industry in 1961, when technological innovations were transforming the industry into a mass-production business and leading to its relocation from the stockyards of Chicago to the cattle-rearing states. By 1980, Iowa Beef was the low-cost leader, running its slaughtering processes at about half the labor cost of its older competitors. Large-scale facilities, highly automated factory line procedures, and integrated transportation enabled Iowa Beef to realize significant economies of scale, yielding it an overall advantage of up to 20 percent of industry average costs.

Although IBP's cost structure remained the best in the industry, competitors narrowed the gap considerably as they made acquisitions to approach IBP's scale and invested in comparable facilities. In addition, the major competitors, ConAgra and Cargill, were diversified into a broader variety of animal proteins and forward integrated into branded products. They also backward integrated into the ownership of feedlots

for livestock. At the same time, market demand was changing as the country became more health conscious and the price of chicken dropped sharply in relation to beef. In response, IBP's only strategic move was entry into the pork industry in 1982.

Thus, while its competitors worked to neutralize IBP's distinctive competence and exploited economies of scope though product diversification and vertical integration, IBP held fast to its old ways. Ironically, IBP's overwhelming success in executing a low-cost strategy and its zeal to maintain distinctive capabilities in that race may have been partially responsible for its failure to cultivate a broader resource base and a more dynamic strategy. When floated on the market by former parent Occidental in 1991, IBP was worth less than $800 million, even though its sales were over $9 billion.

Source: Reprinted from "IBP and the U.S. Meat Industry," by D.J. Collis and N. Donahue, HBS case number 9-391-068. Used by permission of Harvard Business School Publishing Corporation; all rights reserved.

and, in myriad ways, impede firms' attempts to do things differently.[15] Thus, while a source of advantage in a firm's initial strategy, these tightly woven systems and processes often constitute "the dark underside of organizational resources," when core capabilities become **core rigidities.**[16]

In such instances, institutionalized capabilities can lead to **inertia** as the experiences of two companies—Maytag and Iowa Beef—dramatically illustrate. (See "The Advantages and Limitations of Successful Generic Strategies" I and II.) Each of these firms was once very successful pursuing a classic generic strategy: Maytag as a focused-differentiated producer of laundry equipment, and Iowa Beef as the low-cost beef processor. At the peak of its success, each firm had a distinct advantage relative to its rivals.

[15] Richard Rumelt suggests a list of the "five frictions": distorted perception, dulled motivation, failed creative response, action disconnects, and political deadlocks, "Inertia and Transformation," in *Resource-Based and Evolutionary Theories of the Firm: Towards a Synthesis*, ed. Cynthia A. Montgomery (Boston: Kluwer Academic Press, 1995), pp. 101–32.
[16] D. Leonard-Barton, "Core Capabilities and Core Rigidities: A Paradox in Managing New Product Development," *Strategic Management Journal*, 1992, pp. 111–25.

The Advantages and Limitations of Successful Generic Strategies II

MAYTAG

Maytag followed a very different but nonetheless classic generic strategy for many years as a focused differentiated producer. The company enjoyed a reputation as the quality leader in the major home appliance industry for its premium washers and dryers. It succeeded in differentiating its products in terms of durability and reliability, embodying this position in the company's advertisements with "Ol' Lonely," the solitary Maytag repairman who never had any work to do. It also earned number one quality rankings from *Consumer Reports* every year from 1974 to 1983. To capitalize on its perceived differentiation, Maytag typically priced its appliances at a 10–15 percent premium. Accordingly, Maytag's operating structure was geared toward high-quality appliance production.

Over the course of the 10-year period during which Maytag dominated the *Consumer Reports* rankings, the gap in the quality ratings steadily narrowed, while the 10–15 percent price differential remained intact. Partly this was due to the fact that Maytag remained primarily a washer/dryer manufacturer (with some involvement in dishwashers and disposals), while its leading competitors exploited scope economies across a broad line of major home appliances, including dishwashers, refrigerators/freezers, conventional and microwave ovens, ranges, and air conditioners, which they sold, under several brands at multiple price points. Meanwhile, as household saturation levels rose steadily for most appliances, overall industry growth slowed.

In time, Maytag chose to broaden its product line, acquiring brands like Magic Chef and Admiral to establish a presence in a broader range of lower-priced appliances. Reputations and cultures clashed, however, as Maytag struggled to raise quality standards in the new acquisitions. And although Maytag stressed that it had anticipated the need to address quality issues in the newly acquired brands, the difficulties associated with doing so showed up in a 40 percent drop in Maytag's stock price, and a decline in its *Consumer Reports* ratings during the 1980s.

Although the timing and implementation of Maytag's actions can be criticized, on a more fundamental level the firm's experience raises questions about a focused differentiated firm's ability to resist broad-scope competitors and then to leverage its own assets and capabilities across a broad line of products. That is, could a firm that had so closely aligned itself with laundry equipment transfer its brand and expertise to ranges and refrigerators when the competitive dynamics demanded it? How long would such a transition take? Questions such as these underscore the need for a dynamic view of business strategy and firm scope.

In time, however, both were challenged by competitors that matched or nearly matched those original advantages while simultaneously benefiting from scope economies that neither chose to duplicate.

These experiences illustrate the double-edged quality of resources: on a firm's ascendancy, they can shield the firm from competition and make it difficult for rivals to close in on its lead; but when a strategy is eventually challenged, they can block the firm's own ability to respond (see "Darwin and Sticky Strategies").

Darwin and Sticky Strategies

A Darwinian perspective can help us understand firm inertia. Most firms with dominant market positions reached those heights over a number of years. Through experience they developed organizational resources and ways of doing things that proved superior to those of rivals with lesser positions, some of which were forced from the industry. In time, these resources and routines came to embody the firm's competitive advantage and were the very forces that assured its survival. One would not expect, nor necessarily want, such mechanisms to change quickly.

This kind of Darwinian notion is the centerpiece of a stream of research called **population ecology** that applies biological analogies to the growth and survival of populations of firms. As John Freeman explained, this work emphasizes that "all change occurs with friction. Redeploying resources takes effort, effort that cannot be simultaneously used for productive activity, so change is doubly costly. The more fundamental the change, the more effort it takes." Exogenous shifts, such as new technologies, political upheavals, or dramatic demographic changes, threaten whole populations of incumbent firms that were designed to operate under different conditions. Faced with these challenges, "some organizations adjust; others do not. Failure follows. Opportunity comes with it. That is to say, as existing organizations struggle to deal with this changing world, some succeed and make the adjustment. Others cannot adjust and disappear."

Source: John Freeman, "Business Strategy from the Population Level," in *Resource-Based and Evolutionary Theories of the Firm: Towards a Synthesis,* ed. C.A. Montgomery (Boston: Kluwer Academic Publishers, 1995), pp. 219–50.

Practice

The Search for Scale and Scope Effects

Managers often refer to economies of scope as synergy, that enticing mathematical equation in which two plus two equals five. Sadly, this concept has been abused and overused in the business press and in managerial plans as well. Experience has exposed countless instances where synergies, once expected, never materialized. The same may be said for scale effects.

Firms often err by expanding into market segments that appear to be related to their existing businesses, but in fact are quite different. In particular, firms tend to make this mistake when they define relatedness on the basis of product characteristics rather than on resources. While expansion within an industry may sound like an easy route to success, this enthusiasm often masks the fact that segments in an industry can have different key success factors that prevent the exploitation of scale and scope economies.

Earlier, we identified managerial impediments to the achievement of scale and scope economies. Here, we observe the failure of scale and scope effects to materialize because management misjudged their potential from the start. This often occurs when expansion is based on an impressionistic assessment rather than a more careful analysis of the source and magnitude of expected cost savings.

Identifying Scale and Scope Effects

The fact that scale and scope effects are often difficult to estimate cannot be taken as a license for shoddy analysis. Data-driven analyses of the effects of scale, for example, are possible by comparing cost data among plants of different sizes, or using engineering estimates to simulate the cost of a facility that is different from the current size. Such careful work can go a long way to quantify the extent of scale economies in a business. Similarly, experience curves can be constructed and their slope calculated from data on the past output of a firm or industry.

To evaluate the potential for scope economies between two or more business segments, managers also need a systematic process. This analysis should avoid broad generalities and focus on the specific resources and activities that, through combination, may lead to advantage. The value chain, which divides a firm's activities into discrete processes, provides a useful starting point for such an analysis (see "The Value Chain"). Listing all the discrete activities in the value chains of two businesses or segments under consideration allows for an accurate identification of those that are similar enough to be subject to scope economies.

The potential for scale and scope economies will differ among the various activities. Therefore, identifying and isolating those activities where their effect is greatest is an important step. Such activities will either be ones in which a large percentage of the cost structure lies (so that, for example, even a small-scale effect will provide a substantial cost advantage to the largest competitor), or where the magnitude of the scale or scope economies are large.

Using the Value Chain To use the value chain as a tool for identifying scope economies, consider the example of an industrial thermostat company that decided to expand into household thermostats. The firm forecast flat growth in its existing markets, but anticipated an increasing demand in the household market. On that basis, it elected to enter the household market, hoping to capture the growth in that segment.

At first glance, this might appear to be a straightforward example of expansion across industry segments. One might think it would be an eminently sensible move: the firm would remain a thermostat producer, only offering an additional product line. Looking closer, however, one can see that the fit between the two businesses was not at all close.

Although the firm was able to leverage some of its technological know-how in entering the new market, R&D was not a critical success factor in household thermostats, nor did it account for a significant portion of the value added in that market. In contrast, design, product appearance, and packaging were significant selling features in household thermostats, but the firm lacked any experience in these activities. The production and

The Value Chain

To further the analysis of competitive advantage, Michael Porter introduced the value chain as a tool to examine the activities of a business. The value chain disaggregates all of a firm's functions into discrete activities, each of which has its own determinants of cost (called *cost drivers*), and contributes to satisfying different customer needs.

Porter distinguished a firm's support activities from its operational, or primary, activities (see Exhibit 1). The latter contribute directly to the production and delivery of a good or service to a customer. The former are the overhead functions that must be performed to keep the operational activities going. Other approaches, such as McKinsey's business system, generate similar if slightly different categories.

In practice, the activities of the firm can be broken down into an almost infinite list. Manufacturing can be subdivided into assembly and machining; machining can be broken down into the discrete stages in the process; and so on. The level of the analysis should depend on the task at hand. A detailed exercise to benchmark a firm's relative cost position, for example, would require the analysis of a far more disaggregated value chain than would an analysis identifying the key success factors of a strategy. Whatever the purpose, however, the activities should be sufficiently disaggregated so that the scale, experience, and scope drivers of cost and differentiation can be identified within the different activities.

Source: Reprinted with permission of The Free Press, a Division of Simon & Schuster Adult Publishing Group, from *Competative Advantage: Creating and Sustaining Superior Performance* by Michael E. Porter. Copyright ©

EXHIBIT 1   A Generic Value Chain

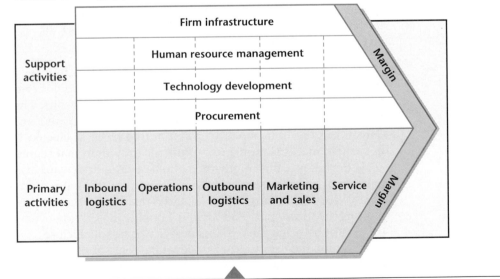

distribution of the products also differed markedly. Industrial thermostats were produced to order, with strict tolerances, and sold by an in-house staff of industrial engineers; household thermostats were mass-produced and distributed through a network of industry representatives to mass marketers and plumbing and heating contractors.

The value chains for the two businesses reveal these critical differences (see Figure 3.4). When placed side by side, it is clear that the resources

FIGURE 3.4
Value Chains for Household and Industrial Thermostats

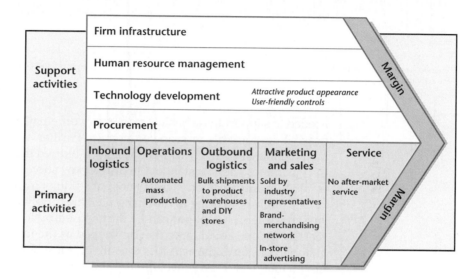

Value chain for household thermostats

Value chain for industrial thermostats

TABLE 3.2   **Relative Importance of Scale and Scope Economies in the Major Appliance Industry**

	R&D	Purchasing	Manufacturing	Distribution	Advertising	Sales	Service	Contract Market
Percentage of cost structure	3%	30%	25%	6%	2%	7%	3%	
Scale within a line	+	+	+++	+	+			
Scope across lines		+		+++	++	+++	+++	+++

Economies of scope are mostly downstream and can only be achieved by sharing costs across multiple products. The volume requirements in these activities are so great that it would be impossible to meet them with a single product line.

needed to support these businesses are very different, and that there are few possibilities for scale or scope economies. Further, when the company attempted to share activities across the lines, it blurred the boundaries between the businesses and lost sight of the distinct key success factors in each. As a result, the company's profitability not only did not improve, it declined.

The plight of Maytag in the changing major appliance industry was discussed earlier. That plight can be illuminated by identifying the specific scale and scope advantages that developed as the industry matured.

Table 3.2 shows the activities that are performed in the industry, beginning with research and development and extending through customer service. Upstream there are few benefits from being a broad-line producer, except for the possibility of sharing some of the more generic elements of research and design. Scope effects, therefore, are modest at this end of the chain. However, there are considerable scale effects in manufacturing individual appliances. All appliances are produced on separate lines, and the size of the minimum efficient scale plant in every instance is considerable.

Downstream, in contrast, scope effects are significant. Distribution, branding, sales, and service are all more efficient when done on a large-scale basis across a full line of products.

Figure 3.5 shows the major industry competitors in the mid-1980s. As their different scopes suggest, the firms pursued a variety of strategies. Design and Manufacture (D&M) was a focused private-label producer of dishwashers. It offered no other product and had no downstream capabilities in distribution, sales, or service. Sears, which commanded the largest market share in the industry, did no manufacturing, but sold and serviced a wide line of products under the Kenmore brand. General Electric (GE), on the other hand, manufactured, distributed, and serviced a full appliance line, although it did no retailing. How could these different strategies, and different firm scopes, exist simultaneously in the industry? And, why, as we saw earlier, did Maytag suffer from its narrow focus?

FIGURE 3.5
Map of Home
Appliance Industry
Players in Product
Space, 1984

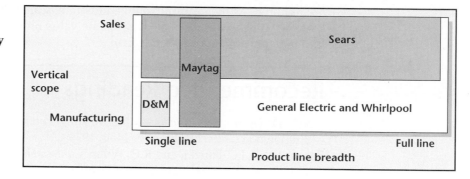

The answer is that each of the successful competitors had access to necessary scale and scope economies throughout the chain, although not always within the boundaries of their own organizations. D&M was large enough to realize significant scale effects in manufacturing dishwashers, but it handed off at that point to large retailers who had access to downstream scope economies. Sears realized significant scope economies in distribution, sales, and service, while buying in large enough volume to support scale-efficient suppliers of each product. GE manufactured multiple product lines, with scale effects in each, and realized economies of scope in distribution, branding, and service. The companies that were disadvantaged in this scenario, were those who, like Maytag, operated in points of the chain where their competitors had scale or scope economies that they lacked.

At a time when the industry was very fragmented, Maytag had built a successful differentiation strategy as a narrow-line producer of laundry equipment, a strategy that necessitated the firm's involvement throughout the value chain to deliver a high-quality product and preserve its high-quality image. As the industry matured and downstream scope economies emerged, Maytag was slow to see the implications. It recognized too late that its narrow product line and extensive vertical scope would be untenable going forward. At that point, its hasty efforts to acquire a handful of marginal producers in order to fill out its product line proved counterproductive. They brought a host of quality problems (anathema to a differentiated firm) and a string of disappointing results.

Conclusion

In summary, vague discussions of scale and scope effects are not only unhelpful, they can be very misleading. General statements such as "substantial cost savings are expected in overhead and marketing" are exceedingly difficult to quantify and do not provoke the kinds of questions that help managers expose inconsistencies in their thinking. Rather, systematic analyses and explicit efforts to assess scale and scope benefits are required. As the examples above illustrate, scale and scope economies have no value in the abstract. They create value only when they translate into material advantages for the firm.

Recommended Readings

Abell, D. *Defining the Business: The Starting Point of Strategic Planning.* Englewood Cliffs, NJ: Prentice Hall, 1979.

Baumol, W.J., J.C. Panzar, and R.D. Willig. *Contestable Markets and the Theory of Industry Structure.* New York: Harcourt Brace Jovanovich, 1982.

Boston Consulting Group. *Perspectives on Experience.* Boston: Boston Consulting Group, Inc., 1968.

Alfred D. Chandler. *Scale and Scope.* Cambridge, MA: Harvard University Press, 1990.

Ghemawat, P. "Building Strategy on the Experience Curve." *Harvard Business Review,* March–April 1985, pp. 143–49.

Hannan, M.T., and J. Freeman. *Organizational Ecology.* Cambridge, MA: Harvard University Press, 1989.

Leonard-Barton, D. "Core Capabilities and Core Rigidities: A Paradox in Managing New Product Development." *Strategic Management Journal,* 1992, pp. 111–25.

Lieberman, M.B. "The Learning Curve and Pricing in the Chemical Processing Industries." *RAND Journal of Economics,* Summer 1984, pp. 213–28.

Montgomery, C.A., and B. Wernerfelt. "Risk Reduction and Umbrella Branding." *Journal of Business,* 1992, pp. 31–50.

Panzar, J.C., and R. Willig. "Economies of Scope." *American Economic Review,* May 1981, pp. 268–272.

Penrose, E. *The Theory of the Growth of the Firm.* London: Basil Blackwell, 1959.

Porter, M.E. *Competitive Advantage.* New York: Free Press, 1985.

Pratten, C.F. *Economies of Scale in Manufacturing Industry.* Cambridge, England: Cambridge University Press, 1971.

Scherer, F.M. *Industrial Market Structure and Economic Performance.* Boston: Houghton Mifflin, 1980.

Scherer, F.M., A. Beckenstein, and R.D. Murphy. *The Economics of Multi-Plant Operations: An International Comparisons Study.* Cambridge, MA: Harvard University Press, 1975.

Shapiro, C., and H.R. Varian. *Information Rules.* Boston: Harvard Business School Press, 1999.

Sutton, J. *Sunk Costs and Market Structure: Price Competition, Advertising, and the Evolution of Concentration.* Boston: MIT Press, 1991.

Teece, D.J. "Economies of Scope and the Scope of the Enterprise." *Journal of Economic Behavior and Organization,* 1980, pp. 223–47.

RESOURCES

BUSINESSES

• VISION

• GOALS & OBJECTIVES

ORGANIZATION

4

DIVERSIFIED EXPANSION

▲ Introduction

Chapter 3 examined the scale and scope of firms within an industry. This chapter will focus on firms that pursue diversified expansion and choose to compete in multiple distinct product markets.[1]

This order of presentation mirrors the growth of many firms: expansion starts within the core industry, and is undertaken to enhance or protect a firm's position in that market. The firm may then move outside its initial industry, often tentatively at first, until over the years it becomes increasingly more diversified (Figure 4.1).

This chapter begins by addressing the motives and vision behind diversified expansion. It then examines the performance implications of various levels and kinds of diversification. The chapter concludes by discussing alternative modes firms use to diversify, including internal growth, acquisitions, and alliances.

Principles

▲ Why Do Firms Diversify?

Firms diversify for many reasons—some inside, and some outside the firm. Edith Penrose referred to these as the external and internal *inducements for growth*.[2]

External inducements are conditions or opportunities in a firm's external environment that draw it into new businesses. These may be attractive opportunities a

---

[1] Portions of this chapter draw from C.A. Montgomery, "Corporate Diversification," *Journal of Economic Perspectives,* Summer 1994, pp. 163–78. Copyright 1994, American Economic Association.
[2] Edith Penrose, *The Theory of the Growth of the Firm* (London: Basil Blackwell, 1959).

FIGURE 4.1
Pattern of
Diversification

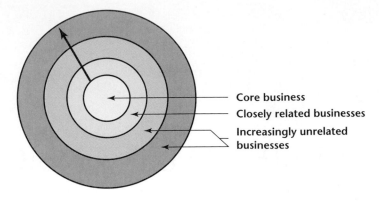

Core business
Closely related businesses
Increasingly unrelated
businesses

firm is well positioned to pursue, such as newspapers entering the business of providing on line information. External inducements can also
come in the form of threats, such as a downward shift in demand in a
firm's primary market that encourages it to seek its fortunes elsewhere.
Defense contractors' recent efforts to deploy their capabilities in private
sector businesses illustrate such a shift. As these examples suggest, external inducements can spawn expansion that is *offensive* or *defensive* in
nature. The same is true of internal inducements.

Internal inducements are conditions within a firm itself that prompt it
to diversify. Defensive diversification, for example, may follow a judgment that a firm's skills are not a good match with the developing needs
in its initial market. Although it was launched as a computer hardware
company, Steve Jobs repositioned Apple in the consumer electronics business with products like the iPod when it became apparent that the firm
could not compete successfully in PCs. Most often, however, internal inducements are offensive in nature and arise from a firm's desire to more
fully employ and exploit its resource base. This is the most typical reason
firms diversify.

At any given time, most firms have some **excess capacity** in their
resource base—resources that are being underutilized. This situation develops for several reasons. First, some resources, and intangible resources
in particular, grow in both value *and capacity* if used judiciously. Brand
names, for example, benefit in this way from ever-widening exposure.
Second, resources are often available only in discrete increments; when
combined in any given business it is unlikely that all of the resources, such
as a specialized piece of test equipment, will simultaneously be used to
their full capacity. Third, in the ordinary processes of operation and
expansion, firms often generate new resources.[3] While doing audits,
for example, Arthur Andersen developed an expertise in information

[3] Penrose, *Theory of the Growth of the Firm.*

systems, which it in turn leveraged into a huge and profitable consulting practice that, as Accenture, survived the demise of the original company.

Many of a firm's most valuable resources are idiosyncratic or deeply embedded in the firm, making it difficult to rent or sell their excess capacity to others. Other resources may be detachable, but due to high transaction costs or unique characteristics, they are worth more in their present setting than they would be elsewhere. Such resources are said to be **immobile** because they are nontradable or less valuable to other users;[4] consequently, they remain in the firm. If leveraging these resources into new businesses will increase the firm's total returns, they become a viable basis for diversified expansion.[5]

Obstacles, inside and outside the firm, often thwart a firm's desire to expand. Although an attractive opportunity may beckon, a firm may lack a necessary resource to succeed, or its board of directors may feel the plan for expansion is too risky. Similarly, plans to deploy a firm's resources in a new market may be blocked by an external obstacle, such as the presence of an entrenched competitor that would pose a formidable threat to a new entrant.

The mix of inducements and obstacles a firm faces will influence not only *whether* expansion will occur, but also the direction and method the expansion will take. For example, a firm that identifies an attractive opportunity but faces the obstacle of an insufficient resource base may elect to proceed through a joint venture or merger. Conversely, the firm may decide to forgo that possibility and pursue another alternative, where internal development would be viable. Ultimately, it is the net effect of the inducements and obstacles to expand that shape a firm's diversification and lay the groundwork for its future profitability.

▲ Guiding Growth

A thousand-mile journey begins with a single step.

Ancient Chinese proverb

Initially, diversification often occurs incidentally, rather than as part of a deliberate plan. However, as complexities increase and businesses abound, the need to guide a firm's growth and make meaningful choices about its portfolio of businesses becomes very important.

This transition can be a critical juncture for a firm. It now needs to consider not only how it will compete in its individual businesses—its business-level strategies—but also how it will function and add value as a whole—its corporate-level strategy.

[4] M.A. Peteraf, "The Cornerstones of Competitive Advantage: A Resource-Based View," *Strategic Management Journal,* 1993, pp.179–91.
[5] The choice between leveraging resources through market contracts or inside the firm is addressed in Chapter 5.

The Growth Idea

Richard Normann made a very useful distinction between what he termed a *business idea* and a *growth idea*. His business idea is analogous to what we have termed *business strategy;* it embodies a firm's means of establishing a competitive advantage within a particular industry.

Normann pointed out that describing a growth idea is far more difficult than describing a business idea; it involves a process whose outcome is continually changing, and best characterized as an emergent process.*

A growth idea begins with a firm's initial endowment of resources and its understanding of the competitive environments it faces or may face in the future. For an established single-business company, these would include everything associated with the business—technology, customers, and competitors, and so forth. Going forward, the question for the firm's management is: How should we use what we have to become something different? This query embodies the essence of a growth idea.

Managing a growth idea involves a dynamic process that is quite different from the kind of goal-directed activity that characterizes many mature planning processes. According to Normann: "Planning for growth cannot therefore be derived logically from a well-defined ultimate goal; it can only proceed step by step. After each step or each measure introduced, the situation must be reconsidered before the next step can be planned or put into effect. Indeed, this kind of planning is characteristic of all learning processes geared to something more than the production of a given final product with the help of some well-known technology, i.e., learning processes aimed at the development of something really new."†

Despite its indistinct nature, it is critical that a vision be linked to concrete and immediate actions. Unless this is done, the vision runs the risk of being "a declaration and nothing more." As these actions are taken, and experience unfolds, each should be scrutinized, not only as an end in itself, but as it relates to the firm's vision and developing strategy.

Due to the complexities involved in positioning or repositioning an entire set of businesses, or developing the resources to support the same, corporate strategies often emerge over a number of years. Even though they may not be born intact, compelling corporate strategies nonetheless are usually forged through such a deliberate and conscientious process.

* H. Mintzberg, "Patterns in Strategy Formulation," *Management Science,* 1978, pp. 934–48.
† From *Management for Growth* by Richard Normann, p. 97. Copyright 1978, © John Wiley & Sons Limited. Reproduced with permission.

Defining a corporate vision and planning for growth across multiple businesses can be very demanding. Almost by definition, it requires an open-ended process. The distinction made in Chapter 1 between visions, which point direction, and goals and objectives, which define milestones, is essential in this regard. Richard Normann captured this distinction when he wrote: "Visions are not goals. They are intuitive ideas of reasonable (although in relation to the present state, sometimes highly deviating) future states of the system, which sometimes only exist as subjective ideas nursed by a few discerning and possibly significant actors in the present system"[6] (see "The Growth Idea").

[6] From *Management for Growth* by Richard Normann, p. 97. Copyright 1978, © John Wiley & Sons Limited. Reproduced with permission.

The process through which a vision is nurtured and refined is critical to a firm's long-term success. Locking into a vision prematurely can artificially narrow a firm's opportunities and prevent ongoing learning. On the other hand, failing to solidify a vision as time goes on can result in an unwillingness to make substantial commitments or a string of actions that are inconsistent with each other. In general, as a firm's experience accumulates, its corporate vision should gain definition. As this is happening, the other elements of the strategy should be taking root. By the time the vision itself is well defined and widely agreed to, the primary building blocks of the diversification strategy are often in place, and the firm has already gone a considerable distance toward its realization.

▲ Choice of Businesses

Matching Resources and Businesses

Central to a corporate vision is the desired fit between the firm's resources and the product markets in which it may compete. These have been described as "two sides of the same coin":

> Most products require the services of several resources and most resources can be used in several products. By specifying the size of the firm's activity in different product markets, it is possible to infer the minimum necessary resource commitments. Conversely, by specifying a resource profile for a firm, it is possible to find the optimal product market activities.[7]

These relationships can be studied through a resource–product matrix, which describes the linkages between a firm's resource and product portfolios (see "Diversification at BIC"). More specifically, to be the basis for an effective diversification strategy, there must be a fit between resources and businesses so that the **resources contribute in an important way to competitive advantage** in the product markets.

Field-based research, for example, reveals that when diversifying, companies often make two systematic miscalculations with respect to resources. They tend to *overestimate the transferability of specific resources*. JC Penney, for example, misjudged the value its retailing skills would bring to the pharmacy business, and was forced to sell its Eckerd Drug subsidiary in 2004. Companies also tend to *overestimate the value of very general resources in creating competitive advantage in a new market.* General Mills, for example, during the seventies, thought its valuable resource was understanding "the needs and wants of the homemaker,"

---

[7] Birger Wernerfelt, "A Resource-Based View of the Firm," *Strategic Management Journal,* 1984, pp. 171–80.

Diversification at BIC

From rather humble beginnings as a manufacturer of disposable ballpoint pens, the BIC Pen Corporation grew into a leading consumer products firm. Its success was due, in part, to its careful management of diversification.

Exhibit 1 shows BIC's resource and product portfolios in 1974. The firm's skills in plastic injection molding and mass marketing, as well as its well-recognized brand name, all stemmed from its initial involvement in the ballpoint pen industry. In a series of sequential moves, BIC leveraged all three resources in its entries into disposable lighters and razors. Notably, each of these skills was a key success factor in these industries.

After this string of successes, BIC's good judgment appeared to lapse when it decided to enter the pantyhose business in the United States. From a product market perspective, it is difficult to argue that the fiercely competitive industry presented an attractive opportunity for expansion. Incumbent players were well established and industry growth was slowing. From a resource perspective, the move was equally disastrous. None of BIC's formidable resources played a valuable role in the industry: the product required a separate distribution system, even within BIC's well-established grocery and drugstore markets;* the BIC brand, recognized for utility and good value, did not transfer well to the fashion-conscious hosiery industry; and BIC's expertise in plastics manufacturing was of no use whatsoever (the hosiery were even sourced from a French company).

In addition to its inability to leverage its existing resources, BIC suffered from a lack of other resources that were instrumental to success in the pantyhose industry. These included a product that met customers' needs (BIC's hosiery were notorious for their poor fit) and a cost-efficient means of producing or procuring that product (BIC's imported hosiery faced stiff import tariffs).

Although BIC's eventual withdrawal from the pantyhose market perhaps came as no surprise, it did come with considerable frustration and great cost. The firm's experience illustrates the challenges even successful diversified firms face in mapping their way forward.

* In drug and grocery stores, hosiery distribution required a dedicated service team to replenish stock on a regular basis.

EXHIBIT 1
Resource-Product Matrix, BIC Pen Corp.

From *Strategic Management Journal,* "A Resource-Based View of the Firm," p. 176, by Birger Wernerfelt. Copyright 1984, © John Wiley & Sons Limited. Reproduced with permission.

Resource \ Market	Plastic injection molding expertise	Mass marketing	Brand name
Disposable pens 1958	◯	◯	◯
Disposable lighters 1973	◯	◯	◯
Disposable razors 1974	◯	◯	◯
Pantyhose 1974			

and so diversified unsuccessfully into fashion retailing, toys, jewelry, and clothing.

To be the basis for diversified expansion, therefore, resources must pass a number of tests. The first is that the resources must be **competitively superior** in the new business. Anheuser-Busch, for example, discovered this was not the case when it tried to leverage its distribution and marketing skills into the startup of its Eagle Snacks business. Unfortunately these resources failed to prove superior to those of Frito-Lay, the entrenched competitor, and Anheuser-Busch was forced to close the business after incurring several hundred million dollars in losses.

Second, the resources being leveraged into the new business must be **key success factors** in that business. Deploying any resource that happens to be better than incumbents' will be unrewarded unless the benefit of that resource to customers is substantial. The chemical company Union Carbide, for example, at one time entered the shoe business believing its superior plastic sole technology would give it a competitive advantage. Not surprisingly, the diversification failed because few customers buy shoes for the quality of their soles!

Third, when entering a new business, the firm must compete on *all* the resources that are required to produce and deliver the product or service. One great resource does not ensure successful diversification, particularly if the firm is disadvantaged on other dimensions. A firm must, therefore, have a strategy in place to reach **competitive parity on the resources it does not possess** that are important to success in the new business.

Fourth, even when a firm's resources could in principle contribute to competitive advantage in a new business, leveraging them into that business must be feasible. Marks & Spencer prided itself on its unparalleled reputation in United Kingdom retailing and its extraordinary domestic supplier network, but neither resource transferred successfully to any of the international markets it entered. Not surprisingly, the factors that prevent resource imitation can also prevent the replication or transfer of a company's own resources. The path dependency behind building customer loyalty, for example, can make it difficult to transfer across countries. Companies must, therefore, confirm that their valuable resources can indeed be **replicated** in new business settings if their diversification strategy is to succeed.

A Sequence of Steps

Although a firm's current resource base often directs its diversified expansion, experience shows that it is neither necessary nor prudent for the firm to consider only its existing resources when making such moves. Fit between a firm's resources and product markets need not always be present at the outset of diversification, if a strategy to develop

FIGURE 4.2
Stepping-Stone
Model

Source: From *Strategic Management Journal*, "A Resource-Based View of the Firm," p. 176, by Birger Wernerfelt. Copyright 1984, © John Wiley & Sons Limited. Reproduced with permission.

Resource / Market	Mass assembly	Consumer marketing	Electronics technology
Semi-conductors	X		X
Consumer electronics	X	X	
Computers			X

the missing resources is in place.[8] In following such a plan, firms can balance the exploitation of existing resources with the development of new ones.

Figure 4.2 illustrates how a market opportunity can spur the development of new capabilities. In this case, the matrix represents the planned evolution of the Japanese electronics industry over several decades. In the 1950s, Japan's Ministry of International Trade & Industry (MITI) reportedly identified an attractive opportunity to make electronics industries the leading edge of economic growth in Japan. At the time, however, Japan was 10 to 15 years behind the West in electronics technology and in the manufacture of electronic goods.[9] Recognizing that Japan lacked the requisite skills to compete in the technologically sophisticated segments of the market such as computers, MITI elected to initially build a base in consumer electronics and to use that as a platform for developing more advanced capabilities.

In time, the semiconductor industry would play a particularly important role in carrying out this strategy. Not only would it serve as a supplier to the consumer electronics firms, it, in turn, would be supported and nourished by that industry's rapidly growing demand. This symbiotic relationship provided both the cash flows and technical expertise the semiconductor firms needed to pursue more advanced applications. Those electronics capabilities in time fostered the development of Japan's four leading mainframe computer makers: NEC, Hitachi, Toshiba, and Fujitsu.

---

[8] Hamel and Prahalad, for example, made much of the importance of stretch in a firm's strategy, of setting the target well beyond the current capabilities. C.K. Prahalad and Gary Hamel, "Strategic Intent," *Harvard Business Review,* May–June 1989, pp. 63–76.

[9] *Business Week,* December 14, 1981, p. 53.

Questions to Ask

A few simple questions about a firm's resources and the industries in which it may compete can be a powerful guide in moving from a business unit to a corporate perspective.

RESOURCES

- On which of the firm's resources could diversification be based?

- Is it likely that those resources would contribute to competitive advantage in another business? Where? How?

- Which resources could be developed further through additional investment or experience?

BUSINESSES

- Are there attractive opportunities for expansion?

- Could a defensible position be built in the business?

- How does the business relate to the firm's existing businesses?

- Would additional resources be required?

- What are the various ways those resources might be acquired, and at what cost?

PLAN

- What is the overall plan?

- Into which markets, and in what sequence, should diversification take place?

Source: From *Strategic Management Journal*, "A Resource-Based View of the Firm," p. 172, by Birger Wernerfelt. Copyright 1984, © John Wiley & Sons Limited. Reproduced with permission.

Hiroyuki Itami argued that a stepping-stone approach is common in many diversified Japanese firms.[10] In his view, it represents the logical development and deployment of a firm's critical resources through time. (See "Questions to Ask.")

Indeed, empirical studies have demonstrated the important role resources play in initiating and directing diversified expansion. There is strong evidence, for example, that internally generated diversification emanates from industries in which R&D-to-sales ratios are unusually high, suggesting that technological know-how fuels the effort.[11] Other research has shown that marketing assets and skills are also important drivers of diversified expansion.[12]

Several studies have also confirmed that most expansion does not occur in random, but in deliberate ways. When expanding, firms tend to diversify into industries that share similar resource characteristics and key success factors. In particular, similarities in R&D intensity, distribution,

---

[10] Hiroyuki Itami, with T.W. Roehl, *Mobilizing Invisible Assets* (Cambridge, MA: Harvard University Press, 1987).

[11] D.J. Ravenscraft and F.M. Scherer, *Mergers, Sell-Offs, and Economic Efficiency* (Washington, DC: The Brookings Institution, 1987).

[12] C.A. Montgomery and S. Hariharan, "Diversified Expansion in Large Established Firms," *Journal of Economic Behavior and Organization,* January 1991, pp. 71–89.

and marketing channels are significant predictors of the network of industries in which a diversified firm will compete.[13]

Resources as a Springboard

As the above discussion suggests, the resources of a firm are at the heart of diversified expansion. Ultimately, the quantity and quality of a firm's resources will have a profound impact on how a firm diversifies and the outcomes it can expect.

Although traditional entry barrier theory emphasized the role incumbents' resources play in restricting entry into highly profitable industries, more recent research has shown that established firms can *vault* their way into such industries if they have the kind of resources and capabilities that are critical to industry success. For these firms, entry barriers do not serve as a deterrent, but as a "gateway," making available opportunities that would not be accessible to most firms.[14]

As we discussed in Chapter 2, resources differ in their degree of **specificity.** To be the basis for a diversified firm, resources must, to some degree, be applicable in more than one business (fungible) but specific enough to provide a competitive advantage in all the businesses in which they are applied. It is this degree of specificity which ultimately determines the range and profitability of a firm's diversification.

Highly specific resources, such as productive skills in biotechnology, may be important to competitive advantage and yield high returns in their initial settings, but often lose value rapidly as they are applied in more distant markets. In contrast, less specific resources, such as teams of general managers or standard milling machines, transfer considerably further, but usually generate lower returns because they are less critical to competitive advantage (Figure 4.3). For example, in countries with well-developed capital markets, access to capital is by itself likely to be a poor basis for diversification due to the generic nature of money. Compared to the number of firms that have had the opportunity to develop general resources, far fewer have had the opportunity to develop specialized resources, thus the relative differences in their availability (scarcity) and hence, value.

Given the inherent differences that exist in firms' resource stocks, the optimal level of diversification will differ across firms. Although all firms should seek to diversify as far as their resources create value, the extent of that diversification, and its expected outcomes, will vary widely.

[13] Andre Lemelin, "Relatedness in the Patterns of Interindustry Diversification," *Review of Economics and Statistics,* November 1982, pp. 179–98; and James M. MacDonald, "R&D and the Direction of Diversification," *Review of Economics and Statistics,* 1985, pp. 583–90; and Moshe Faroun, "Beyond Industry Boundaries: Human Expertise, Diversification and Resource-Related Industry Groups," *Organization Science,* May 1994, pp. 185–99.
[14] This has been proven in studies by George S. Yip, "Gateways to Entry," *Harvard Business Review,* September–October 1982, pp. 85–93, and Montgomery and Hariharan, "Diversified Expansion in Large Established Firms."

FIGURE 4.3
Hypothesized
Relationship
between
Diversification
Distance and
Marginal Rents for
Different Degrees
of Factor Specificity

Source: C.A. Montgomery,
B. Wernerfelt, "Diversi-
fication, Ricardian Rents,
and Tobin's *q*," *RAND
Journal of Economics*, 1988,
pp. 623–32. Copyright ©
1988. Reprinted by
permission of the RAND
Corporation.

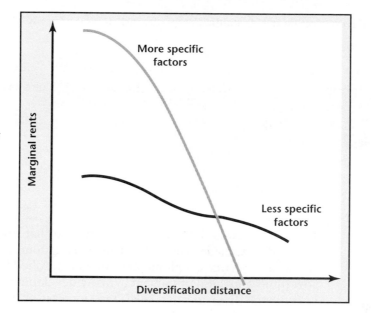

▲ Diversification and Firm Performance

The Extent of Diversification

At any given time, firms are at different places on the path of diversified expansion. Some are just starting out, moving away from their initial businesses. Others are considerably further along, with sets of businesses that may span many industries. Yet others are restructuring and divesting businesses. Although the popular press has highlighted recent divestiture activity among large firms, claiming a "return to the core," changes at the margin must not obscure the fact that many large firms remain remarkably diversified.

When analyzing trends in U.S. manufacturing, for example, Gollop and Monahan concluded that diversification has been "one of the most important structural phenomena" in postwar economic activity.[15]

In 2003 the 500 largest U.S. public companies sold $7.38 trillion worth of goods or services, or approximately 80 percent of the output of all U.S. public companies. On average, these firms competed in 3.7 different industries. These data suggest not only the pervasiveness, but also the economic significance, of diversified firms. (See Table 4.1.)

The United States is not the only country in which diversified companies have a significant role in economic activity. Although recent data are

[15] F.M. Gollop and J. Monahan, "A Generalized Index of Diversification: Trends in U.S. Manufacturing," *Review of Economics and Statistics*, 1991, p. 318.

TABLE 4.1   Diversification in U.S. Public Companies 2002 (Number of SIC Codes Reported)

Source: Reprinted by permission of Compustat.

Number of Firms						
	Mean	1	2 or Less	3 or Less	5 or More	10 or More
Top 500	3.91	61	171	256	157	15
All	2.28	1645	3294	4003	384	20
Percent of Total						
Top 500	3.91	12	34	51	31	3
All	2.28	35	70	85	8	0

difficult to obtain, historical trends indicate that diversification is pronounced in Canada, Japan, the United Kingdom, and other advanced economies.[16] Large conglomerates, often controlled by family groups or government, are also prominent in many developing nations.[17]

Although diversification levels may increase or decrease somewhat in the decades ahead, multibusiness companies will continue to control a majority of corporate assets in many countries for years to come.

Performance Implications

Many researchers have been eager to examine the performance of diversified firms. Conclusions from this research vary widely depending on who is doing the analysis and on the issues being addressed. Unfortunately, much of the research to date has been conducted in pursuit of an unequivocal conclusion that diversification is either universally profitable or universally unprofitable. However, as we saw, the phenomenon is far too complex for such a simple answer.

The complexity surrounding the analysis derives from several factors. First, it is difficult to measure diversification in a way that facilitates comparisons across firms. Second, performance is particularly difficult to measure when looking across industries and over very long periods of time. Third, and most important, the relationship between diversification and firm performance is moderated by a host of other variables, notably the quality and quantity of a firm's underlying resources. To evaluate the efficiency of any diversification, therefore, it is essential to consider the resource endowments and business opportunities that were available to a given firm. (See Figure 4.4.) Examining correlations

[16] These studies were conducted by A. Campbell and M. Goold. *Synergy.* Oxford: Capstone, 1998, respectively. (See recommended readings.)

[17] K. Palepu and T. Khanna, *Corporate Scope and (Severe) Market Imperfections* (Boston: Division of Research, Harvard Business School, 1996).

FIGURE 4.4
The Relationship among Resources, Businesses, and Profitability

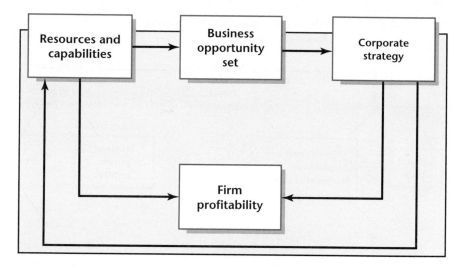

between diversification and performance without considering these underlying conditions can only tell us about the veneer of the relationship, not its inner workings.

Despite these impediments, some notable progress has been made in untangling this very complex relationship. To begin, there is a substantial amount of evidence that diversification and firm performance are negatively correlated when both are measured as continuous, linear variables.[18] Other things being equal, the more diversified the firm, the lower its average profits. Coming upon this result, many have been tempted to conclude that diversification dissipates firm value and is not consistent with profit maximization. However, such a conclusion is not only premature, in many cases it is probably wrong.

Consider that at any given time a firm faces a queue of diversification opportunities, which can be ranked from the most to the least profitable. If the firm pursues the opportunities in that order, as any firm should, and *undertakes only projects with a positive net present value,* its *total* accounting earnings will increase as diversification proceeds, but its *average* accounting earnings will decline. In this scenario, the economic value of the firm will increase as diversification proceeds, so long as expansion stops before undertaking an initiative with a negative net present value. A decline in average accounting earnings, therefore, does not mean that diversification is inconsistent with value maximization.

[18] Robert Comment and Gregg A. Jarrell, "Corporate Focus and Stock Returns," *Journal of Financial Economics,* Vol. 37, 1995, pp. 67–87; Philip G. Berger and Eli Ofek, "Diversification's Effect on Firm Value," *Journal of Financial Economics,* Vol. 37, 1995, pp. 39–65; and L.H.P. Lang and R.E. Stulz, "Tobin's *q,* Corporate Diversification, and Firm Performance," *The Journal of Political Economy,* Vol. 12, No. 6, December 1994, pp. 1248–80.

FIGURE 4.5   Constrained and Linked Diversification

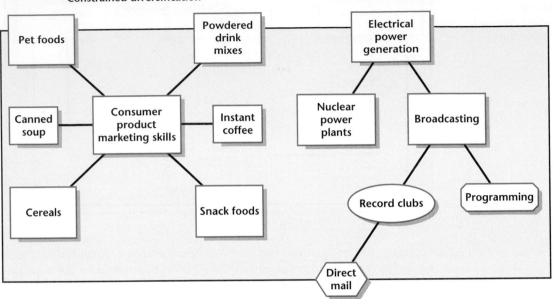

It is also important to consider that the relationship between diversification and firm performance is not necessarily linear, although most tests have assumed this form. Instead of measuring diversification as a continuous variable, Richard Rumelt used a series of objective and subjective criteria to classify firms into nine categories of diversification.[19] In doing so, he made a critical distinction between what he termed "constrained" and "linked" diversification.

In constrained diversifiers, the majority of a firm's businesses share a set of specialized resources, be they in research, operations, or marketing. Linked diversifiers also have connections across their businesses, but their profiles look quite different. In linked diversifiers, new businesses are added to old by building on a variety of connections, such that each new business is related to at least one other business, but the collection as a whole is virtually unrelated (Figure 4.5).

Using various accounting measures, Rumelt found persistent differences in performance across diversification categories. In particular, constrained diversifiers, those that had grown by building on a central

---

[19] Rumelt's nine categories of diversification were single business, dominant constrained, dominant vertical, dominant linked, dominant unrelated, related constrained, related linked, unrelated business, and conglomerate. For a more detailed explanation of the nuances of these categories, see R. Rumelt, *Strategy, Structure, and Economic Performance* (Cambridge, MA: Harvard University Press, 1974).

strength or resource, consistently outperformed all other categories in the sample. Single businesses and linked diversifiers, on average, were middle-of-the-road performers, and unrelated diversifiers were among the worst.[20] These results have been replicated and expanded in a number of other studies.

The Importance of the Industry Effect

In addition to replicating Rumelt's results, subsequent research revealed that the firms in Rumelt's sample differed not only in diversification strategy, but also in the type of industries in which they competed, a well-known influence on firm profitability.[21] In particular, it was shown that the industries in which constrained diversifiers competed were, on average, more profitable than those in which other firms competed, while the industries in which unrelated diversifiers competed were, on average, among the least profitable. This finding suggests that the widely observed correlation between different types of diversification and firm performance is, in part, due to the nature and profitability of the industries in which the firms are located.

This result is not surprising. It is likely that firms that came to follow constrained diversification strategies developed valuable resources in their base industries that gave them the means to enter other profitable markets. In contrast, firms that were not so wise or so lucky had to go further to find opportunities that matched their modest skill sets. Typically this may lead them to a high level of diversification in industries that have lower levels of profitability.

An important rule of diversified expansion is that firms should seek to enter the most profitable industries in which their resources will give them a competitive advantage. Managers who ignore this precept often suffer in the long run. In the late 1960s, for example, many conglomerates attempted to buy their way into highly profitable industries, without having the resources those industries required. Consequently, for these firms the well-recognized positive relationship between firm and industry profitability was reversed: average firm profits decreased, as industry profits increased.[22] In an absolute sense, such firms were shown to be better off

---

[20] For example, see Kurt Christensen and C.A. Montgomery, "Corporate Economic Performance: Diversification Strategy versus Market Structure," *Strategic Management Journal,* October–December 1981, pp. 327–43; D.J. Lecraw, "Diversification Strategy Performance," *Journal of Industrial Economics,* December 1984, pp. 179–98; and P. Rajan Varadarajan and V. Ramanujam, "Diversification and Performance: A Reexamination Using a New Two-Dimensional Conceptualization of Diversity in Firms," *Academy of Management Journal,* June 1987, pp. 380–93.

[21] R.A. Bettis, "Performance Differences in Related and Unrelated Diversified Firms," *Strategic Management Journal,* 1981, pp. 379–94; and Christensen and Montgomery, "Corporate Economic Performance."

[22] C.A. Montgomery and B. Wernerfelt, "Diversification, Ricardian Rents, and Tobin's *q,*" *RAND Journal of Economics,* 1988, pp. 623–32.

when they stayed in industries that, on average, were less profitable but a better fit with their own relatively pedestrian resources.[23]

The "Conglomerate Discount"

In spite of all this theory and evidence, it has become almost an act of faith in the finance discipline that diversified firms trade at a discount to the sum of the value of their parts. The so-called conglomerate discount was first described by Lang and Stulz in 1994.[24] They compared the actual stock market value of diversified companies with the imputed value of their constituent businesses—valuing each separate business at a price calculated for focused firms that only competed in that business. They, and others that followed, argued that the roughly 20 percent discount they found was due to inefficient investment by diversified firms. They demonstrated that such firms tended to subsidize poorly performing business units in ways that stand-alone entities would have been unable to do.[25]

This evidence has been under attack by academics in the strategy field since it was first presented. A number of critiques can be made of the findings and their interpretation, which suggest that the existence of a diversification discount is not as robust as reported. First, the measurement methodology is subject to **survivor bias.** Every single business activity of the diversified firm, successful or otherwise, is included in the corporation's financial results. Yet the sample of companies with which they are compared includes only single business firms that have been publicly quoted and have reached sales of $100 million. Since it is unlikely that the average single business firm is anywhere near as successful as those firms, the comparison is bound to make diversified corporations look bad.

Second, the research is prone to error of **industry definitions.** No statistical research can accurately track the boundaries of a business. One firm offering credit to customers might appear in a database to be diversified into financial services, while another making both fashion shoes and sneakers may appear to be a single business.

Third, and most important, the **direction of causation** is unclear. Even if we accept that there is a negative relationship between market value and diversification, the research has not proved that diversification causes poor performance. Indeed, it is quite likely that the reverse causation is true—that poor performance leads firms to diversify in search of higher profitability. Research by Villalonga, among others, that examines this

---

[23] Sometimes firms use industry entry as a deliberate means to upgrade their resources. If undertaken thoughtfully and with the recognition that the requisite skills will need to be built or acquired, this can be an effective way to slowly lift a firm out of the doldrums of mediocre industries.

[24] L.H.P. Lang and R.E. Stultz, "Tobin's Question, Corporate Diversification, and Firm Performance," *Journal of Political Economy,* Vol. 12, No. 6, December 1994, pp. 1248–50.

[25] See, for example, D.S. Scharfstein and J. Stein, "The Dark Side of Internal Capital Markets: Divisional Rent-Seeking and Inefficient Investment," *Journal of Finance,* Vol. 55, No. 6, December 2000, pp. 2537–64.

FIGURE 4.6
The Relationship between Diversification and Performance

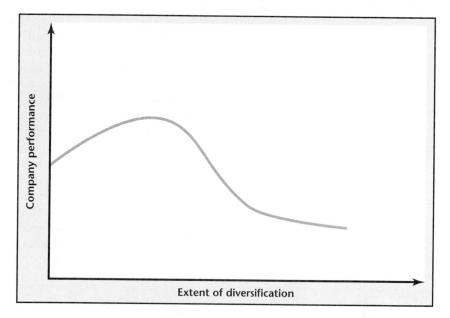

issue by comparing matched firms that were similar before one diversified, in fact suggests that diversification does improve performance.[26] This result supports the earlier research on industry effects that firms in unprofitable industries seek to diversify into higher-profit businesses. The fact that diversified firms tend to be less valuable, therefore, may reflect their unfortunate origins and not the negative effect of diversification.

Summary

The relationship between diversification and firm performance appears to be curvilinear (Figure 4.6). The most profitable firms are those that have diversified around a set of resources that are specialized enough to confer a meaningful competitive advantage in an attractive industry, yet fungible enough to be applied across several such settings; the least profitable are broadly diversified firms whose strategies are built around very general resources that are applied in a wide variety of industries, but are rarely instrumental to competitive advantage in attractive settings.

However, despite the relative success of the constrained diversification strategy, it does not fit all firms. For any given firm, the appropriate strategy is a function of its own resources and opportunities. While a firm with highly specific resources may maximize its profits at a relatively low level of diversification, another firm with more general resources may need to enter far more markets to maximize its profits and may still produce lower absolute returns.

[26] B. Villalonga, "Does Diversification Cause the Diversification Discount?" *Financial Management.*

In light of this evidence, the often-heard adage that firms should stick to their knitting must be interpreted very carefully. Although the foregoing analysis, in effect, supports such advice, arguing that firms should diversify on the basis of what they do well, it also suggests that such strategies will not always result in stellar performance on an absolute basis. In particular, if a firm does its "knitting" with very general resources in pedestrian industries, high profits are unlikely to follow.

Saying that there should be a match between a firm's capabilities and the heights it attempts to scale does not mean that firms with impoverished capabilities are forever relegated to the lowest tier of performers. Rather, it outlines the nature of the challenge such firms face and what they must do to improve their lots. As discussed in Chapter 2 and exemplified in the resource-product matrix, by upgrading their resources, firms can undertake more profitable challenges. However, firms that attempt to shortcut the process and capture the profits without making the requisite investment in resources are unlikely to succeed.

Practice

▲ Mode of Expansion

Firms can implement their diversification strategies through internal development, acquisitions, mergers, joint ventures, alliances, or contracting with external partners. None of these, however, guarantees easy expansion. Choosing among the various modes involves unavoidable trade-offs.

Some would argue, for example, that acquiring a company to gain access to the resources needed to compete in an industry is likely to dissipate future profits. Others would cite the difficulties working across organizational boundaries in joint ventures. On the other hand, internal development can be maddeningly slow and rife with uncertainty. In short, each mode of expansion has its own benefits and costs. Thus, a firm must carefully weigh each alternative against its needs and the exigencies of a particular competitive situation.

Such an analysis is complex. Each mode has itself been the focus of numerous and often very insightful studies. As we cannot cover them all, our purpose here is to provide an overview of the most salient issues in choosing a mode of expansion.

▲ Mergers and Acquisitions

Buying an existing firm is often seen as the easiest way to diversify. Potentially, it enables the firm to obtain immediately the full set of resources required for competitive advantage within an industry. As with other modes of expansion, acquisition has both benefits and drawbacks that make it more appropriate in some circumstances than in others.

Benefits	Drawbacks
Speed	Cost of acquisition
Access to complementary assets	Unnecessary adjunct businesses
Removal of potential competitor	Organizational clashes may impede integration
Upgrade corporate resources	Large commitment

Benefits

A major advantage of acquisitions is that they can quickly position a firm in a new business. By purchasing an existing player, a firm does not have to take the time to establish its presence or develop for itself the resources it does not already possess. This can be particularly important when the critical resources are difficult to imitate or accumulate. The major pharmaceutical companies, for example, have paid billions of dollars to acquire small biotechnology companies and their technological and manufacturing expertise. Building those capabilities in-house might have taken the drug companies 5 or 10 years, with no guarantee that they could generate the kind of patents or knowhow the biotech companies already had.

Acquiring an existing firm also takes a potential competitor out of the market. The internal development required for a firm to reach minimum efficient scale might add substantial capacity to an industry; however, the firm could prevent that increase in rivalry by simply acquiring a competitor that already has the capacity in place. Thus, if the minimum scale of entry is large relative to the market size, acquisition may well be preferred as a means to mitigate intense rivalry within an industry.

Drawbacks

Despite these advantages, acquisitions can have serious drawbacks. First and foremost, acquisitions can be a very expensive way to enter a market. Premiums of 30 percent or more over current share price are frequently required to close a deal. These prices make it possible that whatever value the acquisition creates will be dissipated in the competition to acquire it.

The high bidder in an acquisition is either a firm with extensive private information about the value of the target; a firm that could create unusual value with the acquisition and, therefore, can afford to pay a very high price; or a firm that has neither of these advantages but simply suffers from the "winner curse" (being the one who unluckily happened to value the target company higher than everyone else). Excessively high prices are common when firms get carried away in the bidding process, and

Acquisitions: Rarely a Good Deal for the Acquiring Firm

When making an acquisition, managers often lose sight of the fact that acquisitions are purchased in a market—the market for corporate control—that functions reasonably well. Importantly, the going price for a firm not only reflects the value of the firm as a stand-alone concern, but also incorporates the incremental value the market feels the assets would have to a host of potential acquirers. Unless the winning bidder can use the assets in an unusual way, and create value that other bidders could not, it should not expect to earn economic rent on assets it purchases in the market.

Financial economists have looked at this question in some detail. Their research presents a dramatic challenge to firms that hope to use acquisitions as a means to increase firm value. Exhibit 1 shows that acquirers' risk-adjusted stock prices on average decreased significantly when an acquisition was announced. This means that the market thought their stocks were more valuable before than after the acquisitions.

In contrast to acquirers' decline in value, the stock prices of acquired firms (targets), on average, rise significantly when acquisitions are announced. This suggests that the value created in most mergers is captured by the shareholders of the acquired firms.

EXHIBIT 1   Announcement Period Abnormal Returns by Decade, 1973–1998 (Cumulative Abnormal Return)

	1973–79	1980–89	1990–98	1973–98
Combined (target and acquirer)				
[−1, +1]	1.5%	2.6%[a]	1.4%[a]	1.8%[a]
[−20, close]	0.1%	3.2%	1.6%	1.9%
Target				
[−1, +1]	16.0%[a]	16.0%[a]	15.9%[a]	16.0%[a]
[−20, close]	24.8%[a]	23.9%[a]	23.3%[a]	23.8%[a]
Acquirer				
[−1, +1]	−0.3%	−0.4%	−1.0%	−0.7%
[−20, close]	−4.5%	−3.1%	−3.9%	−3.8%
No. observations	598	1,226	1,864	3,688

Note: Statistical significance at the 5 percent level is denoted by.[a]

Source: G. Andrade, M. Mitchell, and E. Stafford, "New Evidence and Perspectives in Mergers," *Journal of Economic Perspectives*, Vol. 15, No. 2, Spring 2001, pp. 103–20. Used by permission.

winning becomes an object of ego satisfaction rather than economics.[27] Unfortunately, there is a good deal of evidence to suggest that this is frequently the case (see "Acquisitions: Rarely a Good Deal for the Acquiring Firm").

[27] To prevent this irrational but common behavior, it is important for acquirers to specify a reservation price above which they will not go, before the bidding begins.

FIGURE 4.7
Types of
Acquisition
Integration
Approaches

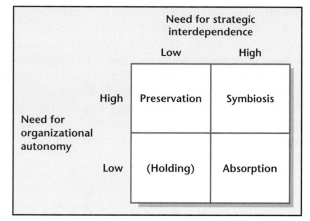

In addition to the likelihood of overbidding, acquisitions pose a number of other challenges. Most targets contain bundles of assets and capabilities, only some of which are of interest to the acquirer. Disposing of unwanted assets or maintaining them in the portfolio is often done at significant cost, either in real terms or in management time. "Selling" a unit yet convincing a buyer that it is not "damaged goods" can be difficult, as can untangling systems and people once they have been integrated into a larger corporation.

Postacquisition Integration Process   Although these obstacles are serious, a number of acquisitions fail on another account: the postacquisition integration process fails. Integrating an acquired company into a corporation is probably one of the most challenging tasks confronting top management. Michael Porter, for example, found that only 45 percent of acquisitions were still retained by the acquirers seven years later.[28] He interpreted this as evidence of the general failure of the acquisition process.

Phillipe Haspeslagh and David Jemison have identified four types of integration that vary according to a unit's need for organizational autonomy and strategic interdependence (Figure 4.7).[29]

The easiest mode of integration to manage is **absorption,** whereby an acquirer merely subsumes the acquisition into its existing structures.

---

[28] M.E. Porter, "From Competitive Advantage to Corporate Strategy," *Harvard Business Review,* May 1987, pp. 43–59.
[29] P.C. Haspeslagh and D.B. Jemison, *Managing Acquisitions: Creating Value through Corporate Renewal* (New York: Free Press, 1991), p. 145. The authors found no examples of one type of acquisition—Holding—in their sample. In this type of acquisition, a firm owns several companies in the same business but makes no attempt to integrate them.

Typically this occurs when a large firm already active in a business acquires a smaller competitor to increase its overall scale.

When seeking to diversify through acquisition, a more common mode of integration is **preservation.** In this instance, the acquired company is more or less left alone to run itself as a discrete entity. Although easy to achieve operationally, this mode of integration begs the question of how value will be added to the acquisition. Haspeslagh and Jemison suggest that this mode is more useful as a way to upgrade corporate resources, when the acquiring firm seeks to learn by example from the acquired firm.

Most typically, if an acquirer attempts to inject its resources into an acquired firm, or vice versa, the integration involves **symbiosis.** In this process, the acquired and acquiring firms are melded together to form a new and different coherent whole. This clearly is the most difficult of the integration modes, and the one on which many acquisitions flounder. Conflicting styles and cultures, a feeling of winners and losers, and operational difficulties in joining systems and people make it extraordinarily difficult to effect this sort of integration.

According to Haspeslagh and Jemison, to work effectively, acquisitions require a gatekeeper who is responsible for managing the interface between the companies. In addition, important decisions have to be made concerning a number of trade-offs, including the speed of integration, equity versus qualification in personnel decisions, operational versus strategic focus in the short term, rationality versus symbolism in decision making, and top-down versus bottom-up decision making.

Many general managers face similar trade-offs in the course of normal operations. In the context of an acquisition, however, these issues can become particularly salient and challenging. As a result, even acquisitions that due diligence suggests are very promising may fail to realize their potential.

▲ Internal Development

Many companies use another mode of expansion, internal development, as they incrementally exploit corporate resources. As with acquisition, internal development has its pros and cons.

Benefits	Drawbacks
Incremental	Slow
Compatible with culture	Need to build new resources
Internalizes learning	Unsuccessful efforts are difficult to recoup
Encourages intrapreneurship	Adds to industry capacity; subscale entry

Drawbacks

The drawbacks of internal development are, typically, the opposite of the benefits of acquisition. Most notably, internal development is a slow process as a firm strives to build resources it did not otherwise possess. In its early phases, the development process can put a firm at risk of being subscale, and it can increase rivalry in an industry through the addition of new capacity.

Internal development also introduces the risk that a project will not turn out as planned. Unfortunately, unlike acquisitions, when failure can often be salvaged by selling off the acquired company, investments in an unsuccessful internal development can be very difficult to recoup. For example, Procter & Gamble never recovered the millions of dollars it spent in advertising its unsuccessful Citrus Hill orange juice. Similarly, Disney lost over $1 billion on Go.com, the website portal it launched in the late 1990s and shut down in 2001, prompting some critics to say Disney had misunderstood the relationship between the Internet and its core business.

Benefits

While acknowledging the inherent risks of internal development, many firms find it also has benefits. Notably, internal development allows for incremental decision making that can accommodate changing environmental conditions and the learning that may occur within the firm itself. In contrast to acquisitions, where the major commitment is made all at once, internal development can reduce risk by allowing a firm to delay certain of its choices over a longer period of time. Further, in the early stages of an industry life cycle, internal development may not only be the best choice, it may be the only choice.

Arguably, the greatest benefit of internal development is that it can be an easier, although by no means easy, way to transfer intangible corporate resources into a new business. Employees who understand the firm's culture and embody its tacit collective knowledge can directly deploy those resources in a new context, where they themselves can shape the business from its onset. This suggests that when the resource a firm wants to leverage is an organizational capability, or an intangible asset, the preferred route is internal development.

There are other benefits of internal development. Through in-house expansion, a firm can capture the externalities of a development process, including the learning and experience that accumulate as a business grows. Through time, this tacit know-how can become a valuable resource in its own right and guide further expansion of the firm.

By growing a business internally, management also signals a commitment to developing and leveraging the resources of the firm. This can foster a culture where intrapreneurship can flourish. Experience suggests that the best way to do so is not to create a separate development unit charged with finding new businesses or screening suggestions made by the divisions, but to encourage new business developments in every business, allowing a champion from that unit to carry the project forward. 3M is, for example, famed for having such a capability.

▲ Alliances

Alliances of all forms, whether joint ventures, franchises, equity participation, or long-term contractual agreements, are designed to capture the benefits of internal development and acquisition while avoiding the drawbacks of both. To some extent, some alliances are successful in doing so, but many others exhibit a number of weaknesses. It is not possible here to review each type of alliance in detail, but we will make some general observations about the managerial implications they raise.

Benefits	Drawbacks
Access to complementary assets	Lack of control
Speed	Assisting potential competitor
	Questionable long-term viability
	Difficult to integrate learning

Benefits

The objectives of every alliance differ. We will focus on those that are formed to combine complementary resources in order to compete in a new business.[30] These alliances generally occur when one firm has some resources that would be valuable in a new business but needs the assets of another firm to effectively carry out its plan. In the 1970s and 1980s, a number of Japanese firms with high-quality products lacked distribution and service networks to enter the U.S. market. Rather than buying a U.S. company or trying to build the networks themselves, many of these firms entered into alliances that matched their products to a domestic firm's distribution and service networks. Similarly, alliances in the biotechnology industry match the technical know-how of start-up enterprises with the distribution channels of established pharmaceutical companies. Through such alliances, the firms involved are able to assemble the full range of resources they need to compete.

---

[30] Alliances have been a topic of much recent writing. We cannot hope to cover all that literature here. Readers are referred to the recommended readings list for a more complete treatment of the issues surrounding alliance formation and management.

Drawbacks

Although attractive on a number of dimensions, alliances present their own challenges. Issues of control and leadership are near the top of this list. What will each partner contribute? How will those contributions be monitored? Who will set the strategy for the business? If these issues are not resolved at the outset, they can come back to haunt the parties at a later date. There is also the risk, of course, that the alliances may develop in a different direction than originally anticipated, challenging the efficacy of the original assumptions and plans.

The legal structure of an alliance can be helpful in addressing these issues, setting the course and parameters of the exchange. However, there are limits to what can be achieved through legal means. Often, closely aligned business interests can be a more powerful mechanism for resolving disputes between firms and setting and maintaining a common course. Thus, understanding the motivation and incentives of all parties, both in the short and the long run, is critical to the formation of any successful alliance.

In particular, it is important to recognize that the needs and aspirations of partners may change over the life of an alliance, and do so in divergent ways. Predicting what the goals and incentives of the various parties will be under various circumstances is a critical part of effective planning. To the dismay of many U.S. firms, countless of their Japanese partners eventually set up their own distribution networks, ending their alliances with U.S. partners. Other contracts may not end but can become quite problematic over time. Franchising agreements, for example, can be effective in building an organization when there is a high degree of environmental stability and agreement on the strategic direction of the firm. In times of turbulence, however, these contracts can hinder a firm's ability to change and can tie together franchisors and franchisees with asymmetric interests. Pizza Hut's franchisees, for example, initially resisted the introduction of home delivery, although the franchisor believed it was a strategic necessity.

Many of these experiences highlight the problems of cooperating with a competitor. In the near term, competition between alliance partners is rarely over the product market (since the two are often collaborating on that dimension) but over who gains most from the alliance.[31] In this sense, a firm is considered a "winner" if it is able to upgrade its capabilities faster than its partners or is successful in building the resources it originally lacked. It has been asserted, for example, that Toyota triumphed in the NUMMI joint venture with General Motors because it learned how to

---

[31] Gary Hamel, Yves Doz, and C.K. Prahalad, "Collaborate with Your Competitors—and Win," *Harvard Business Review,* January–February 1989, pp. 133–39.

build cars in North America; it then went on to build its own plants in Kentucky and Ontario, while GM struggled with how to implement lean production in its other American auto plants.

In their most general terms, then, alliances can be useful in supplementing a firm's resource base; in gaining access to assets and capabilities the firm lacks; or in sharing the costs and risks of a major undertaking. Despite their appeal, many alliances are exceedingly fragile management structures that crumble under the weight of balancing competing objectives and needs. Many alliances, by design or not, are short-lived; others have endured over a number of years and delivered unfailingly on promises envisioned at the start.

Recommended Readings

Bettis, R.A. "Performance Differences in Related and Unrelated Diversified Firms." *Strategic Management Journal*, 1981, pp. 379–94.

Campbell, A., and M. Goold. *Synergy*. Oxford: Capstone, 1998.

Christensen, H. Kurt, and C.A. Montgomery. "Corporate Economic Performance: Diversification Strategy versus Market Structure." *Strategic Management Journal*, October–December 1981, pp. 327–43.

Gomes-Casseres B., with J. Bamford and M. Robinson. "Mastering Alliance Strategy: A Comprehensive Guide to Design, Management and Organization." San Francisco: Jossey-Bass, 2003.

Goold, M., A. Campbell, and M. Alexander. *Corporate-Level Strategy: Creating Value in the Multibusiness Company*. New York: John Wiley & Sons, 1994.

Haspeslagh, P.C., and D.B. Jemison. *Managing Acquisitions: Creating Value through Corporate Renewal*. New York: Free Press, 1991.

Itami, H., with T.W. Roehl. *Mobilizing Invisible Assets*. Cambridge, MA: Harvard University Press, 1987.

Kogut, B. "Joint Ventures: Theoretical and Empirical Perspectives." *Strategic Management Journal*, 1988, pp. 319–22.

Lang, L.H.P., and R.E. Stulz. "Tobin's q, Corporate Diversification, and Firm Performance." *Journal of Political Economy*, Vol. 12, No. 6, December 1994, pp. 1248–80.

Lecraw, D.J. "Diversification Strategy and Performance." *Journal of Industrial Economics*, December 1984, pp. 179–98.

Lippman, S.A., and R.P. Rumelt. "The Payments Perspective: Micro Foundations of Reserve Analysis." *Strategic Management Journal*, Vol. 24, October 2003, pp. 903–28.

Lippman, S.A., and R.P. Rumelt. "A Bargaining Perspective on Resource Advantage." *Strategic Management Journal*, Vol. 24, November 2003, pp. 1069–86.

MacDonald, J.M. "R&D and the Direction of Diversification." *Review of Economics and Statistics,* November 1985, pp. 583–90.

Montgomery, C.A. "Corporate Diversification." *Journal of Economic Perspectives,* Summer 1994, pp. 163–78.

Montgomery, C.A., and S. Hariharan. "Diversified Expansion in Large Established Firms." *Journal of Economic Behavior and Organization,* January 1991, pp. 71–89.

Montgomery, C.A., and B. Wernerfelt. "Diversification, Ricardian Rents, and Tobin's *q.*" *Rand Journal of Economics,* 1988, pp. 623–32.

Normann, R. *Management for Growth.* New York: John Wiley & Sons, 1977.

Penrose, E. *The Theory of the Growth of the Firm.* London: Basil Blackwell, 1959.

Prahalad, C.K., and R. Bettis. "The Dominant Logic: A New Linkage between Diversity and Performance." *Strategic Management Journal,* 1986, pp. 495–511.

Ravenscraft, D.J., and F.M. Scherer. *Mergers, Sell-Offs, and Economic Efficiency.* Washington, DC: The Brookings Institution, 1987.

Rumelt, R. *Strategy, Structure, and Economic Performance.* Cambridge, MA: Harvard University Press, 1974.

Salter, M., and M.S. Weinhold. *Diversification through Acquisition.* New York: Free Press, 1979.

Sirower, M.L. *The Synergy Trap.* New York: Free Press, 1997.

Teece, D.J. "Towards an Economic Theory of the Multiproduct Firm." *Journal of Economic Behavior and Organization,* 1982, pp. 38–63.

Varadarajan, P. Rajan, and V. Ramanujam. "Diversification and Performance: A Reexamination Using a New Two-Dimensional Conceptualization of Diversity in Firms." *Academy of Management Journal,* June 1987, pp. 380–93.

Winter, S. "Understanding Dynamic Capabilities." *Strategic Management Journal,* Vol. 24, October 2003, pp. 991–96.

Yip, G. "Gateways to Entry." *Harvard Business Review,* September–October 1982, pp. 85–93.

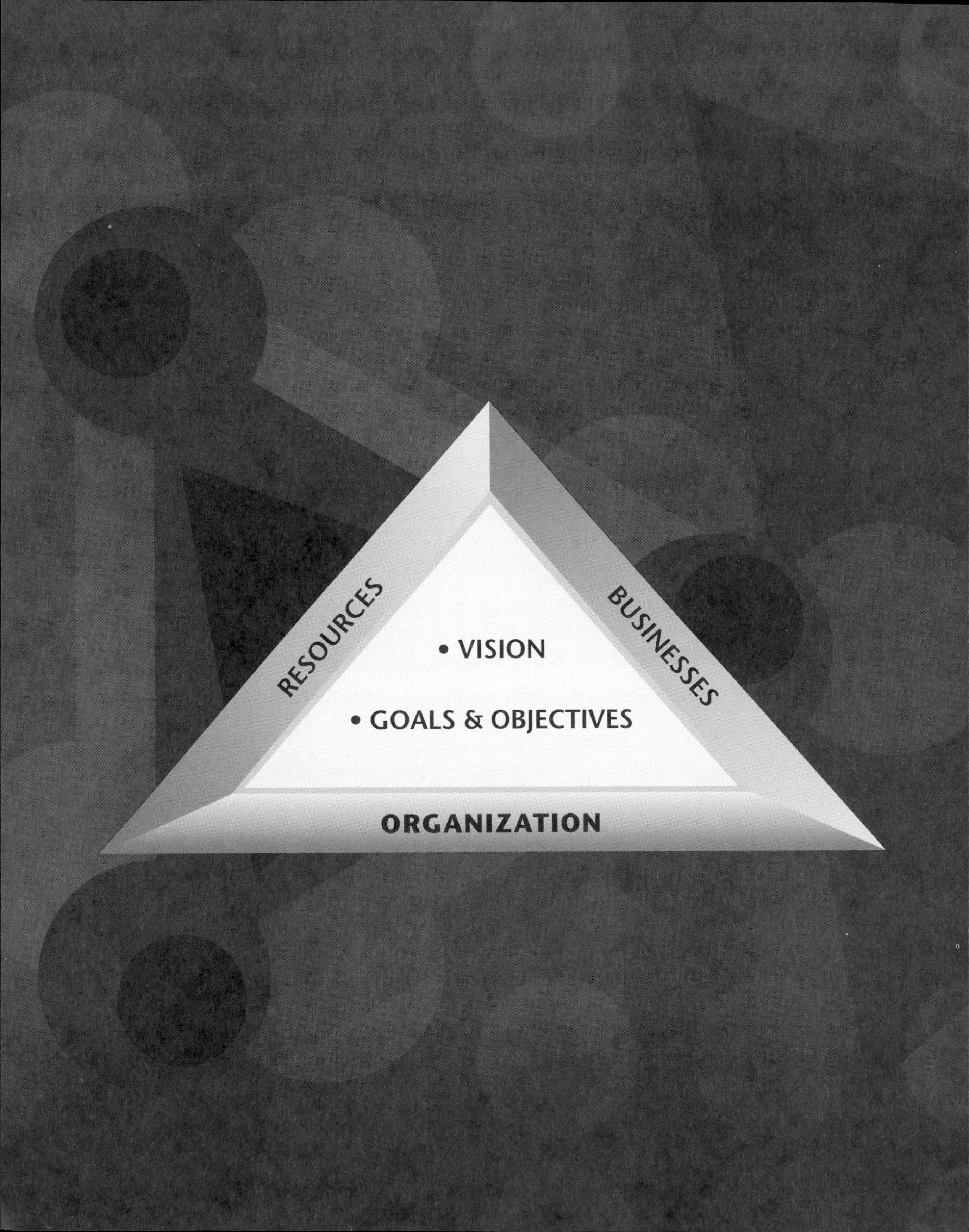
RESOURCES
BUSINESSES
• VISION
• GOALS & OBJECTIVES
ORGANIZATION

5

ORGANIZATIONAL LIMITS TO FIRM SCOPE

▲ Introduction

Many corporations have pursued the strategy of expansion described in the previous two chapters: starting from a single business, expanding scale and scope within that industry, and then branching out into new markets and geographies. As a result, firms today can be found in an enormous variety of sizes and shapes.

But this raises the question: What are the appropriate boundaries for a particular firm? Although many corporations are still expanding, entering new businesses and markets, and becoming ever larger and more complex, others are reducing the scale and **scope** of their activities. Not only are they downsizing the number of employees, they are also decreasing the extent of their diversification across businesses and outsourcing a broad range of activities from gardening to legal and computer services.

Perhaps nothing represents this trend better than the "virtual corporation."[1] Such a firm concentrates on developing and maintaining a few "core competences," performing only the activities directly related to those competences. All other activities and businesses are outsourced or licensed to other firms. The athletic shoe company, Nike, for example, employs around 23,000 people to generate almost $11 billion in revenues. It subcontracts manufacturing to a variety of Far Eastern producers and even relies on outside design houses for many of its product innovations. Nike clothing is supplied by another firm under license.

Another firm responsible for hundreds of millions of dollars of online advertising is run part-time by a single individual. Billing and administration is outsourced to a transactions processing company. Lead generation is performed by a legion of

[1] "The Fall of the Dinosaurs," *Newsweek,* February 8, 1993, pp. 42–53; "The Virtual Corporation," *BusinessWeek,* February 8, 1993, pp. 98–103; "Deconstructing the Computer Industry," *Business-Week,* November 23, 1992, pp. 90–100.

self-employed homeworkers. The purchase of the advertising is done automatically by a computer program that follows complicated algorithms to optimize a customer's presence on the Web. The only task left to the owner (once he or she had written the software) was to negotiate the terms and conditions of the agreement with customers and suppliers.

Such a challenge to the tradition of the fully integrated corporation, and more generally to the wisdom of inexorable corporate expansion, directly questions the limit to the scope of the firm. This chapter addresses that issue by examining which activities and businesses should be retained inside a firm and which should be pursued by other means. To do so, we explicitly introduce **organizational economics** to the analysis of corporate strategy. The term covers a number of different theories that are currently the focus of much research. Although incomplete in a number of important ways, they represent our best understanding of how to rigorously analyze the organizational determinants of firm boundaries.

Principles

▲ Scope of the Firm: Resources and Competitive Advantage

One obvious principle determining whether a firm should perform an activity or compete in a business is whether or not the firm possesses resources that provide a competitive advantage in that activity or business. As the previous chapters illustrated, the motivation for geographic expansion and diversification across product markets is that the firm's resources create value in new markets. When the firm's resources generate no unique value in a business, it should not enter that business. This, after all, is why a metal manufacturing company does not compete in the computer industry.

The same argument is also true in the choice of vertical scope. The essential argument for the virtual corporation, for example, is that it should only perform those activities in which the firm's core competences are valuable; all remaining activities should be outsourced to others, just as Nike outsources manufacturing to East Asian companies. More generally, the reason every firm is not vertically integrated into the manufacture of all the materials and equipment it uses, such as telephones, is that their scale would be so low that the firm would be at a substantial competitive disadvantage if it did so.

Thus, the first determinant of the firm scope is simply whether or not the corporation's resources create a competitive advantage in each business or activity. If they do, the firm should consider competing there. If they do not, the firm should not be active in that business unless other compelling reasons require it.

Questions for Nobel Laureates

At first sight delineating firm boundaries may seem straightforward; however, a closer look reveals that the issue is exceedingly complex. It is at the heart of what economists call the *theory of the firm,* a body of literature that asks fundamental questions about the existence of firms and their ability to achieve things that market transactions alone could not.

Gaining a close understanding of where the lines between markets and firms are drawn is very challenging. Ronald Coase recognized this dilemma in 1937, when he asked, "Why does the entrepreneur not organize one less transaction, or one more?" For this work on the boundaries of firms and other important economic questions, Coase won the Nobel Prize in economics in 1991.

Source: R. Coase, "The Nature of the Firm.," *Economica,* 1937, pp. 386–405.

▲ Scope of the Firm: Market or Hierarchy

Independent of whether there is an underlying economic linkage between businesses or activities, the question still remains: Why should a particular business or activity be performed inside the firm? (See "Questions for Nobel Laureates.")

In the case of diversification, it has to be shown that the best way for a firm to realize value from its resources is to diversify into new businesses itself, rather than just sell or rent its resources to others. Disney, for example, has made a range of choices regarding the scope of its operations along the three dimensions of vertical activities, geography, and product market. The company earns substantial income from many different businesses simply by licensing animated characters, such as the Lion King and Pocahontas. It does not need to compete in the fast-food business to appropriate the profits that its characters create from encouraging children to visit a particular restaurant chain.

Similar issues arise in the other two dimensions of scope. With respect to vertical integration, for example, why should Disney own its cruise ships rather than use franchisees to operate them? In the geographic context, why cannot scale economies be exploited by long-term market contracts? Why, for example, should Disney own the largest share of Disneyland Resort Paris, but only choose to receive a management and license fee for operating Tokyo Disneyland for its Japanese owners?

The choice in each case lies between the two basic forms of economic organization—the **market** and the **hierarchy.** In the former, the price system is used to coordinate the flow of goods and services across separate legal entities. In the latter, goods and services are produced and exchanged within the confines of a firm. Although some activities, such as buying commodities, are very straightforward and easily accomplished through arm's-length market exchanges, the costs of using the price mechanism for others, such as printing a daily newspaper, can be much higher. Organizational economics, therefore, argues that activities should be performed inside the firm, rather than accessed on a market, when administering the activity within the corporate hierarchy is more efficient than conducting it through a market exchange (see "To Print or Not to Print?").

To understand this trade-off, organizational economists examine a basic unit of economic analysis called a **transaction,** which occurs when "a good or service is transferred across a technologically separable interface."[2] For each transaction they then compare the relative costs and benefits of the market and the hierarchy. The costs surrounding a transaction include both the direct costs in producing the good or service and the indirect governance costs associated with completing the transaction, such as the time spent negotiating and enforcing terms of the arrangement. The benefits include the speed and efficiency with which decisions are made, as well as the quality of those decisions.

> The corporate hierarchy will be efficient when it can be shown to be the organizational arrangement that minimizes the sum of production and governance costs. **Production costs** are the direct costs incurred in the physical production and exchange of the item subject to the transaction. **Governance costs** include costs of negotiating, writing, monitoring, enforcing, and possibly also bonding to the terms of the organizational agreement.

Historically, it was believed that production costs were the primary drivers of firm boundaries. An often-cited example was the iron and steel industry, where hot metal was produced in blast furnaces and transported in molten form to an adjacent location to be cast into shapes. The two processes were nearly always owned by the same firm because, it was argued, it would be inefficient for one firm to produce the metal and then let it cool before selling it to another firm to reheat before casting.

More recently, however, attention has been placed on the governance costs of these transactions. In the case of iron and steel, for example, it would be quite possible to maintain a physical flow of molten metal even if separate firms owned the different processes. It would be far more difficult to solve the contractual problems that would be created by transferring the product across corporate lines. If the end product was of inferior quality, who would bear the blame? Who would have the right to order changes in the blast furnace to adjust quality? If the caster had a production problem, how much should the blast furnace operator be compensated for having to temporarily shut down its operations? What if one firm wanted to invest in expanding capacity but the other did not? Questions such as these abound when two production processes are tightly

---

[2] Oliver E. Williamson, "The Economics of Organization: The Transaction Cost Approach," *American Journal of Sociology*, November 1981, pp. 548–77.

To Print or Not to Print?

There is a substantial difference between local daily newspaper and weekly magazine publishers in their ownership of printing presses. The former generally own their own presses. The latter rarely do so, preferring to contract with outside printers for the production of their magazines. Why should this significant difference in scope occur within the same industry?

An obvious reason would seem to be capacity utilization. A weekly magazine, like *Time,* will be printed on the day before publication. This leaves the presses idle for the other six days of the week. In contrast, a local daily newspaper utilizes the presses every night of the week. However, a weekly magazine publisher could, in principle, sell its excess print capacity to others, just as the outside printer does.

One important and valid reason for the vertical integration of newspaper publishers is the difficulty managing the relationship between the publisher and a printer. Few publishers want to be in the printing business—it is a capital-intensive, low-profit business—yet a newspaper publisher has to control its own printing, in part, for fear that it might be held up by a third-party printer at the last moment. We are all familiar with the cry "Stop the presses!"

as a late-breaking story requires redoing the front page. But if an independent printer owned the presses, it could refuse to cooperate unless paid a huge premium. The publisher, with no alternative available that night, might be willing to pay to ensure that the paper had the breaking story on the front page. Other complexities that result from the frequency and time sensitivity of daily newspaper production would lead any market contract between a printer and a publisher to degenerate into continual bickering.

In contrast, it is easier to contract for the printing of a less time-sensitive weekly or monthly magazine. And if performance is unsatisfactory, another printer for the magazine can be sought anywhere in the United States. Unfortunately, a local daily newspaper needs, for obvious logistical reasons, to be published near the town in which it is sold, where the publisher might well find only a single printer capable of printing it.

Such intricate differences explain the different scopes of the two types of publisher and exemplify the complexity surrounding any firm's decision about its scope.

---

linked, yet it is nearly impossible to write contracts that cover all future contingencies that might occur. Having both processes owned by one firm, therefore, saves the costs of continual disputes arising from the market governance of such a production process.

Typically, the costs and benefits of the market and hierarchy are analyzed in the context of vertical integration. However, the same principle of comparing the costs and benefits of various organizational arrangements applies equally to diversification and geographic expansion. For example, as David Teece observed, it is only when the contractual costs of selling or renting excess resources are high that firms themselves can justify diversified expansion into new product markets.[3] Similarly, companies should only become multinational when it is more efficient to perform activities

---

[3] D.J. Teece, "Towards an Economic Theory of the Multiproduct Firm," *Journal of Economic Behavior and Organization* 3, 1982, pp. 39–63.

in a foreign country themselves than to rent their resources, such as brand names, to local firms.[4]

To clarify the factors that determine the choice between the market and the hierarchical organization of production, we next analyze in detail the costs and benefits of each form of organization.[5]

▲ The Market

Benefits of the Market

The argument that the market is the ideal mechanism for the organization of production goes back to Adam Smith. His notion of the "invisible hand" of market forces maximizing the "wealth of nations" has been enshrined in the philosophy of capitalist economies ever since.[6] It has also been formalized in general equilibrium theory, which demonstrates that under certain rather restrictive conditions, an economy of independent agents will optimize social welfare.[7] While both of these abstract macroeconomic approaches ignore many of the realities of the modern industrial economy, their underlying premises describe the two main advantages of the market economy and, therefore, of the market organization of production.

The first of these advantages is that the market is more efficient at **information processing** than the administrative hierarchy. At the extreme this can be considered as the advantage of the market over the centrally planned economy. In the former, independent agents make decentralized production decisions in response to a set of market prices. In the latter, all production decisions are made by a single centralized planning body after it has received all the relevant information.

Although the market can lead to suboptimal outcomes,[8] as recent history has demonstrated, it is a more efficient processor of the information needed to make production decisions than central planning. A planned economy could, in principle, reach the optimal production plan if the central planner knew the production possibilities of all the firms; however, in

---

[4] J.H. Dunning, "Trade, Location of Economic Activities, and the MNE: A Search for an Eclectic Approach," in *The International Allocation of Economy Activity,* ed. B. Ohlin et al. (London: Holmes and Meier, 1977), pp. 395–419.

[5] We will address later the intermediate forms of organization, such as joint ventures, that are neither pure hierarchies nor pure market exchanges.

[6] Adam Smith, *The Wealth of Nations* (Dublin: Whitestone, 1776).

[7] K. Arrow and G. Debreu, "Existence of Equilibrium for a Competitive Economy," *Econometrica* 22 (1954), pp. 265–90.

[8] The inefficiencies of the market organization of production include duplication of effort, as occurred in the Winchester disk drive industry when too many firms invested in a single market opportunity (W.A. Sahlman and H.H. Stevenson, "Capital Market Myopia," *Journal of Business Venturing,* 1985, pp. 7–30) and disequilibrium trades and delays as prices slowly converge on an equilibrium (P. Bolton and J. Farrell, "Decentralisation, Duplication and Delay," *Journal of Political Economy* 98, 1990, pp. 803–26).

practice it would take a lot of time and vast bureaucratic flows of information to achieve this. Indeed, there are many types of information, such as the know-how possessed by a team of craftspeople, that simply cannot be transferred up the hierarchy.[9] In contrast, the market does not require an expensive infrastructure to administer because all information is combined and made available in a set of market prices. Indeed, before its demise, designers of central planning proposed mimicking the price system to economize on the costs of information processing.

This argues that the decentralized and indirect use of information via a price mechanism is more efficient than an administrative hierarchy as a means of transferring the information needed to make production decisions and allocate resources within an economy. By analogy, using a market system to govern production decisions is often more efficient than having those decisions made within a corporate hierarchy.

The second benefit of the market organization of production relates to **incentives.** When production is carried out by independent owners, each receives all the profits from their own endeavors. Thus, each has the incentive to work as hard and as efficiently as possible. Self-interested behavior, therefore, ensures that the market organization of production benefits from high-powered incentives.

In contrast, inefficiencies arise inside the corporate hierarchy because individuals do not receive all the profit they generate. They, therefore, do not have the incentive to maximize corporate profits, but rather to maximize their own welfare. As a result, levels of *ability, effort, and investment* may be lower inside the corporation than in sole proprietorships. Highly skilled workers, for example, may choose to be self-employed because they anticipate earning more money operating their own businesses. Similarly, self-employed workers will probably work harder and take better care of their tools than employees using company tools. Finally, if self-employed salespeople own their customer lists, they will invest more in building and maintaining those lists than if they are employees of a company that owns the list.[10] As a result, lower skill, effort, and investment inside the hierarchy lead to higher production costs. Thus, this perspective argues that the direct production costs of individual proprietors transacting with one another on the market will often be lower than those involving employees inside a corporate hierarchy.

Costs of the Market: Transaction Costs and Market Failure

The original perspective on the scope of the firm, introduced by Coase and called **transaction cost theory,** worked to identify the benefits and costs of

[9] M. Jensen and W.H. Meckling, "Specific and General Knowledge, and Organization Structure," in *Main Currents in Contract Economics,* ed. L. Werin and H. Wijkander (Oxford: Blackwell, 1991), pp. 251–74.
[10] S. Grossman and O. Hart, "The Costs and Benefits of Ownership: A Theory of Vertical and Lateral Integration," *Journal of Political Economy* 94 (1986), pp. 691–719.

market exchange. In particular, it concentrated on identifying the conditions under which markets are very expensive ways to organize transactions or, in the extreme, fail because those costs are so high. Because of the intrinsic merits of markets, transaction cost theory argued that only in such circumstances would the corporate hierarchy become the preferred mode of organization.

A classic example of high transaction costs leading to **market failure** was General Motors' relationship with Fisher Body in the 1920s for the supply of car bodies.[11] GM wanted Fisher Body to build a new plant adjacent to a GM car assembly factory. Fisher Body refused, fearing that once the factory was built, GM could credibly threaten to pay little more than the variable cost of stamping car bodies. At that point, Fisher Body would have no real choice other than to supply GM, because of the costs involved in finding and switching to a new customer (taking out the GM car-body molds, installing new molds, bearing the transportation costs to the new customer's plant, and so forth). Thus, the threat of GM exploiting Fisher Body once it had made the investment led to a market failure. To avoid this, yet to still have the stamping plant built next door to reduce production costs, GM bought Fisher Body and internalized the transaction inside the firm.[12]

This example illustrates many of the conditions that lead to market failure. Specifically, market relationships fail when they are subject to:

- Opportunism

- Asset specificity (small numbers)

- Uncertainty

- High frequency

The premise of transaction cost theory is that because people act in their own self-interest, if the market relationship allows them to do so, they will behave **opportunistically**—that is, they will seek to benefit themselves at the expense of others, just as GM would have taken advantage of Fisher Body (see "Opportunism, Trust, and Reputation"). It is the possibility of firms acting in this way that causes market failure. The other three conditions listed above create the potential for a firm to act opportunistically.

---

[11] B. Klein, R. Crawford, and A. Alchain, "Vertical Integration, Appropriable Rents, and the Competitive Contracting Process," *Journal of Law and Economics* 21 (1978), pp. 297–326.

[12] Note that there are other solutions to this problem. One is trust—Fisher Body remains independent because it trusts GM not to act opportunistically. The other is reputation. GM does not exploit Fisher Body because if it did so other component suppliers may refuse to do business with it in the future. Recent research has examined other motivations for GM buying Fisher Body. Not all of them agree with the analysis above. See R. Casadesus-Masanell and D.F. Spulber, "The Fable of Fisher Body," *Journal of Law and Economics,* Vol. 43, No. 1 (April 2000), pp. 67–104.

Opportunism, Trust, and Reputation

Transaction cost theory views all individuals as self-interested and, therefore, opportunistic. Although this assumption is common to nearly all of organizational economics, it leaves transaction cost theory vulnerable to criticism. If there can be trust in a relationship, so that both parties believe that even when the possibility to behave opportunistically presents itself, the other party will not do so, then the market form of organization need never fail. If one party unfailingly trusts the other to follow the spirit of a contract they have made, no matter what opportunity for self-interested behavior arises, a market contract can be capable of efficiently organizing transactions.

Although trust is not the universal solution to market failure, it can be important in certain situations.

Particularly in less individualistic cultures, such as Japan, trust can be used to explain the existence of markets that transaction theory could not—markets that might in fact be more efficient than hierarchical arrangements. Japanese car manufacturers' relationships with their suppliers, for example, are often portrayed in this light and compared favorably to those of U.S. auto manufacturers.

However, behavior that looks like trust can still be observed in societies where everyone is opportunistic. If a company builds a reputation for acting opportunistically, others will not want to do business with it. Thus, a concern for how reputation may affect future profits can deter firms from acting opportunistically, even when they may be culturally and psychologically predisposed to do so.

Market failure requires **asset specificity,** that is, an asset that is dedicated (specific) to a particular application. In such cases, the party that has made the investment is vulnerable to exploitation because the asset would be worth less in another application. Consider a firm that has customized its production facility to use a particular grade of raw material supplied by only one producer. If the supplier tries to raise the price of the raw material, what alternatives does the buyer have? It can look for a different supplier, but if it does switch it will have to reconfigure its production facility for the new grade of material, which would be expensive. The firm, then, would be prepared to pay an amount equal to the reconfiguration cost, over and above the original price for the raw material, before it would consider switching suppliers.

Types of asset specificity include location, physical, and human capital:[13]

- **Location specificity** occurs when buyers and sellers locate fixed assets in close proximity to minimize transport and inventory costs.

- **Physical asset specificity** occurs when one party or both parties to a transaction invest in equipment that is dedicated to a particular, limited use.

- **Human capital specificity** occurs when employees develop skills that are specialized to a particular relationship or a given organization.

[13] O.E. Williamson, *The Economic Institutions of Capitalism* (New York: Free Press, 1985).

The frequent occurrence of such investments suggests that the phenomenon of asset specificity is actually quite common. Building a power plant next to a coal mine to minimize transport costs is an example of location specificity. Customizing a plant to a particular grade of material is an example of physical specificity. The network of personal relationships that managers develop inside a firm, which makes their working elsewhere less efficient, is an example of human capital specificity.

As Oliver Williamson argued, investments such as these that are specific to an application create a small numbers bargaining problem. After making such an investment, the purchasing firm is unable to negotiate freely and equally with other potential suppliers, as might well have been possible before the investment was made; instead, a firm is locked into buying from only a few suppliers, and often only one. This gives the supplier bargaining power that allows it to act opportunistically and so leads to the market failure.[14]

The obvious solution to the problem of one party acting opportunistically would be to write a contract for the duration of the asset that simply prevents such behavior. Why doesn't Fisher Body just set a contract price for the supply of car bodies that GM cannot renegotiate? This is when the condition of **uncertainty** comes into play. It would be impossible to write a comprehensive long-term contract if the nature of the transaction is such that all possible future eventualities cannot be written down. If the contract would have to cover an enormous number of clauses, such as, "if demand for the product increases 10 percent in less than one month, the supplier is entitled to deliver only 8 percent more product," it becomes prohibitively expensive to write and enforce.[15] The more uncertainties there are, the more difficult it is to write a long-term contract that covers all possible contingencies, and the more likely that the market will fail.

Finally, it is argued that **high transaction frequency** increases the likelihood of market failure. Frequent transactions repeatedly expose a firm to holdup, so that haggling and negotiation occur more often. To eliminate these costs, and remedy the market failure, vertical integration is often necessary. In contrast, for one time or occasional transactions, such as a public construction project, vertical integration is unlikely.

Many empirical tests have been conducted to demonstrate the validity of transaction cost theory, particularly in the context of vertical integration.

[14] Note, however, that asset specificity almost always leads to a bilateral threat of holdup. In principle, Fisher Body could have held up GM, just as easily as GM could hold up Fisher Body. Once GM had negotiated a price with Fisher Body and installed the molds at its factory, Fisher Body could raise the price. GM would be powerless to object because it would have to remove the molds, install them in another supplier, and potentially lose several months of car production.

[15] Indeed, given "bounded rationality"—physical limits to what the mind can process—it will most likely be impossible. R.M. Cyert, and J.G. March, *A Behavioral Theory of the Firm* (Englewood Cliffs, NJ: Prentice Hall, 1963).

For example, asset specificity (measured by the amount of customized engineering required) has been shown to be an important determinant of vertical integration in the auto components industry.[16] Likewise, the link between physical site specificity and ownership, in the cases of electricity generating stations owning their suppliers of coal and alumina smelters owning their suppliers of bauxite, has also been demonstrated.[17] The same research also found evidence of the effects of frequency and uncertainty on the presence of market versus hierarchical arrangements.

In summary, transaction cost theory identifies durable relationships involving asset specificity, uncertainty, and high frequency of transactions as conditions for market failure. Whenever market exchange for the sale (or purchase) of a good or service fails, a firm will have to establish some form of hierarchical control over the transaction.

Other Sources of Market Failure

Even without the specific investments that are critical to transactions cost theory, there are other situations in which markets fail. One such instance is **inseparability**—the impossibility of separating one resource from others within a firm.[18] For example, vacationers who perceive lodging as an integral part of their Disney World experience are unable to separate their hotel stay from their overall perception of the Disney brand name. To preserve the latter, Disney believes it must operate the former, and so does not contract out the management of its Disneyworld hotels.

Other failures can arise in the **market for information.**[19] When information can be easily conveyed to others, there may still be a classic paradox over its sale. Buyers don't want to pay for information without knowing its content, but sellers don't want to reveal their information before being paid. As a result, when individuals or firms have valuable information, such as the location of a new motorway, they often use it themselves rather than selling it on the market.

Other failures arise when information simply cannot be transferred. This is the case of **tacit knowledge**—knowledge that cannot be written down in a set of blueprints or equations.[20] Archetypal examples are riding a bicycle

[16] D.J. Teece and K. Monteverde, "Supplier Switching Costs and Vertical Integration in the Automobile Industry," *Bell Journal of Economics* 25 (1979), pp. 833–48; and G. Walker and D. Weber, "A Transaction Cost Approach to Make-or-Buy Decisions," *Administrative Science Quarterly,* September 1984, pp. 373–91.

[17] P. Joskow, "Vertical Integration and Long-Term Contracts: The Case of Coal-Burning Electric Generating Plants," *Journal of Law, Economics, and Organization,* Spring 1985, pp. 33–80; and J. A. Stuckey, *Vertical Integration and Joint Ventures in the Aluminum Industry* (Cambridge, MA: Ballinger, 1987), pp. 185–220.

[18] D. J. Teece, "Economies of Scope and the Scope of the Enterprises," *Journal of Economic Behavior and Organization,* September 1980, pp. 373–91.

[19] K. Arrow, *Economics of Information* (Cambridge, MA: Belknap Press, 1984).

[20] M. Polyani, *Personal Knowledge* (New York: Harper Torchbooks, 1962).

and shooting pool. However much physics you have studied, you cannot actually ride a bike or pocket a pool ball unless you have practiced how to to it. Thus, tacit knowledge is difficult to sell because it cannot be transferred in written form, it can only be re-created by an individual or firm learning the skill for itself.[21]

Resources that involve tacit knowledge, such as a unique consumer marketing capability that resides in a management team, therefore, are particularly vulnerable to market failure. Indeed such informational resources are the basis for many corporate strategies or diversification. David Teece, for example, found that oil companies were more likely to diversify into markets for alternative fuels that shared proprietary know-how.[22]

A final cause of market failure is not due to efficiency considerations, as are all the previous arguments, but to the exercise of **market power.** More specifically, markets can fail when a firm achieves the *vertical foreclosure* of competitors. This was the idea that Rockefeller exploited in building Standard Oil in the late 19th century. His insight was that by controlling the railroad and pipeline transportation of oil, he could squeeze out his competitors in the oil business, a strategy later made illegal by the Sherman Antitrust Act of 1890. Rockefeller first exploited the benefits of the large size of Standard Oil (by 1869, Standard's Cleveland oil refinery was the largest in the world) to gain leverage with the railroads and later with pipelines. By controlling both the oil production and railroad transportation businesses, Rockefeller then locked production-only competitors out of the market. He could then acquire the firms that Standard wanted at distress prices and drive out of the oil business those firms that it did not need. To avoid being foreclosed from the market, competitors would have had to vertically integrate into the transportation of their own oil. Rockefeller's control of oil transportation, therefore, effectively led to the failure of that market.

This is a dramatic example of a phenomenon that by definition can only be found in concentrated industries, or when a dominant player exists.

Summary

Theory can explain the existence and scope of the firm from the perspective of market failure. Recognizing the potential information processing and incentive advantages of markets, it argues that a firm's activities should be limited to those involving transactions for which the costs of market exchange are extremely high. However, it is also possible to explain the boundaries of the firm from the opposite perspective—considering the advantages and disadvantages of the hierarchy.

---

[21] Tacit knowledge is an example of path dependency in the accumulation of a resource, and so is often a valuable and inimitable resource (see Chapter 2).
[22] Teece, "Economies of Scope and the Scope of the Enterprise," pp. 223–47.

▲ The Hierarchy

Benefits of the Hierarchy

The benefits of the corporate hierarchy, which allow it to efficiently organize transactions when the market fails, lie in the nature of the hierarchical relationship and the unified ownership structure of the firm.[23]

Unlike a market relationship, where no one has **authority** over anyone else, inside the firm superiors are vested with the power, both legal and cultural, to tell employees what to do within broad bounds set out by the employment contract and societal norms. Thus, opportunism and the unproductive bargaining that cause the market to fail can be reduced when corporate executives mandate behavior and then monitor subordinates. **Unified ownership** can also reduce the pursuit of local goals, unambiguously determine a clear corporate goal, and provide easier access to the relevant information needed to settle disputes.[24]

The hierarchy is particularly effective when there is an ongoing need for intense **coordination** among parties to a transaction.[25] This occurs whenever tasks are mutually dependent and appropriate actions by each party depend on what others do. The need for coordination is perhaps easiest to see in the design of a complex product that does not have well-defined interfaces between components—what Milgrom and Roberts called *design interconnectedness*.[26] In this context, a hierarchy is more likely to produce the optimal system design rather than one that reflects the sum of the best individual component designs. Moreover, a hierarchy minimizes the continual bargaining over each unit's profit (the share of the pie), that can prevent the best overall design (the size of the pie) from

---

[23] Note that the hierarchy itself involves a contractual relationship—the employment relation. Thus, the distinguishing aspect of a firm as a "nexus of contracts" is that it defines residual rights of control (who decides what happens when contracts do not precisely specify behavior) and residual property rights (who retains the profits after all participants have received their contractual payments).

[24] Transaction cost theory, somewhat controversially, argues that the hierarchy can monitor and audit behavior at a lower cost than the market (Williamson, *Economic Institutions of Capitalism,* p. 155). Another theoretical perspective within organizational economics, imperfect decision making, examines the circumstances under which hierarchies are preferable because they allow for the overseeing of individuals, who, however well intentioned and thorough their analyses, will occasionally make incorrect decisions (R. K. Sah and J. E. Stiglitz, "Human Fallibility and Economic Organization," *American Economic Review,* May–June 1985, pp. 292–97).

[25] Alchian and Demsetz argued that a firm must exist when coordination involves team production where the effort of each individual cannot be measured (A. Alchian and H. Demsetz, "Production, Information Costs and Economic Organization," *American Economic Review,* December 1972, pp. 777–95).

[26] P. Milgrom and J. Roberts, *Economics, Organization and Management* (Englewood Cliffs, NJ: Prentice Hall, 1992).

Influence Costs

One set of costs associated with the hierarchy has recently received a lot of attention. Termed **influence costs,** they are closely related but not identical to agency costs.[29] Their premise is that a lot of activity inside corporations is wastefully directed toward influencing the decisions of the firm in ways that will produce favorable results for the individual involved. The simplest example would be people lobbying to get the biggest office in the building. This sort of activity, while prevalent in large corporations and immediately recognizable as internal office politics, is, of course, pure waste.

Influence costs inside firms do not presume divergent interests between owners and employees or superiors and subordinates. They will be incurred whenever there is jockeying for position among participants inside an organization. Competition among peers for the distribution of the wealth available to the workforce, rather than overt conflict between principals and subordinates, are the principal concern of influence costs.[30]

emerging.[27] For example, an independent manufacturer of auto emission catalysts is less likely to suggest a change in the design of the exhaust system if it leads to less use of catalysts.[28] Although these coordination problems do not completely disappear inside the hierarchy, they are usually reduced.

Costs of the Hierarchy

The exercise of authority inside the corporate hierarchy does not come without costs. If it did, the corporation could extend its scope indefinitely through what is called *selective intervention*—letting divisions make all their own decisions except those that require corporatewide coordination.

The costs of the hierarchy include the drawbacks typically associated with the **bureaucracy** of large-scale organizations that impede efficient information processing: the expense of layers of management in the corporate hierarchy; the slowness and inflexibility of bureaucratic decision making; the difficulties corporate executives have in controlling businesses that may have different dominant logics; and the waste incurred in office politics (see "Influence Costs"). All are costs of performing activities inside the firm.

[27] This is the argument surrounding incomplete contracts. See Grossman and Hart, op. cit (footnote 10).
[28] The argument that firms should vertically integrate to maximize profitability by setting marginal revenue equal to the sum of marginal costs at each stage in the chain, rather than simply the marginal cost of the last player in the chain, is similar. Without vertical integration, profitability in the whole chain is reduced because participants at each stage try to maximize their own profit.
[29] P. Milgrom and J. Roberts, *Economics, Organization and Management* (Englewood Cliffs, NJ: Prentice Hall, 1992).
[30] Influence costs have more typically been examined in the context of public policy, where individuals, and groups lobby for legislation that favors their own interests.

Agency Costs

Agency costs arise from the failure of the hierarchical relationship between the principal (typically thought of as the owner of the firm) and the agent (typically an employee). They include the production costs resulting from self-interested behavior by agents and the governance costs of writing, monitoring, and bonding to any systems put in place to reduce the principal's losses from that behavior.

The underlying conditions for the existence of agency costs are:

- **Asymmetric Interests.** Agents act to maximize their personal welfare and do not automatically act in the interest of principals.

- **Private Information.** Because principals do not have access to all of the same information as agents, they incur monitoring costs and have difficulty accessing the skill and effort of agents.

- **Uncertainty.** Since performance is often affected by unpredictable, exogenous events, the observed outcomes of agents' behavior may not be an accurate reflection of their skill and effort.

Probably the greatest costs of the corporate hierarchy involve what are called **agency costs.** These are the costs that arise when individuals act in their own self-interest, rather than acting to maximize corporate performance (see "Agency Costs").[31] Agency costs are therefore prevalent throughout an organization whenever there is a divergence of interests between shareholders and managers,[32] superiors and subordinates, or, as we will use to illustrate, the corporate office and divisional executives.[33]

In its starkest form (the so-called **moral hazard** problem), the argument of agency theory is that because corporate executives do not have access to exactly the same information as divisional management and cannot monitor their every action, divisional managers will pursue their own interests. The resulting behavior may involve simply slacking on the job, such as playing golf on Friday afternoons; but it will more likely involve actions, such as divisional managers acting to reach targets that trigger their bonuses even at the expense of corporate profits; fudging the numbers in favor of investments that expand the size of their own divisions; or refusing to transfer a highly regarded executive to another division. Such

---

[31] M. Jensen and W. H. Meckling, "Theory of the Firm," *Journal of Financial Economics* 3, No. 4 (1976), pp. 305–60, and K. M. Eisenhardt, "Agency Theory: An Assessment and Review," *Academy of Management Review* 14, No. 1 (1989), pp. 57–74.

[32] The implications of agency costs between shareholders and managers are examined in the chapter on corporate governance (Chapter 8).

[33] One reason for the divergence of interest between principals and agents is their respective attitudes toward risk. Agents whose careers depend on the performance of the company are typically assumed to be risk averse while principals for whom the firm is only one of many investments are typically assumed to be risk neutral.

Human Nature

Some critics of agency theory argue that its premises are unrealistic because they are based on a flawed view of human nature.[35] These critics argue that if people are not treated as individualistic, but, at least partly, as altruistic, and if they value things other than money, then a basic assumption of agency theory is violated.

This is not correct. Agency theory assumes nothing more about human nature than that people are calculating rational actors who respond to incentives in order to maximize whatever they value. Agency theory does not specify what individuals value. It is quite possible for individuals to be altruistic. It is also quite feasible in agency theory to have individuals derive pleasure from peer praise, self-esteem, position in the hierarchy, quality of lifestyle, and so forth. All of these variables can be included in the payoffs that individuals seek to maximize.

Although such an argument bolsters agency theory, real life complicates the reduction of agency costs because we never know exactly what any particular individual values, nor can most incentive systems be fine-tuned to each individual's motivation.

behavior incurs both direct production costs—resulting, for example, from the lower effort put out by divisional managers and their inappropriate decisions—as well as the governance costs of the monitoring and control systems, such as budgets, capital expenditure approvals, and HR reviews that are put in place to prevent such behavior. These are costs of the hierarchical mode of organization.

Other agency costs of the corporate hierarchy result from **adverse selection.** Although similar to moral hazard in that it also arises from the inability of superiors in a hierarchy to observe something about their subordinates, moral hazard reflects *hidden actions* whereas adverse selection refers to *hidden qualities*. An example is the inability of the firm to select desirable workers when it cannot accurately distinguish their intrinsic quality before hiring them.[34] For example, start-up firms in Silicon Valley would like to hire innovative, entrepreneurial managers. They would even be willing to pay such individuals more than the average salary

---

[34] The costs of adverse selection can also lead to market failures. This was demonstrated in a classic article on the market for used cars (G. Akerlof, "The Market for Lemons: Qualitative Uncertainty and the Market Mechanism," *Quarterly Journal of Economics* 84 (1970), pp. 488–500). The authors argued that most used cars that are for sale will be of poor quality because any owner who knows that his or her car is reliable will choose (select) to keep driving it. Even if owners want to sell, buyers, who cannot accurately determine a car's quality even in an inspection, will be skeptical that it is reliable and so won't pay much for it. This provides another reason for owners of good-quality cars to keep them off the market. In turn, this reduces the average quality of used cars that are sold, so lowering the price a buyer will pay, leading fewer people with good cars to sell them, and so on until, at the extreme, no market for used cars exists.

[35] Michael J. Brennan, "Incentives, Rationality, and Society," *Journal of Applied Corporate Finance,* Summer 1994, pp. 31–39.

because they would create more value. However, since companies are limited in their ability to distinguish such workers from others before they hire them, they cannot offer to pay those individuals their true worth. Therefore, individuals who know they have desirable skills but cannot credibly convey that information will choose to establish their own businesses, if they are able to do so, knowing that they will earn more than the salary offered.[36] While an incentive scheme, such as giving managers phantom stock in their divisions, rather than a straight salary, will alleviate some of the problem (arguably only those with confidence in their own entrepreneurial skills will seek out such a compensation scheme), it cannot completely eliminate the costs of adverse selection.

Minimizing Agency Costs   To minimize self-interested behavior that cannot be prevented by direct monitoring (see "Human Nature"), corporate executives usually install an incentive scheme that attempts to align the interests of division managers as closely as possible with those of the corporate office. They might, for example, reward division managers on the performance of the whole company as well as their own divisions. Such an incentive scheme can reduce, but will never eliminate, the cost of self-interested behavior: the more division managers are rewarded on corporate pay, for example, the less incentive they will have to maximize their own division's performance. In addition, there are always expenses involved in the design and operation of any incentive scheme.

If the managerial behavior itself, or an outcome measure that is tightly correlated with managerial skills and effort, can be **cheaply and accurately monitored,** it will be easy to design an incentive system that produces the desired behavior, and agency costs will be low.[37] The quality of store managers' contributions, for example, can often be accurately measured by their stores' profitability, so that a profit-based incentive scheme ensures that they will not be able to slack without paying the penalty. In contrast, when it is difficult to directly observe the behavior of managers, or use performance of their units as a surrogate, incentive systems will be less effective and agency costs will be higher. It is notoriously difficult, for example, to assess the effectiveness of an R&D team because the link between their effort and the success of a project is often weak. In this

[36] The critical condition for the existence of adverse selection and moral hazard is asymmetric information. The individual has private information about how entrepreneurial he or she is, which the firm cannot verify. One solution to adverse selection, therefore, involves the individual incurring costs to acquire a "signal" of those dimensions of quality that cannot objectively be evaluated (A.M. Spence, *Market Signalling: Information Transfer in Hiring and Related Processes* [Cambridge, MA: Harvard University Press, 1973]). The fact that most readers of this book are acquiring MBAs partly reflects their desire to learn something about management, but also, in part, reflects the importance of the MBA as a signal of inherent quality.

[37] Eisenhardt, "Agency Theory;" and W.G. Ouchi, "A Conceptual Framework for the Design of Organizational Control Mechanisms," *Management Science* 25 (1979), pp. 833–48.

setting, incentive schemes that are too tightly tied to performance may be demotivating. Not doing so, however, creates slack that allows R&D managers to shirk or pursue their own interests.

When employees' skills and efforts have a **substantial impact on performance,** the absence of an effective incentive system can be particularly costly. The quality of the contribution of senior managers, for example, can dramatically affect their firm's long-run performance. As a result, the costs of any self-interested behavior that does occur may be high. In contrast, even if a night watchman sleeps on the job, it may have little effect on firm performance.

Summary

Although hierarchies have the advantage of authority and unified ownership, they inevitably incur agency costs. Theory suggests these costs will be highest when an employee's skill and effort are important, but difficult to measure accurately. Under these circumstances, the expense of the hierarchy may limit the scope of the firm.

It is for these reasons, for example, that most large corporations do not have in-house advertising departments. The skill and effort of creative talent is critical to the development of a good advertisement, yet creative work is very difficult to monitor. In particular, evaluating the performance of an advertising campaign is hard. Moreover, talented advertising executives have the choice of establishing their own companies. Thus, rather than incur the agency costs of operating an advertising department inside the corporate hierarchy, most corporations, including those like Unilever that once had their own advertising staffs, now employ outside agencies.

▲ Conclusion: The Choice between Market and Hierarchy

Neither the market nor the hierarchy is the ideal form of organization. If either was, the economy would be dominated by one firm or made up exclusively of self-employed individuals. Instead, each form of organization has its costs and each has its benefits. (See Figure 5.1.) In most cases, it will be obvious when a business or activity is best conducted inside a firm or on the market. However, there will be many instances when there is neither a clear market failure, nor overwhelmingly high agency costs inside the firm. In such cases, there is ultimately a trade-off between the market and the hierarchy as mechanisms for the organization of production.

The market benefits from high-powered incentives and efficient information processing because individuals receive the profits from their work and respond to decentralized market prices. However, the market can fail when conditions surrounding an exchange lead to high transaction costs or the exercise of market power.

FIGURE 5.1
Cost and Benefit of
the Market and
Hierarchy

	Market	Hierarchy
Benefits	Informational efficiency High-powered incentives	Authority Coordination
Costs	Transaction costs Market power	Bureaucracy Agency costs

Conversely, the hierarchy is often more effective than the market in coordinating activity because it can define routines and exert authority that workers, within bounds, will obey. However, the hierarchy incurs the bureaucratic and agency costs that result from self-interested behavior by subordinates.

The most complex decisions concerning mode of organization often come down to a trade-off between incentives and coordination. When providing high-powered incentives to individuals is important because of the effect their skill and effort have on performance, the market may ultimately be preferred. When there is a need for continual coordination of activities, the hierarchy may be more efficient.

In principle, a firm should include within its corporate hierarchy only those businesses and activities where the benefit of ownership is greater than the costs (to the left of A in Figure 5.2). However, since the costs of the hierarchy will increase with broadening scope, if for no other reason than the span of control is increasing, while the market transaction costs are more or less independent of firm scope, the organizational boundary of the firm (B) often comes before this point.[38] Indeed, it is usually the relative costs of administering a business or transaction within the firm or in a market exchange that determine the scope of the firm.

These trade-offs can be observed in the debate over the effect that the Internet will have on the scope of the firm. Some argue that firm scope will contract with faster and more ubiquitous communications because the cost of external market contracting will be reduced. A small factory in Shanghai, for example, can be in direct real-time contact with a retailer in France. As a result, it is now substantially cheaper and more effective for that retailer to outsource manufacturing. However, those exact same arguments also apply inside the hierarchy! Monitoring the behavior and

[38] In practice, the costs of the hierarchy and the market are not continuous with expansions of scope (as they appear to be in Figure 5.2). Rather, as the previous discussion demonstrated, they vary with each individual business or activity.

FIGURE 5.2
The Limit to Firm Scope

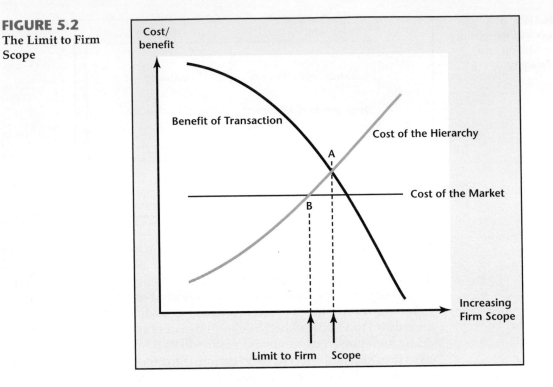

Intermediate Forms of Organization

performance of an overseas manufacturing facility becomes much easier as communications improve. Whether the scope of the firm increases or decreases, therefore, cannot be predicted with certainty. As Figure 5.2 illustrates, if both hierarchical costs and market transaction costs are reduced, the resulting effect on the scope of the firm is indeterminate.

Intermediate Forms of Organization

A problem with the analysis so far is the assumption that the choice of organizational form is binary—either the market or the hierarchy. In fact, the range of alternatives more closely resembles a long and varied spectrum (see Figure 5.3). At one extreme is the market, which refers to a well-organized spot market where goods and services are bought and sold at arm's length. At the other extreme is the corporate hierarchy where all the activities are ensconced within the legal boundaries of a firm. In between are a variety of alternative ways to organize a given transaction. Some of these, such as joint

FIGURE 5.3 **A Spectrum of Governance Structures**

ventures, more closely resemble the corporate hierarchy. Others, such as long-term market contracts, are market-based alternatives, although they differ considerably from spot market transactions. Indeed, Hennart has gone so far as to call these intermediate forms of governance "the swollen middle" to indicate how common they are in practice.[39]

We do not have space to go into the details of all the intermediate organizational forms. In general, these forms, to greater or lesser extent, combine the strengths and weaknesses of the archetypes. Therefore, the principles determining the costs and benefits of the market and hierarchy, as outlined above, remain appropriate for the analysis of intermediate forms and demonstrate that no form of organization is universally superior.

Williamson, for example, matched governance structures and the attributes of transactions to predict which types of transactions can efficiently employ so-called mixed modes of governance. In essence, he predicted that standardized transactions (whatever the frequency) will be handled through the market (classical contracting procedures). In contrast, transactions involving repeated asset specific investments will be done under the firm hierarchy (unified governance). In between, a host of intermediate solutions will be based on structures where the autonomy of the parties is maintained (such as joint ventures), or where there are specific third-party mechanisms for resolving disputes (for example, arbitration).

Practice

▲ Choosing the Scope of the Firm

Although the principles outlined above apply to decisions about the boundary of the firm in all three dimensions of scope, the ideal place to apply them is to the analysis of vertical integration—the make-or-buy decision. This dimension of scope is currently subject to much examination as firms look to outsource many activities and services that were previously unquestioningly accepted as part of the corporate hierarchy.

Bias to the Market

The underlying premise behind this analysis is that activities should be performed outside rather than inside the firm unless there are compelling reasons to the contrary. The arguments for this bias are the production cost benefits that independent suppliers can exploit and the governance cost benefits of high-powered incentives and decentralized information processing. In addition, a corporate hierarchy inevitably incurs agency costs. Thus, the burden of proof in the analysis of vertical integration will be on

---

[39] Jean-Francois Hennart, "Explaining the Swollen Middle: Why Most Transactions Are a Mix of 'Market' and 'Hierarchy,'" *Organization Science* 4, No. 4, pp. 529–47.

justifying why the firm itself should perform a given activity. This principle is contrary to traditional practice in many large companies for whom the bias has been to perform activities in-house. Such companies tend to overestimate the costs of market exchange while simultaneously overestimating the benefits of the hierarchy.

Indeed, an increasing number of firms are today using market contracting, rather than vertical integration, to coordinate production. One such company is Benetton, the Italian clothing manufacturer whose brand achieved great popularity.[40] Historically, 99 percent of its knitting, all of its assembly, and most of its finishing were carried out by several hundred small independent contractors, while all its products were sold through independently owned shops. Only a substantial amount of dyeing was done in-house. The whole system was coordinated by a sophisticated management information capability that linked stores, production scheduling, and contractors. As a result, Benetton was able to adapt flexibly to uncertain fashion demand without bearing the fixed costs of its own manufacturing capacity.

Given the viability of this model of independent market contracting, the historical bias to perform activities inside the firm can be problematic. Adjusting to the new principle will require a fundamental shift in thinking about the appropriate scope of many companies and a careful assessment of the production and governance costs of the two modes of organization at every stage in their activities (see "When Not to Vertically Integrate").

▲ A Decision Process

On the basis of the principles outlined earlier, we can propose a process that can be applied to decisions about the vertical scope of the firm. The process involves a logical sequence of steps that lead to a conclusion about whether or not a firm should vertically integrate into a particular activity. It should be stressed, however, that issues concerning the organizational boundaries of a firm are some of the most complicated facing the corporate strategist and that there are often no easy answers.

Step 1: Disaggregate the Industry Value Chain

The analysis of vertical integration can only proceed after the industry value chain has been disaggregated into all the steps that are physically capable of being separated. Too broad a definition of activities can lead firms to compete in an activity simply because of its adjacency to another activity they perform well. For example, many firms historically developed their own computer programs for production control, arguing that

[40] J.L. Heskett, "Benetton Group," Harvard Business School Case no. 396–177.

When Not to Vertically Integrate

There are many fallacies about when vertical integration makes sense. One is that physical linkages in the production process, such as those between different processing stages in an oil refinery, require vertical integration. Although often true because of the need for intense coordination, on some occasions such separate processes may be carried out by different firms.

Another fallacy is that it is necessary to backward (or forward) integrate to secure favorable prices in a cyclical industry. This is incorrect. If a firm supplies itself at a price below market value, it is forgoing the high prices it could charge others for those supplies. While this may be of benefit to the purchasing unit, the supplying unit will suffer relative to its independent peers.

A third fallacy is that it is good to forward integrate into higher-value-added parts of the value chain. This too is often incorrect. Value added and profitability often do not correlate. Moreover, a firm's resources do not necessarily transfer across adjacent activities or businesses. A competitive advantage in one stage may arise from completely different factors and conditions than competitive advantage at another stage.

A last fallacy is that a firm should backward integrate simply because it is a large purchaser and can exploit manufacturing scale economies. While firms may be above minimum efficient scale for the production of a particular component, specialist outside suppliers who are also above that scale often benefit from efficiencies across a full range of activities, from R&D to service. Further, compared to vertically integrated firms, focused suppliers often are more successful in realizing dynamic innovations.

these were integral to their production process. However, outside programs were often better because they were developed by software experts. Determining the appropriate level of disaggregation of activities is therefore an important prerequisite to analyzing the desired degree of vertical integration.

The intrinsic structural attractiveness of each activity in the industry value chain should then be analyzed. Each can be thought of, at least conceptually, as a discrete business whose profit potential varies according to its underlying structure. In the Australian concrete industry, for example, most of the industry profit is captured in cement production and stone and sand quarrying (see Figure 5.4). More competitive stages of the industry, such as concrete mixing, cover cash costs and provide a fair return on invested capital but create no economic profit.

Having mapped out the separate stages in an industry and determined their expected average profit potential, firms can now apply a set of questions to decide whether or not they should compete in any given stage. The result of decisions made at each stage will ultimately determine the overall scope of the firm.

The analysis begins by assuming there are efficiently functioning markets at every stage in the industry value chain. Subsequent steps will address situations where this is not the case.

FIGURE 5.4
Australian Concrete Industry Value Chain

Source: Reprinted from "When and When Not to Vertically Integrate" by J. A. Stuckey and D. White, MIT *Sloan Management Review*, (Spring 1993), p. 77, by permission of publisher. Copyright © 1993 by Massachusetts Institute of Technology. All rights reserved.

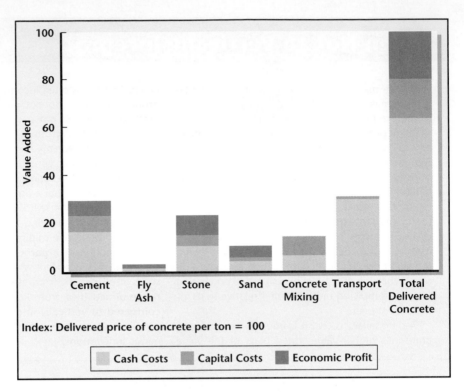

Index: Delivered price of concrete per ton = 100

Step 2: Competitive Advantage

Do you have a competitive advantage in the performance of the activity?

When efficient markets are available for transactions between each stage of an industry, decisions to participate in a given stage depend simply on whether or not it would be profitable for the firm to do so. That is, could the firm earn a return above its cost of capital? This depends on the fundamental attractiveness of the business and whether or not the firm possesses a competitive advantage that would enable it to make the product (or perform the service) more efficiently than outside suppliers.

Indeed, when there are perfect markets, the firms that own the valuable resources in an industry should be able to appropriate most of the profit, without having to compete in all stages of the industry. In the personal computer (PC) industry, for example, Intel and Microsoft are able to appropriate about three-quarters of industry profits just by providing the microprocessor and the operating system, respectively. They are not vertically integrated into the manufacture and sale of PCs themselves.

This is the argument behind the virtual corporation. Performing only one or two critical activities, while accessing other goods and services from competitive markets, the virtual corporation is presumed to be able to capture most of the profits from an industry and may also use its flexibility and low fixed costs as a source of competitive advantage. The Internet has enabled many companies to successfully operate as virtual organizations, using market transactions to provide many of the activities necessary to complete the production and delivery of a product or service. For example, eBay, the online auction site, which does little more than provide a Web site, has a market value of $ 57.1 billion. Vendors list the product, describing its features and providing photographs if necessary. Purchasers send the funds directly to the vendor, and delivery is usually completed by UPS or the U. S. Postal Service. So eBay never takes physical possession of the product or the money; it merely acts as the electronic intermediary.

One unusual and more traditional example of this is Sulzer, a Swiss machinery manufacturer.[41] For many years, Sulzer was the world leader in marine diesel engines, even though it came from a mountainous and landlocked country and did not even make the engines itself. The explanation for Sulzer's success was that it designed the world's most reliable engine. Because the cost of downtime for shipowners is very high, an engine that is more reliable can justify a substantial price premium. Sulzer marketed the merits of its engines to shipowners, provided 24-hour worldwide delivery of spare parts, and manufactured only a few of the most critical engine parts. Shipowners then specified Sulzer engines for their vessels, while shipyards, using local contractors to manufacture the remaining parts, installed the engines. In this way, Sulzer was responsible for perhaps 20 percent of the total engine cost. Its design expertise, however, was so valuable that it could make substantial margins while other participants in the value chain made only normal returns.

In many instances, the analysis is more complex because industry profit is not captured by one particular resource or activity. Indeed, profit commonly accrues to a system of assets employed together, for which individual markets do not function adequately or even exist. In these situations, firms might have to extend their scope into markets where they do not necessarily have a competitive advantage to overcome market failures or to exploit the systemic advantages of coordination. Consider, for example, Zara—the fashionable Spanish clothes manufacturer and retailer. Unlike Benetton, Zara owns all its own stores and does nearly all its own manufacturing around its Galician headquarters, arguing that the rapid coordination between stores and production facilities reduces cost and ensures

[41] Richard R. Rawlinson, "Sulzer Brothers Limited," Harvard Business School Case no. 386–021, 1986.

in-stock availability.[42] Indeed, this vertically integrated model with tight interconnectedness currently appears to be more successful than Benetton's disaggregated model.

Step 3: Market Failure

Is there a market failure? Are the costs of market governance extremely high? Can dominant firms exercise market foreclosure?

Steps 1 and 2 of the analysis explicitly assumed that efficient markets existed at all stages in the industry. When this is not the case, a firm may have to vertically integrate into those activities for which there are no viable markets. To determine when this is necessary, the firm must examine each activity for conditions that transactions cost theory identifies as leading to high market governance costs and hence to market failure.

Consider, for example, whether a baseball team should own the stadium in which it plays. First, there is a long-term relationship involved. The stadium itself will last a long time (Fenway Park, the oldest in major league baseball, was built in 1912). Second, the stadium is a **specific asset,** designed for the baseball business. Although outdoor concerts could be held there, no other activity may generate the summer attendance that baseball does. Similarly, a team that has built local fan loyalty will be loath to move to another city. Thus, the stadium represents an asset that is committed to one baseball team, and so creates the potential for opportunistic behavior. Once the stadium is built, the team can threaten to pay $1 for the use of the facilities, and the stadium's owner seemingly has no choice but to accept the offer. Conversely, the stadium owner can charge $20 million for a year's usage, and the team seemingly has little option but to pay up.

Given this situation, can a contract be written to prevent opportunism over the life of the stadium? This is problematic given the future **uncertainty.** In principle, it would seem feasible to write a contract that sets a price today and includes an escalator clause. But what if the television contract for baseball quadruples in value? What if the rules of baseball change in 40 years' time and the stadium needs to be expanded? The list of possible contingencies is very long, and writing a foolproof contract is almost impossible. As a consequence, many stadiums are owned by the teams that play there. Those that are not are usually owned by a municipality that covers the expense through tax revenues.

Transaction costs surrounding the transfer of tacit knowledge are also high, and so can lead to market failure. When valuable skills or knowledge cannot be written down, firms may have to extend their scope so that knowledge can be directly deployed by those with the relevant experience. In biotechnology, for example, the tacit expertise of researchers is

---

[42] See P. Ghemawat and J.L. Nueno, "ZARA: Fast Fashion" Harvard Business School Case no. 9-703-497, 2003.

often critical to bringing a manufacturing facility onstream. Because such information cannot be transferred on a market, the R&D function in this case cannot be separated from manufacturing.

In addition, market failures may be due to the exercise of market power. When there are a limited number of firms at any stage in an industry, an opportunity may exist to use their bargaining power to extract profit from upstream or downstream players, or (within legal bounds) to lock out competitors at other stages. This threat can force firms to vertically integrate into activities in which they do not have a competitive advantage. (See "The Exercise of Market Power.")

Problems with market power can be particularly acute in the case of **cospecialized assets.**[43] These are a set of assets that are specific to each other, yet because of their rarity, each possesses market power. Consider three firms: one owns a patent for a new arthritic drug; another, one of a few specialized biotech manufacturing facilities that could make the drug; and a third controls a distribution channel to rheumatologists. Each is a valuable resource, but when deployed in combination, they are likely to create substantially more value than when used separately. However, the intense bargaining over the profit created by the combination may produce market failure. As a result, cospecialized assets often end up under common ownership, or in joint venture arrangements.[44]

Market failures arising from high transaction costs or the exercise of market power are, in fact, quite common. As a result, they are a major influence on choice of firm scope.

Step 4: Need for Coordination

Is there an ongoing need for intensive coordination? Are continual and integrated changes required? Is there a distinct interface between activities?

Even if there are no obvious market failures, the benefits that can be achieved from coordination inside the hierarchy might still lead a firm to vertically integrate. Whenever a transaction requires **continual mutual adaptation** by both parties, the benefits of authority and unified ownership may require a firm to perform an activity, even though efficient independent suppliers exist.[45]

---

[43] D.J. Teece, "Profiting from Technological Innovation: Implications for Integration, Collaboration, Licensing, and Public Policy," in *The Competitive Challenge,* ed. D.J. Teece (Cambridge, MA: Ballinger, 1987), pp. 185–220.

[44] G. Pisano, "The Governance of Innovation: Vertical Integration and Collaborative Arrangements in the Biotechnology Industry," *Research Policy* 1991, pp. 237–49.

[45] A long-term contractual relationship in which both parties stake their reputations on abstaining from self-interested behavior is also a feasible solution. Relationships such as Japanese keiretsu supplier relations that place the long-term relationship above short-term gain can be thought of as pseudo-vertical integration.

The Exercise of Market Power

Pragmatically, the exercise of market power suggests that vertical integration can be valuable as a competitive tool.

First, it can raise *industry entry barriers.* Major trucking firms, for example, are trying to improve their profitability by taking responsibility for the management of customers' logistics. This service is very difficult for smaller firms to provide. As a result, they can no longer compete for the transportation business of companies wanting the bundled service.

Second, dominant firms can backward or forward integrate to *offset supplier or buyer power.* Because of their size, even partial integration into an adjacent business can discipline trading partners and keep their profits to a minimum.

Third, a dominant firm may vertically integrate to *pioneer a new market* that otherwise might not be developed. Fragmented downstream firms may be reluctant to make early stage investments that educate customers, if the benefits of those investments will spill over to competitors and suppliers. Instead, as occurred in the introduction of aluminum foil, it was an upstream supplier, Reynolds, who made the necessary investments in market development.

Indeed, the argument for maintaining many of the functional activities inside a firm is the ongoing need for coordination. A marketing group may need to change tactics continually and reallocate resources as new products are developed. Similarly, a manufacturing plant may need to adjust output and reschedule production as orders are received, and so on. This simple need to coordinate the response of functional activities to shifting business requirements can lead to prohibitive recontracting costs, and thus justify vertical integration beyond the limited activities the firm performs uniquely well.

Furthermore, performing a coordinated set of activities can give a firm an advantage it does not possess in any single activity. Sharp Corporation, for example, considers itself neither a components supplier nor an end products firm; instead, its advantage comes from its ability to coordinate across these activities. Even though it is not a leading producer of semiconductors, the firm has found that its presence in that business dramatically improves its ability to rapidly introduce innovative consumer electronics products. Other firms that believe their competitive advantages come from the integration of a system of activities may be similarly reluctant to outsource them.

However, the viability of the market mode of organization, as exemplified by Benetton, forces a careful evaluation of these apparent coordination needs. In most cases, the discriminating factor in favor of the market is whether activities or businesses have **clear interfaces** between them, behind which each can work without mutual adjustments. Gardening, for example, can easily be outsourced because its operation has no effect on other corporate decisions. In contrast, the design of a new product can rarely be "thrown over the wall" from R&D to manufacturing, but must continually be adjusted to accommodate the needs of both. This blurring of the interface between activities gives rise to the need for explicit coordination, and so may favor the hierarchy.

Step 5: Importance of Incentives

How high are agency costs inside the hierarchy? How much do worker skill and effort affect outcomes? Can an effective incentive scheme be designed? Which is more important: coordination or high-powered incentives?

The presence of agency costs inside the hierarchy can be a compelling argument to limit the scope of the firm's activities. In particular, achieving the benefits of coordination inside the corporate hierarchy often involves a **trade-off** with exploiting the power of market incentives. Although pay for performance schemes inside corporations can go a long way toward mimicking market incentives, they can never completely replicate them, and they also incur monitoring costs. Thus, when skill and effort are critical to the performance of an activity and effective incentive systems are hard to implement, there is a powerful argument to establish some form of market relationship that exploits high-powered incentives.

Often, the organizational limit to the scope of a firm is ultimately determined in this trade-off between coordination and incentives. When coordination needs are high, and when the importance of incentives is low because the contribution of individual effort is immaterial or monitoring is easy, the firm should be vertically integrated. In contrast, if individual effort is critical to performance, and monitoring is difficult, the market is more likely to be the preferred form of organization. Although the balance in the trade-off can shift over time, as competitive and technological conditions change, it remains central to the decision to vertically integrate in cases that have not been resolved by the analyses in the previous steps.

The Example of Franchising Franchising, one of the fastest-growing forms of corporate organization, is an illustration of this trade-off.[46] Franchises are typically used in geographically dispersed service or retail businesses to provide high-powered incentives for individual unit owners (the franchisees). In the retailing environment, this is often necessary because the skill and effort of the store manager are major determinants of how well a store performs. Further, monitoring the operations of hundreds of stores across the country for 12 hours a day would be very expensive. Conversely, there is limited need for coordination because standardization of the product offering provides a clear interface between the store and the franchisor.

[46] J.A. Brickley, and F.H. Dark. "The Choice of Organizational Form: The Case of Franchising," *Journal of Financial Economics* 18 (1987), pp. 401–20.

Other Explanations for Franchising

There is another possible explanation for franchising that has much validity in the early years of a franchise organization: resource scarcity.[47]

For many businesses that are suitable for franchising, there are important first mover advantages and scale economies to exploit. The first successful chain of fresh bread bakeries, for example, will build a brand name and lock up desirable locations. There is, therefore, great pressure on new firms in such businesses to grow quickly. Since opening a new location will be expensive and the access to the capital market for a start-up firm is limited, franchising, which uses the franchisee's capital for most investments, facilitates the strategically important rapid expansion.

For these reasons, a franchise, which is essentially a long-term market contract, is often the preferred arrangement for the governance of the relation between the individual store and a chain (see "Other Explanations for Franchising"). A pure market exchange would probably be inappropriate because there are often asset-specific investments involved (think, for example, of the McDonald's restaurant building, which would require substantial investment to be adapted to another fast-food chain).

However, franchising is not always the ideal organizational arrangement. It can produce misaligned incentives between two independent parties that lead to substantial problems. Consider the use of franchising in the soft-drink bottling industry. PepsiCo and Coca-Cola earn their profit on the sale of concentrate to the bottler, and so want to sell as much volume as they can. Their interest, therefore, is to introduce a wide variety of soft drinks and to have as broad distribution as possible, including, for example, in every student's dorm room.

The incentives for franchised bottlers are very different. They bear the costs of manufacturing new varieties of soft drink (extra bottling lines, more SKUs in inventory, and so on), and of distributing the bottles and cans to every outlet. Their concern is with the profitability of each line extension, not simply with whether it sells another ounce of concentrate. Thus, there is an inherent conflict between the concentrate producers and their bottler franchisees over decisions such as product line expansions and retail price wars, which are difficult to fully specify in advance.

It was the prevalence of such misaligned incentives that hampered coordination between soft-drink producers and bottlers, which led PepsiCo and Coca-Cola to buy back many of their bottler franchises in the eighties. However, the balance between coordination and incentives altered over time. The name of the game in the soft-drink industry in the eighties was product proliferation to stimulate market growth and to squeeze out

[47] M. Carney and E. Gedajlovic, "Vertical Integration in Franchise Systems: Agency Theory and Resources Explanations," *Strategic Management Journal* 12 (1991), pp. 607–29.

competitors by filling shelf space. By the nineties competitors' optimum number of varieties was established, and the attention of the soft-drink companies shifted. Both leading firms deintegrated, and, in doing so, capitalized on the incentives of franchised bottlers to improve efficiency. The experience all parties had had with the introduction of new varieties also made it somewhat easier to write contracts governing the introduction of any new flavors. In turn, this reduced the governance cost surrounding the franchise arrangement and tilted the balance in favor of the market organization of bottling. In 1999, PepsiCo spun off its bottling operations as the PepsiCo Bottling Group (PBG). PBG's streamlined focus and high-powered incentive is expressed in its three-word mission statement: "We sell soda." If history is any indication, however, this balance will likely shift again as the market changes.

Summary

The pragmatic analysis described above suggests that there is a sequential flow to the decision of whether or not to vertically integrate. If the answer to a particular step in the process is to conduct the transaction inside the firm, the analysis can stop there. If the answer to that step is that vertical integration is not required, the analysis can move to the next set of questions. (See Figure 5.5.)

The logic behind the process is that firms should be vertically integrated into those activities where their resources are the source of value creation (Step 2). Even if a firm is not able to earn above-normal returns from an activity, it should be performed inside the firm if there are asset-specific investments involved or other market failures (Step 3). Similarly, an activity should be performed inside the hierarchy if there are substantial

FIGURE 5.5
Choosing the Scope
of the Firm

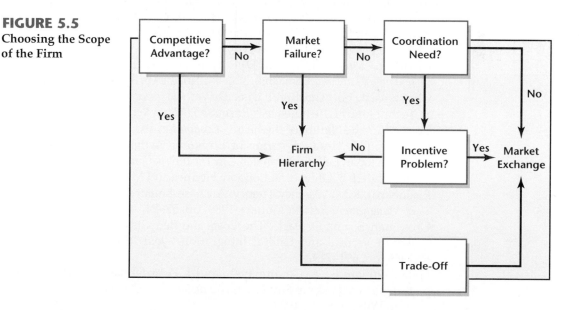

requirements for ongoing coordination (Step 4). Failing that, or if there is a need for high-powered incentives, the activity should be performed by an independent firm (Step 5).

Even though we began this section by arguing that the default assumption should be to perform activities through market exchange, the analysis provides many justifications for performing activities inside the corporate hierarchy. It should come as no surprise, given the prevalence of the corporate form of organization, that the traditional hierarchical mode of governance is indeed efficient in many circumstances.

However, careful analysis along the lines laid out above will probably lead to a reduction in the vertical scope of most corporations. The simple fact is that too many firms have inherited a particular vertical scope from an era of higher market governance costs and of greater desire for corporate size and control. Starting from the assumption that the market is the preferred arrangement of production will lead to the continuing outsourcing of many corporate activities.

Recommended Readings

Akerlof, G. "The Market for Lemons: Qualitative Uncertainty and the Market Mechanism." *Quarterly Journal of Economics*, 1970, pp. 488–500.

Arrow, K. *Economics of Information*. Cambridge, MA: Belknap Press, 1984.

Banford, J., B. Gomes-Cassares, and M. Robinson, *Mastering Alliance Strategy*. San Francisco; Jossey-Bass, 2003.

Baumol, W.J., J. Panzer, and R. Willig. *Contestable Markets and the Theory of Industry Structure*. New York: Harcourt Brace Jovanovich, 1982.

Bolton, P., and Farrell, J. "Decentralisation, Duplication, and Delay."*Journal of Political Economy*, 1990, pp. 803–26.

Casadesus-Masanell, R., and D. F. Spulber. "The Fable of Fisher Body." *Journal of Law and Economics*, Vol. 43, No. 1 (April 2000), pp. 67–104.

Christensen, C. "The Rigid Disk Drive: A History of Commercial and Technological Turbulence." *Business History Review*, 1993, pp. 531–88.

Coase, R. "The Nature of the Firm." *Economica*, 1937, pp. 386–405.

Dunning, J.H. "Trade, Location of Economic Activities, and the MNE: A Search for an Eclectic Approach." In *The International Allocation of Economic Activity*, ed. B. Ohlin et al. London: Holmes and Meier, 1977, pp. 395–419.

Eisenhardt, K.M. "Agency Theory: An Assessment and Review." *Academy of Management Review*, January 1989, pp. 57–74.

Grossman, S., and O. Hart. "The Costs and Benefits of Ownership: A Theory of Vertical and Lateral Integration." *Journal of Political Economy*, 1986, pp. 691–719.

Halal, William E., A. Geranmayeh, and J. Pourdehnad. *Internal Markets: Bringing the Power of Free Enterprise inside Your Organization*. New York: John Wiley & Sons, 1993.

Harrigan K. *Strategies for Vertical Integration.* Lexington, MA: DC Heath & Company, 1983.

Hayek, F.A. "The Use of Knowledge in Society." *American Economic Review,* 1945, pp. 519–30.

Jensen, M., and W.H. Meckling, "Specific and General Knowledge, and Organization Structure." In *Main Currents in Contract Economics,* ed. L. Werin and H. Wijkander. Oxford: Blackwell, 1991, pp. 251–74.

Jensen, M., and W.H. Meckling, "Theory of the Firm." *Journal of Financial Economics,* 1976, pp. 305–60.

Joskow, P. "Vertical Integration and Long-Term Contracts: The Case of Coal-Burning Electric Generating Plants." *Journal of Law, Economics, and Organization,* Spring 1985, pp. 33–80.

Klein, B., R. Crawford, and A. Alchian, "Vertical Integration, Appropriable Rents, and the Competitive Contracting Process." *Journal of Law and Economics,* 1978, pp. 297–326.

Marschak, J., and R. Radner, *Economic Theory of Teams.* New Haven: Yale University Press, 1972.

Milgrom, P., and J. Roberts, *Economics, Organization and Management.* Englewood Cliffs, NJ: Prentice Hall, 1992.

Ouchi, W.G. "A Conceptual Framework for the Design of Organization Control Mechanisms." *Management Science,* 1979, pp. 833–48.

Polyani, M. *Personal Knowledge.* New York: Harper Torchbooks, 1962.

Simon, H. *Administrative Behavior.* Macmillan, 1957.

Spence A.M. *Market Signaling: Transfer in Hiring and Related Processes.* Cambridge, MA: Harvard University Press, 1973.

Stuckey, J.A. *Vertical Integration in the Aluminum Industry.* Cambridge, MA: Harvard University Press, 1983.

Stuckey, J.A., and D. White, "When and When *Not* to Vertically Integrate." *Sloan Management Review,* Spring 1993, pp. 71–83.

Teece, D.J. "Profiting from Technological Innovation: Implications for Integration, Collaboration, Licensing, and Public Policy." In *The Competitive Challenge,* ed. D.J. Teece. Cambridge, MA: Ballinger, 1987, pp. 185–220.

Teece, D.J. "Economics of Scope and the Scope of the Enterprise." *Journal of Economic Behavior and Organization,* 1980, pp. 223–47.

Teece, D.J., and K. Monteverde, "Supplier Switching Costs and Vertical Integration in the Automobile Industry." *Bell Journal of Economics,* Spring 1982, pp. 206–13.

Walker, G., and D. Weber, "A Transaction Cost Approach to Make-or-Buy Decisions." *Administrative Science Quarterly,* September, 1984, pp. 373–91.

Williamson, O.E. *The Economic Institutions of Capitalism.* New York: Free Press, 1985.

Williamson, O.E. Markets and Hierarchies: Analysis and Antitrust Implications. Free Press, 1975.

RESOURCES

BUSINESSES

• VISION

• GOALS & OBJECTIVES

ORGANIZATION

6

MANAGING THE MULTIBUSINESS CORPORATION

▲ Introduction

Managing a multibusiness corporation is perhaps the most difficult corporate strategy challenge. Conceptualizing a strategy can be analytically demanding, but putting the mechanisms in place to bring it to fruition and operating the company on a day-to-day basis can be even more daunting.

Part of this struggle comes from difficulties implementing strategy at any level in an organization. A team of executives must be selected, an appropriate organization design and reward system put in place, a culture created, and so forth. However, executives in charge of corporate strategy face additional challenges unique to multibusiness corporations. In particular, they must **maintain control** of the diverse and often autonomous set of businesses in the portfolio and **provide coherence** to the entity as a whole. Only by doing so will they create value and justify the firm's existence as a multibusiness corporation.

This chapter addresses the third side of the Corporate Strategy Triangle—the organizational structure, systems, and processes management can use to implement a strategy. The chapter cannot provide a comprehensive guide to organization theory, nor even to the use of particular organizational mechanisms.[1] Rather, it will draw on aspects of relevant theories to illuminate the management of multibusiness firms and the operation of the corporate office in that setting.

---

[1] See, for example, Robert H. Miles, *Macro Organizational Behavior* (Santa Monica, CA: Goodyear Publishing Co., 1980), and Henry Mintzberg, *The Structure of Organizations: The Synthesis of the Research* (Englewood Cliffs, NJ: Prentice Hall, 1978).

Principles

▲ The Administrative Context

In managing a multibusiness corporation, senior executives must recognize that they cannot make all the decisions in the firm themselves. The sheer number of complex issues in large diversified companies, quite apart from the impossibility of being fully informed of the circumstances surrounding each one, makes it impractical for corporate executives even to make all the critical strategic decisions. How, then, do such executives "manage" the firm?

In a classic examination of this issue, Joseph Bower studied the capital budgeting process in a large diversified chemical company.[2] Initially, it appeared to him that corporate management was unable to influence even vitally important resource allocation decisions. He noted that nearly all investment proposals were initiated by the divisions, not the corporate office, and that the corporate team evaluating the requests was dependent on the financial projections and market information supplied by the divisions. Further, nearly all the proposals that reached top management were eventually approved.

On closer observation, however, Bower discovered that corporate management did in fact have a very powerful influence on the pattern of corporate investment. By shaping the **administrative context** within which such decisions were made, corporate management's impact was not limited to just the final rubber-stamp approval of an investment; it extended throughout the entire process. Functional managers in the divisions identified investment projects, midlevel managers decided which of the proposed projects they would support, and senior managers approved projects, all in response to a very complex set of constraints and incentives established by the organization structure, the measurement and reward systems, the strategic planning process, and so forth, which corporate management had put in place.

This principle underlies the management of multibusiness corporations. Corporate executives do not directly make many of the important business-level decisions. Rather, they impact the firm by establishing an administrative context that shapes the definition, championing, and approval of decisions by managers throughout the organization.

Included in the administrative context are all the elements of structure, systems, and processes that influence delegated decision making in large, complex organizations. The McKinsey Seven-S framework—strategy, structure, systems, style, superordinate goals, staff, and symbols[3]—

---

[2] Joseph H. Bower, *Managing the Resource Allocation Process* (Cambridge, MA: Harvard University Press, 1970).
[3] Richard Tanner Pascale and Anthony G. Athos, *The Art of Japanese Management* (New York: Simon and Schuster, 1981).

FIGURE 6.1 The Elements of Organization Design

Organization Structure	Planning and Control Systems
• Organization chart • Corporate functions • Ad hoc teams • Conflict resolution mechanisms	• Strategic planning • Budgeting • MIS • Resource allocation, capital budgeting • Transfer prices
Human Resource Management	**Culture and Style**
• Personnel selection and training • Reward/incentive schemes • Measurement variables	• Top management role • Culture • Symbolic actions • Management style

is representative of the many typologies that describe the range of elements senior management uses to implement strategy. As Figure 6.1 indicates, the list of such elements is long and includes both formal and informal aspects.[4]

Designing the Context

Traditionally, two overarching principles have governed the design of the administrative context. The first is the principle of **internal alignment,** the simple notion that each element of organizational structure, systems, and processes needs to be designed to reinforce rather than conflict with the signals and motivations provided to managers by other aspects of the administrative context. For example, if the incentive system rewards only divisional performance while the corporate culture attempts to foster cooperative behavior, there will be cognitive dissonance within the organization. Managerial behavior results from the complex interplay of all the organizational elements that affect individual motivations. These must, therefore, be designed as a consistent system so that their impact is interactive and mutually reinforcing.

The second overarching principle governing the design of the administrative context is that of **contingent design.** Organization theory has long recognized that no single design is optimal for every corporation or strategy. Instead, it has argued that the internal characteristics of an effective organization should be contingent upon the tasks it must perform interacting with its environment.[5] For a multibusiness firm, contingency theory

[4] It is impossible to produce a list of the elements of administrative context that is exhaustive and mutually exclusive. The list presented here is, therefore, illustrative rather than definitive.
[5] J. W. Lorsch and S.A. Allen, *Managing Diversity and Interdependence* (Boston: Harvard Business School, Division of Research, 1973), p. 171. See also P.R. Lawrence and J.W. Lorsch, *Organizations and Environment* (Boston: Harvard Business School, Division of Research, 1967).

Form and Function

C.K. Prahalad and Gary Hamel suggested the analogy of a corporation as a tree (see Figure 6.2).[6] The set of businesses in the corporate portfolio are represented by the branches of the tree, the "core competences" of the firm are its trunk, and the resources of the firm are the roots that nurture the tree's growth. Extending the analogy, the firm's organizational structure can be interpreted as the tree's shape, while its systems and processes are the vital biological functions that maintain the efficient functioning of the entire system.

The tree analogy is useful. All trees share the same biological processes of photosynthesis and nutrient extraction, even though the precise forms of species differ widely. Similarly, all companies have systems for budgeting, capital expenditures, and compensation, even though their details differ enormously. However, just as the structures and processes of each species of tree are optimized for its particular habitat—trees that grow tall have deep roots, evergreens have thin needles filled with pitch to survive the winter, and so forth—so organizational structures, systems, and processes must be optimized according to each firm's strategy for success in its habitat—the resources it employs and the set of businesses in which it competes.

FIGURE 6.2
Core Competence Tree for Ciba-Corning Diagnostics

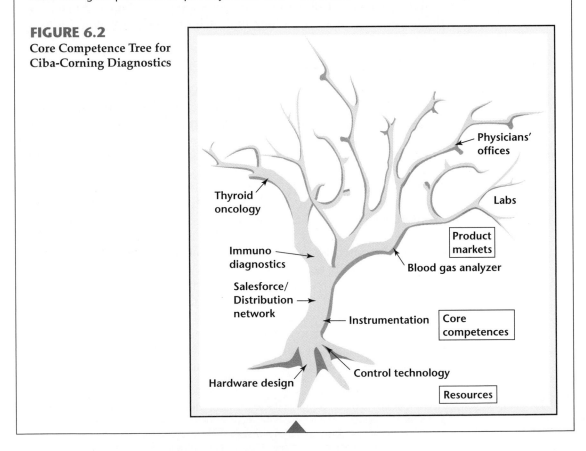

[6] C.K. Prahalad and Gary Hamel, "The Core Competence of the Corporation," *Harvard Business Review* 68, No. 3 (May–June 1990), pp. 79–91.

The Informational Advantage of the Firm

One argument for the value of diversification is the informational advantage that the corporate hierarchy has over the market.[7] The capital market, for example, may be an inefficient mechanism for the allocation of capital if firms are reticent to release confidential strategic information publicly. In such cases, the corporation, acting as an internal capital market with complete information, may be able to make more efficient investment decisions. The same argument can also be made with respect to the allocation of labor. Since the corporate office will have access to confidential information on employee performance, it can more cheaply and efficiently allocate employees than can the external labor market. These advantages, it is argued, can give validity to multibusiness corporations as economically efficient entities.

Although correct in observing the potentially superior informational characteristics of the hierarchy, proponents often fail to recognize the agency costs that can arise with the internal allocation of resources.[8] For example, when not subject to market pressures, CEOs can subsidize poorly performing businesses. Moreover, if the informational advantage of the corporation comes from the rights to confidential information, in principle any firm could own any business. Indeed, one giant conglomerate could efficiently run the whole economy. Clearly, there is a trade-off between the efficiency of internal and external markets as allocators of resources. The availability of information is only one component to be considered in that trade-off.

suggests that the administrative context should be driven by the other elements of a firm's corporate strategy—its resources and set of businesses (see "Form and Function"). These determine the particular tasks the corporation must fulfill to create value and should, therefore, directly shape the firm's overall design.

Despite their conceptual power, the principles of internal alignment and contingency theory offer little specific advice about how to design the context for a particular firm that will produce the desired behavior (best decisions) at the lowest possible administrative cost. Neither principle addresses the enormous range of elements that influence managerial behavior or the wide variety of options that firms have when implementing each element, such as a budgeting system. To move beyond these general principles, we need to know specifically how the configuration of a particular structure or system affects managerial behavior, and the decisions and costs which, in turn, result from that behavior (see Figure 6.3). In achieving this, we draw on the underlying theories of modern organizational economics—particularly information and agency theory—to enlighten our understanding of these relationships and so further our ability to design effective organizations (see "The Informational Advantage of the Firm").

[7] K.N.M. Dundas and P.R. Richardson, "Corporate Strategy and the Concept of Market Failure," *Strategic Management Journal* 1, No. 2 (April/June 1980), pp. 177–88.
[8] Julia P. Liebeskind, Internal Capital Markets in Diversified Firms: Benefits versus Costs (unpublished manuscript), June 1995.

FIGURE 6.3
Strategy
Implementation

Applying Organizational Economics

Information theory argues that there are costs associated with transferring information within the firm. It also accepts that, because of human limitations, it is infeasible for any individual to assimilate, yet alone act upon, all the information that could be cheaply transferred to them.[9] As a result, Jensen and Meckling suggest the locus of decision-making authority in firms should vary according to the nature of the information and knowledge involved in each decision.[10] Following Hayek,[11] they argued that there are two types of knowledge: **general knowledge** that can cheaply and easily be transferred up an organizational hierarchy, and **specific knowledge** that is difficult and costly to transfer even with modern information systems. Specific knowledge, which includes, for example, the know-how of skilled craftsmen and experienced managers, is often tacit and so cannot be written down in blueprints or easily communicated to other people.[12] Jensen and Meckling argue that decisions that depend on specific knowledge should usually be delegated to those who possess the requisite know-how and information. Only decisions that rest on general knowledge can potentially be made higher up the corporate hierarchy.

Agency theory tempers this view. It argues that, when given decision rights, self-interested managers may act in ways that maximize their own welfare at the expense of the corporate good. As a result, any firm with delegated decision making may incur the adverse consequences of self-interested behavior. Organizational design must therefore mitigate the agency costs that result from delegated decision making by introducing monitoring and control systems to deter such behavior.

Combining these theories, we can identify three "rules of the game" that determine behavior inside the firm:[13]

[9] Herbert A. Simon, *Administrative Behavior* (New York: Free Press, 1976). See also R. Cyert and J. March, *A Behavioral Theory of the Firm* (Englewood Cliffs, NJ: Prentice Hall, 1963).
[10] M.C. Jensen and W. H. Meckling, "Specific and General Knowledge, and Organization Structure," in *Main Currents in Contract Economies,* ed. L. Werin and H. Wijkander. (London: Basil Blackwell, 1991), pp. 251–74.
[11] F.A. Hayek, "The Use of Knowledge in Society," *American Economic Review* 35, No. 4 (September 1945).
[12] M. Polyani, *Personal Knowledge* (New York: Harper Torch Books, 1962).
[13] Jensen and Meckling, "Specific and General Knowledge."

- The allocation of decision rights.

- The information structure.

- The set of measurement and reward schemes, or more generally, the incentive structure.

These *organizational rules* collapse the myriad complicated relationships among all elements of the administrative context into a parsimonious but nevertheless comprehensive model of the firm. They identify who will be making a decision, the information that person will possess, and how he or she will be rewarded for the outcome of the decision. With this information, and knowledge of individual endowments and preferences,[14] one could in principle predict all of a firm's decisions.

In practice, of course, using this framework to design an administrative context is impossible. One can never isolate or directly control these three aspects of organizational configuration, nor is there a strict correspondence between the design of particular structures and systems and performance outcomes. While an elegant theoretical description of the firm, this model can never be used pragmatically.

Nevertheless, the approach does identify the critical parameters that shape managerial behavior. When configuring the more traditional elements of organizational design that can be directly determined by corporate executives—**structure, systems, and processes**—it is, therefore, important to recognize that their effect can be usefully interpreted through their impact on these three rules of the game.

▲ Organization Structure

Formal structure was the traditional concern of organization theory and is probably the element of organization design that has been most studied. Initially much of this research was undertaken with the hope that, for any given strategy, the perfect organization structure could be identified (see "Structure Follows Strategy"). More recently, it has been recognized that organization structures are rarely optimal; rather, the challenge for managers is to identify the structure that best fits the current needs of their corporation.

Most effective organization structures have in common the division of the organization into **discrete subunits** that have substantial authority for their own decisions. These subunits may be defined by function, by business, or by geography.

The advantages of such delegated decision making are that it allows decisions to be made by those who possess the relevant knowledge, while minimizing the amount of information transfer up the hierarchy. The

[14] These, together with the production possibilities facing the firm, are the standard data required for general equilibrium analysis.

Structure Follows Strategy

The seminal research on organization structure in multibusiness firms was conducted by the business historian Alfred Chandler. He documented how the rise of the **multidivisional structure (M-form)** in corporate America was a response to the strategy of corporate diversification. Indeed, his observation that "structure follows strategy" was perhaps one of the first statements of contingency theory in the managerial literature.

By studying Du Pont, Sears, General Motors, and Standard Oil, Chandler observed how the traditional functional organization became overloaded when these companies expanded into multiple businesses in the early 20th century. When this happened, such firms adopted a structure in which each division controlled almost the complete set of functional activities for the production, marketing, and delivery of its products.[15] Allowing divisions to take on operating responsibility freed the corporate office to plan strategy and allocate resources among the various businesses. Chandler argued that this partition of the workload solved the information overload problem faced by senior corporate managers when they competed in multiple businesses with a functional organization structure.

Following Chandler's work, there were a host of empirical studies of the adoption of the multidivisional structure in companies around the world.[16] These studies revealed that, although at different rates, most companies in developed countries switched to multidivisional structures as their degree of diversification increased. Empirical studies also verified that corporations improved performance by choosing the appropriate organizational form.[17] Diversified corporations that adopted the multidivisional form, for example, were more profitable than ones that remained functionally organized.

presence of specific knowledge about manufacturing facilities, for example, usually explains why it is more effective for business, rather than corporate, managers to make operating decisions.

When the corporation is divided into discrete units, each can also be **specialized** to succeed in its own competitive environment.[18] In particular, it can develop and tailor its resources and shape the details of its own organization to fit its unique tasks. For example, the culture of a high-technology division can and should be different from that of a capital-intensive commodity business. Moreover, specialized units that are focused on a particular activity such as distribution, can, through repeated experience, increase their efficiency over time.

[15] A.D. Chandler, *Strategy and Structure* (Cambridge, MA: MIT Press, 1962).

[16] D. Channon, *The Strategy and Structure of British Enterprise* (London: MacMillan, 1973); and G. Pooley-Dyas, "Strategy and Structure of French Enterprise," Ph.D. dissertation, Harvard Business School, 1972.

[17] H. Armour and D. Teece, "Organization Structure and Economic Performance: A Test of the Multidivisional Hypothesis," *Bell Journal of Economics* 9 (1978), pp. 106–22; and R.E. Hoskisson, "Multidivisional Structure and Performance," *Academy of Management Journal* 30 (1987), pp. 625–44.

[18] In the original research on this topic, Lawrence and Lorsch (*Organizations and Environment,* Harvard Business School, 1967) and Lorsch and Allen (*Managing Diversity and Interdependence,* Harvard Business School, 1973) described this as the advantages of differentiation.

The alignment of managerial authority with responsibility and rewards, which is possible when decision making is delegated to discrete units, satisfies one of the basic tenets of agency theory and increases organizational efficiency by providing powerful incentives. The resulting sense of ownership also builds managerial commitment, with corresponding increases in effort and initiative. It is also expected that the motivation of managers who are given control of an entire unit will be high, particularly when they are directly rewarded for the performance of that unit.

There are countless variants of organization structures for multibusiness corporations that capitalize on the benefits of discrete subunits (see Figure 6.4). The choice of which to adopt for a particular firm is usually determined by the need to combine those activities that are most

FIGURE 6.4 **A Range of Organization Types**

Source: J. Galbraith, *Competing with Flexible Lateral Organizations,* 2nd ed. (Reading, MA: Addison-Wesley, 1994), p. 57.

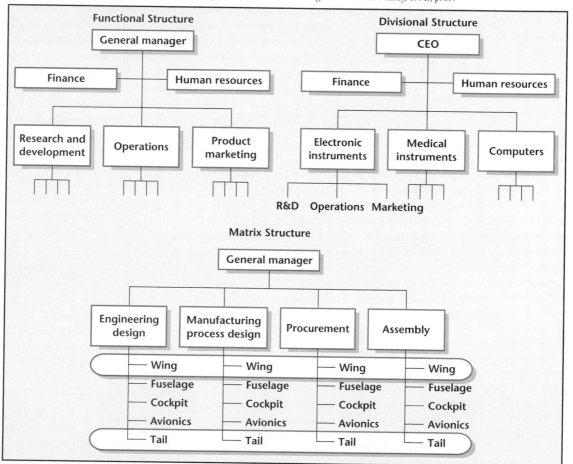

interdependent in order to minimize the number of informational linkages across units, and to **align authority with responsibility.**[19]

Today, the predominant organizational form in multibusiness corporations in the West is a structure of autonomous and discrete product divisions. This will be the efficient structure when the critical resources and most important needs for integration are located *within the businesses* themselves. However, when the resources in most intense interdependencies are contained *within a function or geographic region,* organizations divided along those dimensions will be more efficient. Many consumer packaged goods companies, for example, are organized around business functions, so that they can realize economies of scale in their critical sales and marketing activities. In contrast, many professional service organizations, such as law and accounting firms, are configured around independent geographic offices so that they can efficiently offer a full range of services to local clients.

Since many diversified firms have important interdependencies along multiple dimensions, there often is no clear-cut structure that is appropriate. Adopting a functional structure, for example, may lead to problems coordinating product strategy, but a product-division structure may lead to inefficient functional activities, perhaps with multiple sales forces calling on the same customer. (See "Matrix and Network Organizations" for a discussion of structures designed to simultaneously manage several interdependencies.)

More generally, none of these organization structures will perfectly implement a corporate strategy. Every structure featuring delegated decision making in discrete and differentiated subunits will have drawbacks because of the inherent conflicts that arise in multibusiness corporations over integration of specialized units.

Ultimately, we have to recognize the **principle of organizational suboptimality**—that no structure is ideal for all firms, nor even for a particular firm at a point in time. Therefore, managers should divide the firm into discrete subunits whose activities rely most heavily on one another, and use the other elements of administrative context to support and enhance the chosen structure.

▲ Systems and Processes

Organization structure alone does not define a firm's administrative context. Systems and processes, both formal and informal, also influence the incentive structure facing managers, the allocation of decision rights, and the distribution of information inside a firm.

---

[19] P.R. Nayyar, and R.K. Kazanjian, "Organizing to Attain Potential Benefits from Informational Assymetries and Economies of Scope in Related Diversified Firms," *Academy of Management Review* 18 (1993), pp. 735–59; and R. Antle, and J.S. Demski, "The Controlling Principle in Responsibility Accounting," *Accounting Review* LXII (October 1988), pp. 700–18.

Matrix and Network Organizations

One structure that promised to solve the trade-off between organizing along different dimensions was the **matrix** organization. In this structure, employees report to two superiors—a function and a division manager, for example; or, in the case of many multinational firms, a division and a country manager. The hope was that these dual reporting structures would accommodate and blend both viewpoints and so provide for the efficient utilization of resources while integrating their deployment across units.[20]

In practice, however, matrix organizations internalized the trade-off in individuals who had to balance the demands of two bosses. The resulting ambiguity and complexity often produced insurmountable problems. Rather than optimally satisfying the needs of both superiors, individuals often ended up satisfying neither.

A more recent innovation in organization structure has been the **network** organization.[21] Rather than using a formal organizational structure, the firm takes on a loose and shifting set of relationships both internally—among teams that, for example,

focus on customers or reengineered processes—and externally, with suppliers, customers, and even competitors. The advantages of such a structure are argued to be the flexibility and the adaptability to reconfigure the firm rapidly and cheaply in response to changing circumstances.

The network organization is almost the antithesis of structure; it depends on informal processes to hold the company together. Indeed, in the guise of boundaryless and learning organizations,[22] it suggests that the right set of processes alone can overcome the trade-offs endemic to contemporary organizations.[23] Attractive as this vision is, an exclusive reliance on informal processes can lead to chaos in large, complex companies. Further, network organizations optimistically assume that a context can be generated in which employees act in the best interests of the corporation. In practice, self-interested behavior—the focus of organizational economics—validates the need for the formal aspects of organizational structure and systems, such as incentive schemes.

We cannot here discuss how the design of all a corporation's systems and processes, from compensation to capital expenditure and strategic planning, can be used to complement the chosen organization structure.[24] Rather, we will focus on how that set of systems and processes can be used to address the two challenges corporate executives face in managing multibusiness firms—how to maintain **control** over delegated decision

---

[20] J.R. Galbraith and R.K. Kazanjian, *Strategy Implementation: Structure, Systems and Process* (St. Paul: West Publishing, 1985).

[21] R.G. Eccles, and N. Nohria, eds., *Networks in Organizations* (Boston, MA: Harvard Business School Press, 1992).

[22] Ron Ashkenas, D. Ulrich, T. Jick, and S. Kerr, *The Boundaryless Organization* (San Francisco, CA: Jossey-Bass Publishers, 1995); Peter M. Senge, *The Fifth Discipline* (New York: Doubleday/ Currency, 1990); I. Nonaka and H. Takeuchi, *The Knowledge Creating Company* (Oxford: Oxford University Press, 1995).

[23] S. Ghoshal and C.A. Bartlett, *The Individualized Corporation,* (New York: HarperCollins, 1997).

[24] Robert Simons, *Levers of Control* (Boston, MA: Harvard Business School Press, 1995); and P. Milgrom, and J. Roberts, *Economics, Organization and Management* (Englewood Cliffs, NJ: Prentice Hall, 1992).

making within otherwise autonomous units, and how to provide **coherence** to the corporation by deploying resources across otherwise structurally differentiated units.

Control

Embedded in every organization structure is the need to maintain control over delegated decision making. Agency theory highlights the adverse consequences of delegation and warns that without appropriate systems, the corporate office can quickly lose its ability to determine corporate direction and performance. While independent units, as far as possible, must be allowed to operate autonomously if they are to maximize their own performance, there must be some measure of corporate control to prevent them pursuing their self-interest to the detriment of the company as a whole.

Historically, discussion of how to balance the trade-off between delegation and control of decision rights focused on a **centralization-decentralization continuum.** This described where control lay between corporate headquarters and the divisions for numerous decisions such as pricing, hiring, facility locations, and so forth. Research, however, revealed that this simple distinction could be quite misleading.[25] For example, a firm could centralize financial policies and retain strategic control at headquarters, but might freely delegate operational control to the divisions. Indeed, there are so many elements to the relationship between the divisions and the corporate office that the whole network of interactions cannot easily be collapsed into a single measure of decentralization. One element of the relationship might be decentralized and another centralized, and the success of a strategy could depend on just such careful differentiation.

More recently, attention has turned to the design of the systems and processes needed to resolve the agency problem created by delegated decision rights. Rather than being concerned only with who has the power to make a given decision, it recognizes that some delegated decision making will exist in all firms, and suggests rewards and measurement systems that can mitigate its adverse effects.

Designing the control systems to minimize agency costs is not a simple task. In the case of operating performance, for example, corporate management may have trouble distinguishing between the effects of exogenous industry events and managerial skill and effort on performance. Thus, when evaluating divisional performance, they may not know whether it was due to poor (good) decisions, adverse (positive) exogenous market conditions, or lack of (a lot of) hard work by

---

[25] R.F. Vancil, *Decentralization: Managerial Ambiguity by Design* (Burr Ridge, IL: Irwin, 1978).

managers.[26] The difficulty of sorting out these effects may allow divisional managers to act in their own self-interest and blame the resulting poor performance on events beyond their control.

To prevent this from occurring, corporate managers can monitor and reward either the outcomes or the behaviors that they observe,[27] depending on which is correlated more cost-effectively and accurately with the subordinate's skill and effort.[28] If, for example, the current financial results of a bakery are a reasonably accurate measure of how effective management was, outcome control is appropriate. In a high-technology business, in contrast, short-term financial performance may be a very poor indicator of both underlying strategic position and managerial effectiveness. In that case, a much broader set of variables will need to be evaluated, many of which require qualitative judgments and most of which concern the specific decisions made by managers.

This suggests that there will be important differences in organizational systems and processes between firms practicing **outcome control** and **behavior control**.[29] Both rely on delegated decision making. The underlying difference is that outcome control concentrates on monitoring results while behavior control concentrates on prescribing and evaluating actions as means of setting the incentives for subordinates. (See "Clan Control" for a third type of control.)

Outcome control typically rewards divisional managers on their unit's financial performance. It, therefore, influences divisional decision making indirectly by aligning divisional managers' incentives with corporate goals. Generally outcome control requires little interference by the corporate office in the daily affairs of the division. The archetypal modern example is the LBO that holds managers accountable for a limited number

---

[26] Sophisticated, and probably more realistic, versions of agency theory argue that agency costs are not so much due to slacking but to inappropriate decisions. A division manager, for example, is more likely to propose an investment that generates certain but low returns, rather than an investment in a high-risk, high-return R&D project, even if the expected value of the R&D investment is higher. The personal risk if the project fails (dismissal) may be sufficiently great to deter the manager from supporting the higher-expected-value strategy that corporate executives would prefer.

[27] Theoretically, the outcomes or behaviors have to be both observable and legally contractible.

[28] Agency theory demonstrates that no incentive scheme can entirely eliminate agency costs. Any scheme is, therefore, what economists call "second best." Prime among these second best solutions is a "tournament." In this, managers are rewarded not for their absolute performance, but for performance relative to their peers. This incentive scheme, would, for example, promote the best-selling regional sales manager to national manager. When all peers are subject to the same exogenous events, such a scheme controls for the effect an event such as a recession may have on performance.

[29] K.M. Eisenhardt, "Control: Organizational and Economical Approaches," *Management Science* 31 (1985), pp. 134–49; and W.G. Ouchi, "A Conceptual Framework for Design of Organization Control Mechanisms," *Management Science* 25 (1979), pp. 833–48.

Clan Control

A third type of control is **clan control.**[30] This type of control may eliminate agency problems inside organizations if subordinates have deeply internalized the goals of the organization. When this happens they interpret their own self-interest in terms of the organization's interests. Examples of this type of control are typically found in nonprofit, religious, and political organizations, whose goals are more ideological than material, and where it is believable that individuals will abdicate their self-interest for a superordinate goal.

Some economic organizations appear to get close to this sort of control system. Cooperatives and small firms run by charismatic entrepreneurs, such as Apple in its early days, are examples. But the occurrence of the sort of messianic purpose that is required for effective clan control is rarely, if ever, found in large multibusiness organizations. Only in cultures in which collectivism rather than individualism is a more accepted philosophy can clan control be expected to solve the control problem for an extended period of time.

of financial targets, usually related to cash flow, but does not intervene in or intensively monitor the means by which those targets are met.

For pure outcome control to be viable, there must be very tight links between effort and skill and financial outcomes, with very little interference from uncertain exogenous events. This implies that outcome control is appropriate in mature, stable, and predictable industries (as opposed to rapidly changing and highly competitive industries); in addition, divisions should be unrelated and self-contained, sharing few important activities so that they are not reliant on others for their own performance.

Behavior control, in contrast, more directly prescribes and evaluates divisional managers' actions. Typically, this kind of control is practiced by corporations, such as Ford Motor Company, that view themselves as operating companies. Corporate executives rarely make divisional decisions themselves, but will be sufficiently well informed to evaluate divisional managers on those decisions, rather than on just their financial results.

Behavior control is therefore appropriate under different conditions. First, when corporate managers have detailed industry-specific expertise, judging the actions of divisional executives is possible. In such cases, corporate executives may know to focus on certain operating behaviors that are keys to success in the business, or perhaps asking certain questions allows them to advise on and evaluate appropriate behavior. Second, behavior control can be used when it is difficult to find single summary measures of strategic performance. In some industries, for example, cash flow may be a fair representation of divisional performance, but in many others such simple outcome measures are unreliable. In those cases,

[30] W.G. Ouchi, "A Conceptual Framework for Design of Organization Control Mechanisms," *Management Science* 25 (1979), pp. 833–48.

corporate managers must continuously monitor a broad range of behaviors and qualitative performance measures to evaluate the performance of divisional managers fairly.

Because of the differences between these modes of control, the choice between them is contingent on the other elements of a firm's corporate strategy. Both the set of businesses in which the firm is active (which will, for example, affect the availability of a good outcome measure) and the resources underlying corporate advantage (for example, the particular expertise of senior management) will determine the appropriate method for controlling delegated decision making in a given company. (The Practice section expands on the specific design of the systems required to implement outcome and behavior control.)

Coherence

Merely controlling the operation of autonomous divisions is rarely enough to justify the existence of a corporation as a multibusiness entity. Although units need to be differentiated and specialized if they are to serve their own markets efficiently, valuable resources must also be deployed throughout those units to provide coherence to the corporation. Some degree of integration across otherwise differentiated units is therefore required if the corporate performance is to be more than merely the sum of what the individual divisions could achieve alone.

As described in Chapters 3 and 4, the advantages of corporate coherence can arise in almost all the value-creating activities of a business, and from any of its common assets or capabilities. The specific source of the benefits can be anything from simple economies of scale and experience curve effects, to coordinating product market positions and competitive responses. For example, by using a single corporate sales force, rather than allowing each of its many divisions to have its own, Johnson & Johnson exploits scale efficiencies in providing one-stop shopping to hospitals.

It is tempting to think that autonomous divisions will willingly cooperate to achieve the benefits of corporate coherence. However, there is a limit to the circumstances under which they will do so. Opportunities for integration across divisions that are win/win for all divisions (Pareto optimal) will always be realized (Figure 6.5). However, self-interested managers will not be able to reach agreement on an action that benefits the corporation as a whole if that gain is accompanied by a loss for any division.

Much can be done by the corporate office to extend the range of issues on which otherwise autonomous divisions will cooperate. Managers, after all, behave in response to their incentives. In principle, therefore, the corporation can create incentives for managers to act in the interests of a broader entity, such as a group of related businesses or the corporation as a whole, by partially rewarding them for the performance of that larger

FIGURE 6.5
Cooperation and
Corporate
Performance

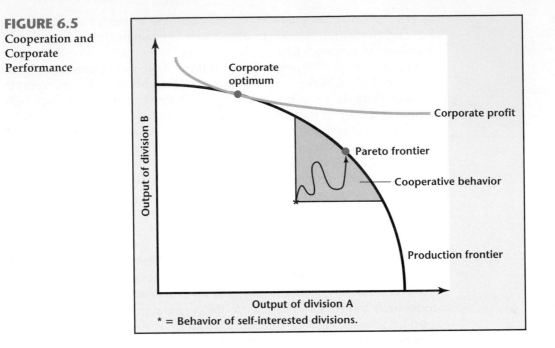

unit.[31] However, there are intrinsic limits to the ability of financial incentives alone to achieve the desired degree of coherence. Managers may now be held accountable for actions beyond their responsibility. The precision of the incentive system will, therefore, decline and agency costs will increase.[32]

To achieve the desired degree of coherence, therefore, corporations not only have to alter incentives, but also employ other systems and processes that potentially supplant divisional autonomy. These mechanisms for leveraging resources throughout the corporation involve the **transfer of skills and resources** and the **coordination of activities.** Transferring skills and resources involves the development and maintenance of a resource or skill that is made available to and then independently used by different divisions. Coordinating activities involves some degree of direct sharing in the performance of an activity by multiple divisions.

---

[31] The ultimate obstacle to self-interested coordination comes back to the very existence of the corporation as a multibusiness entity. If some form of self-interested behavior could achieve all the desirable cooperation, the firm would not be able to justify its existence.
[32] A.K. Gupta and S. Seshadri, "Horizontal Resource Sharing: A Principal Agent Approach," *Academy of Management Best Papers,* August 1994, pp. 37–41. One solution that encourages autonomous divisions to realize the benefits of coherence, even when it is detrimental to a particular unit, is to allow side payments. Informal versions of these payments involving agreements to "scratch your back if you scratch mine" are often implicit inside many companies, but explicit payoffs, such as crediting one division with a negotiated share of another division's profit, are rare.

The choice between the two modes for achieving corporate coherence is primarily contingent on the resource that is being deployed across the various businesses. In particular, the choice between transferring a skill and coordinating an activity depends on whether the valuable resource can be used simultaneously by several divisions without affecting its employment in each. When a resource is a public good, such as a best demonstrated practice in sales force management, the mechanism used will be the deployment of a skill. However, when the resource is an asset, such as a computer or plant, whose use by one division inevitably leads to conflict with other divisions, the mode chosen must be the coordination of activities.

The transfer of a corporate-level resource often requires little intervention in divisional affairs. The corporate office takes responsibility for managing the valuable resource, such as a corporate brand name or governance structure, and makes that resource available to the divisions, which can operate more or less freely with it. In transferring skills, the corporate office focuses on improving the quality of the skill and disseminating that knowledge among the divisions. In principle, it is possible to do this with minimal interference in the autonomy of business units because the resource can often be used simultaneously by many divisions. At Danaher Corp., for example, manufacturing practices and processes are transferred among divisions without their use in one division precluding their use in another.

Generally speaking, coordinating activities requires more explicit corporate intervention. To compel divisions to give up their autonomy and manage the conflicts that necessarily accompany joint activity requires some form of overt corporate coordination. Although sharing activities, such as purchasing or a sales force, may be the largest and most obvious source of synergy in multibusiness corporations, to a greater or lesser extent the process incurs all the costs that result from divisions losing authority over some of their activities.

Whether transferring skills and resources or coordinating activities across operating units, the pursuit of corporate coherence involves inevitable costs. Not only does it raise the cost of corporate overhead (which must ultimately be borne by the divisions), it can violate the sanctity of divisional differentiation and autonomy (see "Costs of Coherence"). The CEO of a very successful multinational lubricants company, for example, referred to synergy as the "enemy of focus." This is a serious charge. To be of net benefit to the firm, the costs of pursuing coherence must be lower than the benefits it generates, or the strategy is misguided. For managers, the challenge is how to design the systems and processes that create the desired degree of integration at minimal cost. (See Appendix C for a detailed description of mechanisms for achieving coherence.)

Summary: Linking Administrative Context to Purpose

The choice of administrative context for managing a multibusiness corporation is complex and involves a number of difficult trade-offs. However,

Costs of Coherence

There are five types of cost incurred when integrating otherwise discrete units.[33]

Compromise costs result from suboptimal decisions. Since two different businesses are sharing some activity or skill, one may be disappointed in the level of service provision. Consider a company, such as Marriott, that maintains hotel chains at several different price points. If the chains share a computer reservation system, one or another may have to compromise, either by paying more for a higher-quality system than it needs or by receiving lower-quality service than it desires. No solution is likely to perfectly satisfy all the chains.

Inflexibility costs are those associated with the loss of control over all the business's activities. If one division wishes to switch to just-in-time delivery to improve its production process, it may be impossible to agree to a revised schedule with another division for deliveries from common suppliers. Slower speed of response is another cost of inflexibility.

Coordination costs refer to the time and effort that managers spend working with their peers in other divisions to coordinate joint activities. It simply takes time—in meetings, on the phone, writing memos, and so forth—to reach agreement, and none of that would be incurred if the division alone could decide on all its own activities.

Incentive costs occur when a division no longer has authority over all its own activities. Blurred accountability reduces the clarity of incentives and may demotivate managers and even lead to shirking.

Complexity costs arise because the overhead costs of managing a shared activity often increase exponentially. Production scheduling, for example, might no longer be done in a plant manager's head, but could require a separate department. Inventory management becomes more complex and may require new, expensive systems. The simplicity of discrete and focused divisions disappears when the complexity of achieving coherence is introduced.

---

the guiding principle is that a firm's structure, systems, and processes should flow from its overall strategic vision and the key tasks that must be performed to fulfill that vision.

Traditionally, differences in administrative contexts were captured in the dichotomy between corporate strategies of related and unrelated diversification. Generally speaking, unrelated diversifiers were seen as needing organizational designs that separated business units into discrete product divisions with little corporate intervention. In contrast, the prescription for related diversifiers was to adopt functional organizations or have substantial corporate staffs to coordinate divisional activities.[34] As a result, unrelated diversifiers were commonly thought of as requiring decentralized management systems, whereas related diversifiers would need to be considerably more centralized.[35]

More recently, Charles Hill and others have drawn a similar distinction between cooperative corporate strategies, where divisions are related and

---

[33] These draw on M. Porter, *Competitive Advantage* (New York: Free Press, 1985), Chapter 9.
[34] Norm Berg, "What's Different about Conglomerate Management?" *Harvard Business Review* 47 (1969) pp. 112–20.
[35] Vancil, *Decentralization*.

benefit from sharing with one another, and competitive corporate strategies, where the corporate office merely allocates capital between unrelated product divisions that are in effect competing for that capital.[36]

In our corporate strategy framework, differences (and similarities) among administrative contexts are driven by the resources that firms possess and the businesses in which they compete. It is those aspects of the corporate strategy that largely dictate how a firm will choose to control and integrate the activities of its businesses.

Practice

▲ Roles of the Corporate Office

Being a CEO responsible for managing a multibusiness corporation is a task that shares many aspects of any general manager's job. We do not describe that job in this chapter, even though we recognize that in multibusiness corporations, just like any other, having the charismatic leadership and managerial skills of Michael Eisner in his early years at Disney or Jack Welch at GE may create as much shareholder value as any particular strategic move Disney or GE could make.[37] Here, we will focus on the unique management challenges of a multibusiness firm and the roles of the corporate office in meeting those challenges.

There are four roles that the corporate office of any public multibusiness company must perform. The first is to articulate and adhere to the **vision** for the corporation. The second is to act as the **guardian of resources** in the corporation. The third is to fulfill the **general overhead functions** of the corporation, such as the legal reporting requirements. The fourth is to set the **administrative context** for the firm by choosing the structure, systems, and processes to control the various units and achieve coherence across them (see Figure 6.6).

FIGURE 6.6
Roles of the
Corporate Office

- Set vision
- Guardian of resources
- General overhead functions
- Set administrative context

[36] C.W.L. Hill, M.A. Hitt, and R.E. Hoskisson, "Cooperative versus Competitive Structures in Related and Unrelated Diversified Firms," *Organization Science* 3 (1992), pp. 501–21.
[37] For useful discussions, see S. Ghoshal and C.A. Bartlett, "Changing the Role of Top Management: Beyond Structure to Processes," *Harvard Business Review,* January–February 1995. See also H. Mintzberg, *The Nature of Managerial Work* (New York: Harper & Row, 1973).

▲ Vision

All CEOs have a responsibility to articulate and communicate a strategy for their companies. As described in Chapter 1, this involves the identification of the unique Corporate Strategy Triangle they believe will create a corporate advantage. Here we do not want to reiterate the elements of that Triangle; rather, we want to emphasize the importance of an overarching vision for the corporation.

Some believe that this is the most critical aspect of the CEO's task—to identify what Goold, Alexander, and Campbell called the "parenting insight"[38] and what Prahalad and Doz referred to as the "value creation logic,"[39] the differentiating way in which the corporate entity can add value to its businesses. For multibusiness corporations, conceiving this insight can be vital to success. Surfacing the logic that underpins a strategy not only facilitates its implementation but provides a powerful check on the consistency of a firm's actions.

It is important to note that setting the corporate vision and strategy does not necessarily involve specifying strategy for each of the business units. The final choice of business-unit strategy may be constrained by the corporate strategy, or influenced by the guidance of corporate management, but ultimately the initiation, selection, and commitment to a particular business-unit strategy should ultimately be the responsibility of its own managers.

▲ Resource Guardian

In Chapter 2 we said that it is the responsibility of the corporate office to develop a resource-based strategy. In that chapter, we focused on the critical tasks of identifying, investing in, and leveraging a **set of valuable resources.** These duties are among the most important responsibilities of senior management.

As resource guardian, the corporate office must also be concerned with the allocation of those resources. Once there is more than one business in the corporate portfolio someone has to decide on the distribution of resources among them. In fact, choosing which businesses to compete in—**portfolio selection**—and which projects to invest in—**capital budgeting**—is a critical function in multibusiness corporations. It is for this purpose that portfolio-planning techniques, introduced in the seventies (see Appendix A), were

---

[38] M.C. Goold, M. Alexander, and A. Campbell, *Corporate Level Strategy: Creating Value in the Multibusiness Company* (New York: John Wiley & Sons, 1994).
[39] C.K. Prahalad and Yves L. Doz, "CEO: A Visible Hand in Wealth Creation?" (preliminary draft), September 1995.

developed, along with the more traditional tools of capital expenditure, long-term planning, and annual budgets.

The challenge of resource allocation at the corporate level is twofold. The first is to ensure that while allocating resources to individual divisions, the performance of the corporation as a whole is optimized. What may seem to be a good investment to a particular division may in fact weaken the overall position of a company. The corporate office is the entity charged with maintaining overall performance and so has to balance a holistic perspective with the more narrow interests of individual product divisions. Second, in providing for the sustainable growth of the corporation, the corporate office must allocate resources in a way that maintains a balance between short-term profitability and long-term growth.

Because of the intrinsic trade-offs among these different objectives, there will never be easy recipes for achieving a balance in allocating a corporation's resources. Nor are simplistic pictorial representations of the portfolio adequate to capture the complexity of the trade-offs. Only a multidimensional assessment of the strategic and financial consequences of different investment patterns can lead to effective resource allocation decisions over time.

▲ General Overhead Functions

Every firm must conform with regulations concerning the **legal reporting requirements** of its particular governance structure—incorporated, partnership, publicly quoted, and so forth. These requirements are for both taxation and capital market purposes and involve the IRS, the SEC, and external auditors. If nothing else, therefore, the aggregation and reporting of consolidated financial results for the various businesses of a corporation has to be performed at the corporate level. Every company will have a corporate staff to fulfill these requirements and to oversee the performance of the reporting activity in the divisions.

Other corporate functions that verge on being required include activities such as public relations, external communications, government relations, and corporate giving. These activities are pure overhead costs of doing business as a public company; they rarely are important sources of value creation. Beyond the attempt to perform these functions as efficiently and accurately as possible, little more remains to be said, as few things differentiate these activities across corporations.

Many corporations also centralize the treasury function or computer operations, such as payroll and benefits administration, at the corporate level, or maintain all their lawyers in a corporate staff function. Such corporate units are not performing public company functions; they are acting as service providers of **scalable overhead functions** for the divisions. This is a perfectly valid role for a corporate center to perform if it is a more cost-effective provider of those services than either the divisions themselves or an outside supplier.

Some firms are beginning to apply exactly this market test to corporate activities that involve the provision of overhead services. As a result, they are structuring some corporate functions to be arm's-length suppliers to divisions that are allowed to choose whether or not to use the services provided by the corporate unit. This imposes a market discipline and allows the divisions to choose the level of service appropriate for them. As a corollary, the corporate unit is often allowed to compete for outside business. This not only demonstrates that the unit is cost effective, but also increases its scale.

The result of this approach has been the **outsourcing** of many corporate services, such as data processing and legal affairs, when third-party suppliers are found to be more efficient and responsive than an internally focused corporate unit. Offshoring—the movement of administrative functions, particularly related to IT and call centers—to India and other developing countries is an extension of outsourcing to domestic third parties. In addition, the approach has led to the **decentralizing** of many overhead functions to the divisions. For example, as part of restructuring at ABB, the European electrical equipment company in the nineties, Chairman Percy Barnevik dealt with corporate functions according to a "30/30/30/10 rule"—30 percent of the employees were laid off because their activities were outsourced; 30 percent were transferred to divisions as their activities were decentralized; 30 percent were moved to units that charged for their services; and only 10 percent remained at headquarters.[40]

Such actions can be entirely appropriate. When it is cheaper to outsource or decentralize an overhead function, or when the service provided by the division or external supplier is more responsive and flexible, there is no longer any reason to maintain a central corporate unit. Outsourcing such opportunities can not only lead to cost reductions, it can force a firm to reconsider the means by which it adds value to its units.

▲ Setting the Administrative Context

The major influence the corporate office has on the implementation of its corporate strategy is by establishing the administrative context within which delegated decisions are made. As described in the Principles section, the administrative context defines the information structure, the allocation of decision rights, and the incentive structure inside the firm. More pragmatically, in a multibusiness corporation that context is created from the design of the organization structure and the systems and processes used to achieve control and coherence of the units established by that structure.

[40] R.L. Simons and C.A. Bartlett, "Asea Brown Boveri," Harvard Business School, Case no. 192–139, 1992.

Structure

As was discussed in the Principles section, organizational designs are rarely ideal for any corporation. No matter how complex the design, every organizational structure will have weaknesses. This does not mean that CEOs should throw up their hands and walk away from structuring their organizations. Rather, it implies that organizational design should be contingent on the immediate task at hand and that managers should be prepared to expect some degree of conflict around, and discomfort within, any organization. Particular designs are not solutions for eternity; rather, they are appropriate at a point in time.

This suggests that a degree of organizational change at reasonable intervals is probably appropriate. The corporation should adopt what currently seems to be the best choice, stick with it for a while to give it a chance to affect behavior, and then make changes as circumstances demand. As a simple example, in transformational processes corporations are often broken into smaller units to improve efficiencies within those units. At a later stage, the units may be recombined under a single manager in order to exploit the underlying synergies among the businesses. No organizational design can achieve both goals simultaneously, so firms choose different structures to achieve these goals *sequentially*.[41]

Control

Corporate control systems are often seen as the necessary evil of large organizations. They prevent abuse of delegated decision-making authority by autonomous divisions (minimize agency costs) but may add interfering layers of bureaucracy to the entrepreneurial activities of those divisions. Although the old-fashioned "command and control" hierarchy may not be popular today, the corporate office still has a responsibility to monitor and regulate divisional activities. Further, in a more positive light, such systems can be seen as a powerful discipline for divisions, providing the structure within which creativity may take place.

Most multidivisional corporations ultimately employ some form of hierarchical control by a corporate executive or, in very large corporations, by a number of group vice presidents who reduce the span of control of the CEO to whom they report. Control is also exerted through the selection and replacement of senior divisional personnel. For example, choosing a manager with a particular set of skills, such as cost-cutting experience, is a simple way to ensure that a division will attempt to achieve a particular objective. Similarly, replacing the president of a division is the most immediate way to correct unsatisfactory performance.

[41] Richard P. Rumelt, "Inertia and Transformation," in *Resource-Based and Evolutionary Theories of the Firm: Towards a Synthesis,* ed. C.A. Montgomery (Boston, MA: Kluwer Academic Publishers, 1995), pp. 100–32.

Yet the most pervasive form of corporate control is the use of a set of systems and processes that continually monitor and regulate the behavior and performance of the divisions. Typically, these are the budgeting, strategic planning, capital expenditure, and measurement and reward schemes installed by corporate managers. Their value lies in setting the incentive structure for managers by defining performance and behavior targets, monitoring progress toward those targets, rewarding and motivating managers to meet the targets, and including mechanisms to intervene when performance deviates from acceptable bounds.

As noted in the Principles section, control systems can be differentiated by an emphasis on outcome or behavior control. Each approach serves different strategic needs and has different organizational requirements.

Implementing Outcome Control   Outcome control is most appropriate when: (1) a single measure of current financial performance, such as cash flow, is a good surrogate for the health of a business; (2) when few exogenous influences intervene between managerial behavior and a business outcome; and (3) when a firm's business units have little need for coordination. Outcome control, therefore, is most often found in mature businesses with low technology, where unprecedented competitive changes are rare.

When implementing an outcome control system, the first task is to structure the organization into **autonomous and self-contained business units.** Managers evaluated on outcome control will be improperly incentivized and demotivated if they are held accountable for events and actions beyond their control. The organizational structure, therefore, must align managerial authority and responsibility as closely as possible.

The next step is to select an appropriate performance measure. Most firms use one or very **few financial measures of performance** to evaluate divisional executives. Some focus on measures of accounting profitability, such as return on investment (ROI), while others, more recently, have installed value-based measures.[42] Many of the incentive schemes are highly leveraged so that managers who do exceed their targets are handsomely compensated. In LBO firms, for example, where incentives are tied to equity stakes, managers have the potential to become very wealthy if their buyout succeeds. Even in more traditional corporate hierarchies, the slope of the incentive payment is often very steep, and the size of the bonus payment relative to base salary is large.

When using outcome control, the critical management system is the **annual budget.** The budget sets goals that divisional managers must meet and is often the basis for most interactions between the divisions and the

[42] J.M. MacTaggart, P. Kontes, and M.C. Mankins, *The Value Imperative: Managing for Superior Shareholder Returns* (New York: Free Press, 1994); and T. Copeland, T. Koller, and J. Murrin, *Valuation: Measuring and Managing the Value of Companies* (New York: John Wiley & Sons, 1990)

corporate office. To preserve the integrity of the budgeting system, it is particularly important to avoid gaming by divisional managers around their performance targets. This may be done by holding all divisions accountable to one standard, even if external circumstances change, or by locking managers into the division in which they are currently employed so that if they increase profit today at the expense of profit tomorrow, they themselves will bear the consequences of that action. If a particular division does not meet its target over a sustained period, corporate management is likely to replace the unit's managers or sell the division rather than adjust its goal or attempt to assist in a turnaround. In companies that rely on outcome control, corporate managers are simply unlikely to have the level of specific expertise that more active involvement would require.

Due to their limited involvement in divisional affairs, firms that rely on outcome control typically have **small corporate staffs. Controllers** fulfill a critical function in these firms and are usually corporate staff employees. Even though they may be assigned to a particular division, they will be independent from divisional management in matters of financial reporting. In fact, they will often be the most powerful managers inside the company, and many of them will become senior corporate executives.

Not surprisingly, the **accounting system** may well be the only uniform system throughout the entire corporation. Since it is important to hold all divisions to a similar standard, it is critical to have one set of accounts that makes assessment fair and comparisons easy. Divisions may choose the format of their own strategic plans, although the emphasis will always be on the financial implications. Capital budgeting will typically impose a tight discipline on the divisions since investment is, in the short run, the enemy of performance. In fact, some of the more extreme exponents of outcome control have very low capital spending limits as a direct check on cash flow.

The clearest examples of outcome control are associated with the classic conglomerates, like ITT under Harold Geneen, which evaluated performance and allocated resources on the basis of divisional ROI. Today, many successful corporations, like General Electric, essentially employ outcome control. Although many of these firms may appear to take a more active role in the management of their divisions, a closer look often reveals that the primary relationship between headquarters and the divisions is one of arm's-length monitoring of financial results.

Implementing Behavior Control   Unlike outcome control, behavior control solves the agency problem inside the corporation by directly evaluating the behavior of divisional managers, not their results. This system of control is particularly appropriate in companies with **complex interdependencies among divisions,** where outcome control is less feasible.

In these companies, corporate managers usually monitor **multiple operating and financial measures of performance.** In particular, attention is paid to critical operating data, such as reject rates, delivery lead times, and sales conversion statistics. Indeed, corporate managers in companies practicing behavior control may be presented with monthly reports that contain up to 200 line items on divisional performance. Managerial assessment in this setting may be flexible, and involve a number of **quantitative and qualitative goals.** The trade-offs among these targets may not be fully specified, and the evaluation and incentive scheme may resemble more of an implicit contract than a simple objective target. Short-term financial rewards are often less important as an incentive than long-term career progression in such companies.

In practice, for corporate managers to utilize behavior control effectively, they have to **know the businesses in the portfolio.** As a result, managers often come from within the firm, or at least from the industries in which the firm operates. When this mode of control is working properly, the role of the corporate officers becomes more of a coach than a monitor. They do not necessarily make decisions for divisional managers, but their industry experience allows them to offer advice and critique behavior in a constructive way that improves the decisions of divisional managers. Consequently, although businesses in the corporate portfolio need not produce similar products, they do need to share similar managerial characteristics; that is, have the same "dominant logic."

Not surprisingly, behavior control typically necessitates active corporate involvement in **many management systems.** The strategic and the capital budgeting processes, for example, will often be interactive and involve corporate initiatives because the corporate managers have something of value to contribute. These processes are also likely to be standardized across divisions so that corporate management can readily understand detailed divisional operating and financial data. Business units will usually have a common culture so that managers can move freely and easily among them.

Finally, although behavior control often requires a **larger corporate staff** than outcome control, it does not necessarily demand an enormous corporate infrastructure. If corporate managers are familiar with the industries they are overseeing, it is quite possible for them to be adequately informed without a vast support system.

A Blending of Control Systems   Although the two modes of control are often treated as a dichotomy, they are more accurately portrayed as a range. Most firms use elements of both: corporate offices, for example, often evaluate divisional managers on financial performance, but also monitor and evaluate more specific behaviors. Nevertheless, the administrative imperatives of each, and the contingencies that determine when each type of control is appropriate, are sufficiently different that corporations do have to choose a relative emphasis on one or the other.

Coherence

The second set of systems and processes that the corporate office must design to support a given organization structure are those that provide coherence to the activities of the differentiated business units. It has been in this regard that corporate strategy has too often failed. Yet it is exactly this role that is critical to the effective implementation of any corporate strategy. If the corporation cannot be organized to leverage valuable corporate resources across the divisions, it will not be able to justify its existence as a multibusiness corporation.

In the Principles section we suggested that valuable resources could be leveraged through transfer or coordination. *Transferring resources and skills* across businesses can be a powerful way to create value while minimizing the interference in the autonomy of divisions. Many corporations, for example, move highly skilled managers, or replicate best demonstrated practices, such as supply chain management, across all the businesses in the firm's portfolio.

Other firms may have the potential to exploit their multibusiness nature by *coordinating* activities across businesses. Some firms may jointly purchase common raw materials to take advantage of purchasing scale economies. Others may share a sales force, a common component manufacturing facility, or a joint distribution system. Coordinating activities may not only reduce costs, it may also provide direct benefits to the customer, such as a single point of contact.

To leverage valuable resources across business units, a firm has to follow one or both of these approaches to achieve coherence. However, the two are not mutually exclusive; the necessary systems and processes can be customized for each resource that is being shared. Not surprisingly, therefore, many corporations employ both methods as they exploit their corporate advantages. (See Appendix C, "Mechanisms for Achieving Corporate Coherence.")

Transferring Skills   In transferring resources or skills across divisions where they will be used independently, the corporate office faces two basic decisions, identified by Andrew Campbell.[43] These are **where to develop the resource** (at the corporate or divisional level), and who has **authority over its transfer** (the corporate office or the divisions).

In choosing where to develop a resource, the advantage of centralization in a corporate unit lies in exploiting economies of scale and being of a sufficient size to support specialists. It also avoids the duplication of effort that ensues when multiple divisions make investments in similar resources or skills. This, for example, is why basic R&D is usually concentrated in a

---

[43] Andrew Campbell and Kathleen Sommers Luchs, *Strategic Synergy* (Oxford: Butterworth-Heinemann Ltd., 1992).

corporate unit. Conversely, the amount of experimentation is increased by allowing divisions to individually develop new knowledge, processes, and practices before selecting the best that emerges. In between these extremes lie a range of alternatives, such as nominating individual divisions to take the lead for a particular innovation, in much the way that multinationals select lead countries for developing particular new products or management practices.

After it has been decided where a resource should be developed, a choice has to be made about how much corporate intervention will be involved in transferring that resource or skill across businesses. At one extreme, transfers can be entirely left to the self-interest of the divisions. Divisions wishing to adopt a best practice, for example, can seek out individuals in other divisions who are identified as possessing state-of-the-art knowledge and ask them to act as temporary consultants. At the other extreme, the corporate office can mandate that all divisions adopt a particular set of policies and practices, which can even be set down in detail in a manual of procedures.

It is important to note that companies can choose how to deploy each resource or skill differently. Ideally, most would be transferred in a way that does not violate the autonomy of the divisions. The imposition of more centralized procedures should occur only when those with less intervention fail to achieve the desired degree of coherence.

Coordination of Activities　Despite the many benefits of transferring resources across autonomous divisions, some of the most highly valued benefits of synergy can only be achieved by coordinating activities across businesses.

Because introducing coordination to previously stand-alone businesses can be difficult, it is important to first be **selective** about the activities to be coordinated. This is best done at a disaggregated level. Rather than treating all purchasing as a single activity, for example, it can be disaggregated into discrete processes that can be managed differently. Divisions may be given authority to arrange their own logistics and to select vendors, while the corporate purchasing department is made responsible for approving vendors, establishing standard terms for suppliers, and negotiating prices.

Activities that are a **large part of the cost structure,** or those that have little impact on the differentiation of an individual division's products, are often coordinated because sharing brings substantial benefits. At banks, for example, it is the backroom operations that are shared between consumer, commercial, and large business accounts because they involve substantial costs, are subject to scale economies, and their performance is invisible to the customer. Smaller, or more sensitive activities, such as the issuance of credit, are often left under the control of each product line.

After identification of the activities that should be shared, the next step is to choose the mechanism by which coordination will be achieved. Options for doing so can be arrayed along a **hierarchy of coordination.** This extends

Introducing Coordination

The corporate office can play a pivotal role in managing a transition to more intensive coordination. Some of its more important activities include:

- *Selling* the benefits by preaching the quantifiable gains that the corporation will make from cooperation and reiterating the importance of optimizing corporate, not divisional, performance.

- *Encouraging* the mechanisms that are appropriate at each stage in the change process.

- *Facilitating* the transition by removing barriers, whether these are organizational structures or high-performing managers who do not accept the process.

- *Validating* the outcomes from the new organization. This involves supporting initiatives that come out of these structures, and publicly and repeatedly applauding progress.

from actions guided by self-interested behavior to a formalized process in which a superior is imposed to directly coordinate divisional activities.

To be sure, introducing coordination in previously autonomous businesses can be difficult because it requires a change in attitudes and behavior. Nonetheless, as corporations remain under pressure to justify their existence as multibusiness entities, it will be increasingly important for them to take advantage of opportunities for sharing resources.

There are no universal solutions for the process of introducing coordination to an organization, and trade-offs abound (see "Introducing Coordination"). Moreover, all corporations have to be sensitive to their own unique administrative heritage. However, the preferred approach appears to be incremental. By gradually working up from the synergies that are in all divisions' interests, a firm can "pick the low-hanging fruit" first and address the more difficult and contentious issues later. At that point, a firm may have clarified its intentions and built sufficient commitment to the process to impose solutions on those parts of the organization that still resist.

Summary: The Size of the Corporate Office

Although all corporate offices perform the four roles described above, their implementation is very different across firms. How executives actually manage their organizations depends fundamentally on the corporate strategy they are pursuing. As a result, the range and nature of activities carried out at headquarters, and the appropriate size of the office itself, will differ radically across firms (see Figure 6.7).

Research suggests that the average cost of the corporate office is between .66 percent and .75 percent of corporate assets,[44] or perhaps 1 percent of total

---

[44] Copeland et al. *Valuation: Measuring and Managing the Value of Companies.*

FIGURE 6.7
Size of Corporate
Office in Various
Companies

Company	Assets ($ billions)	Employees in Corporate Office
Sharp	16	1,500
Cooper Industries	5	300
Newell	1.5	250
KKR	40	90

corporate revenue.[45] This compares with the expense of 0.22 percent of asset value that a mutual fund charges for investing in an indexed portfolio of stocks, and the 0.70 percent that Fidelity, one of the largest actively managed mutual fund company, charges for its Magellan Fund. Since the corporate office in a multibusiness firm is, if nothing else, acting like a mutual fund, that comparison provides a minimum benchmark for corporate expenses.

As a more pragmatic benchmark, European data reveal that the typical multinational consumer goods company employing just over 10,000 people had a staff of 100, or 1.0 percent of employees, in its head office.[46] This is, however, a purely descriptive statistic. The United States, for example, has substantially larger headquarters.[47] It carries no normative implications. Deciding whether the number is too large or too small requires an understanding of how to implement the roles of the corporate office for a chosen strategy. As Figure 6.7 shows, the appropriate number can vary broadly.

Corporate costs will continue to be under scrutiny as companies look for ways to increase their organizational efficiency. As these efforts proceed, however, it is critical that they are not decoupled from an understanding of a firm's corporate strategy. It is the strategy, after all, that determines the means by which a firm will add value to its businesses and the range of functions that its headquarters should perform. Once these decisions have been made, attention should be given to carrying them out in the most cost-efficient manner.

Recommended Readings

Armour, H., and D.J. Teece, "Organization Structure and Economic Performance: A Test of the Multidivisional Hypothesis." *Bell Journal of Economics* 9 (1978), pp. 106–22.

[45] D. Young et al., *Corporate Headquarters* (London: Pearson, 2000).
[46] D. Young, *The Headquarters Fact Book* (London: Ashridge Strategic Management Centre, 1993).
[47] See D. J. Collis, D. Young, and M. Goold, "The Size, Structure, and Performance of Corporate Headquarters," Harvard Business School Strategy Unit Working Paper no. 03-096, 2003.

Bartlett, C., and S. Ghoshal. *Managing across Borders.* Boston, MA: Harvard Business School Press, 1989.

Berg, N. "What's Different about Conglomerate Management?" *Harvard Business Review* 47 (1969), pp. 112–20.

Bower, J.H. *Managing the Resource Allocation Process.* Cambridge, MA: Harvard University Press, 1970.

Brickley, J., C. Smith, Jr., and J. Zimmerman, *Managerial Economics and Organizational Architecture.* New York: McGraw-Hill, 2004.

Chandler, A.D. *Strategy and Structure.* Cambridge, MA: MIT Press, 1962.

Copeland, T., T. Koller, and J. Murrin. *Valuation: Measuring and Managing the Value of Companies.* New York: John Wiley & Sons, 1990.

Cyert, R., and J. March. *A Behavioral Theory of the Firm.* Englewood Cliffs, NJ: Prentice Hall, 1963.

Eccles, R.G.N., and N. Nohria, eds. *Networks in Organizations.* Boston, MA: Harvard Business School Press, 1992.

Eisenhardt, K.M. "Agency Theory: An Assessment and Review." *Academy of Management Review* (1989), pp. 57–74.

Galbraith, J. R., and R.K. Kazanjian. *Strategy Implementation: Structure, Systems and Process.* St. Paul, MN: West Publishing, 1985.

Ghoshal, S., and C. Bartlett, *The Individualized Corporation.* New York: HarperCollins, 1997.

Goold, M.C., M. Alexander, and A. Campbell. *Corporate-Level Strategy: Creating Value in the Multibusiness Company.* New York: John Wiley & Sons, 1994.

Goold, M., and A. Campbell, *Organizing Effective Organizations.* San Francisco: Jossey-Bass, 2002.

Gupta, A.K., and S. Seshadri. "Horizontal Resource Sharing: A Principal Agent Approach." *Academy of Management Best Papers*, 1994, pp. 37–41.

Halal, W.E., A. Geranmayeh, and J. Pourdehnad. *Internal Markets: Bringing the Power of Free Enterprise inside Your Organization.* New York: John Wiley & Sons, 1993.

Hill, C.W.L., M.A. Hitt, and R.E. Hoskisson. "Cooperative versus Competitive Structures in Related and Unrelated Diversified Firms." *Organization Science* 3 (1992), pp. 501–21.

Jensen, M.C. *Foundations of Organizational Strategy.* Cambridge, MA: Harvard University Press, 1998.

Jensen, M.C., and W.H. Meckling. "Specific and General Knowledge, and Organization Structure." In *Main Currents in Contract Economics,* ed., L. Werin and H. Wijkander. London: Basil Blackwell, 1991, pp. 251–74.

Lawrence, P.R., and J.W. Lorsch. *Organizations and Environment.* Boston: Harvard Business School Press, 1967.

Lorsch, J.W., and S.A. Allen. *Managing Diversity and Interdependence.* Boston: Harvard Business School Press, 1973.

MacTaggart, J.M., P. Kontes, and M.C. Mankins. *The Value Imperative: Managing for Superior Shareholder Returns.* New York: Free Press, 1994.

Nayyar, P.R., and R.K. Kazanjian. "Organizing to Attain Potential Benefits from Information Assymetries and Economies of Scope in Related Diversified Firms." *Academy of Management Review* 18 (1993), pp. 735–59.

Nonaka, I., and H. Takeuchi. *The Knowledge Creating Company.* Oxford: Oxford University Press, 1995.

Ouchi, W.G. "A Conceptual Framework for the Design of Organization Control Mechanisms." *Management Science* 25 (1979), pp. 833–48.

Porter, M.E.. "From Competitive Advantage to Corporate Strategy." *Harvard Business Review* 65, No. 3 (May–June 1987), pp. 43–59.

Porter, M.E. *Competitive Advantage.* New York: Free Press, 1985.

Simons, R. *Levers of Control.* Boston, MA: Harvard Business School Press, 1995.

Vancil, R.F. *Decentralization: Managerial Ambiguity by Design.* Burr Ridge, IL: Irwin, 1978.

Young, D., M. Goold, G. Blanc, R. Bühner, D. Collis, J. Eppink, T. Kagono, and G.J. Seminario, *Corporate Headquarters.* London: Pearson, 2000.

Appendix C

Mechanisms for Achieving Corporate Coherence

The Principles and Practice sections of Chapter 6 outlined an approach to designing the administrative context for a multibusiness corporation. Here we describe in detail the systems and processes that can be used to effectively achieve coherence in such organizations.

Transferring Resources and Skills

Transferring resources and skills across organizational units can produce important synergies. At the same time, it often is a relatively low-cost, low-risk way of achieving coherence.

As we discussed in Chapter 6, the corporate office must decide where a resource should be developed—at the corporate or divisional level—and who should have authority over its transfer.

Andrew Campbell has developed a matrix that portrays these options (Figure C.1).

Quadrant 1

Corporate-level resources that are the "crown jewels" of a company merit a high degree of corporate involvement in their deployment. To the extent that an umbrella brand name or technical knowledge, for example, is critical to the corporate strategy, the corporate office must be particularly vigilant in overseeing its development and judicious usage. As a result, the optimum way to deploy these resources across businesses is to adopt systems and processes from Quadrant 1 of the grid. In particular, the task of the corporate office includes investing in the valuable resources; making them available to the divisions to use as they want; and maintaining quality control over their usage by the divisions.

FIGURE C.1
Transferring
Resources and
Skills

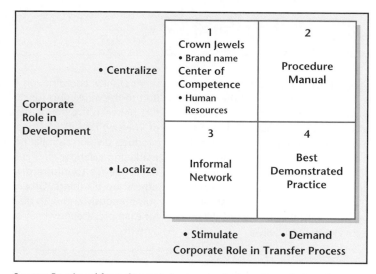

Source: Reprinted from *Strategic Synergy,* by Andrew Campbell and Kathleen Luchs, p. 185, Copyright 1992, with permission from Elsevier.

The corporate office must be in charge of the development of, and investment in, such critical resources. Divisions might well underinvest in these resources because many are public goods in which each division wishes to free ride on the investments of others.[1] In the case of R&D, for example, even if divisions will voluntarily pay for a certain amount of central research, the corporation as a whole will often be better off if it spends more than the sum of divisional research requests. Moreover, individual divisions may have conflicting priorities: one division, for example, might want the corporate brand reputation to appeal more to younger consumers, while another division might prefer an older age profile. The corporate office must, therefore, have control over both the level of investment and the specific nature of the resource that is being developed.

Since divisions will ideally regard the firm's crown jewels as vital to their own competitive advantage, they will voluntarily seek transfer of those resources to their businesses. Every division at Disney, for example, wants to use the latest cartoon character in its operations (see "Disney's Crown Jewels"). As a result, divisions by and large can be allowed to choose how to deploy the resources in their daily operations. As the intra-firm linkages provide little constraint, if any, on their autonomous operations, a few specific conflict resolution mechanisms and a strong-minded corporate arbitration policy are often sufficient to resolve divisional differences.

The exception is the need for quality control in the use of the resource. A division may, for example, be tempted to offer poor products to maximize its profits, knowing that they will sell because of the corporation's overall brand name or reputation for technical prowess. To prevent this degrading of the corporate resource, the corporate office must monitor the quality of divisional activities.

Many successful corporate staffs today are evolving into **centers of competence** (which fit under Quadrant 1), as central developers of a specific

[1] The market for a public good fails because each user has the incentive to underinvest in, or overexploit, the public good. When one division invests, for example, all other divisions benefit, so that the marginal private return to investing is below the social return. Formally, this occurs when the residual rights of control and the residual returns are not vested in the same entity [P. Milgrom and J. Roberts, *Economics, Organization and Management* (Englewood Cliffs, NJ: Prentice Hall, 1992), Chapter 9]. The solution is to give one entity (i.e., the corporation) property rights to the public good.

Disney's Crown Jewels

Disney essentially provides its library of cartoon characters as a central resource to otherwise autonomous divisions—theme parks, studio, and consumer products. Disney's chairman, Michael Eisner, invests in one new full-length animated feature film per year, but exactly what the theme park or consumer products divisions do with Simba from *The Lion King* is up to them. Eisner is more concerned with tightly controlling the quality of what the divisions do, rather than with the specifics of the product or service they choose to deliver.

At Disney, coordination among divisions is limited to the marketing function. This prevents conflict between the theme park division's promotion of *The Lion King* at McDonald's and the consumer products division's similar promotion at Wendy's. A marketing calendar is, therefore, used as a coordination device to inform divisions of the programs others are planning. Otherwise, divisions operate autonomously and with no coordination, utilizing, for example, their own pay scales and management systems.

skill or a particular pool of knowledge, such as supply chain management for batch manufacturing, that can be transferred to divisions as they request it.[2] In this role, corporate staffs can become valuable resources that businesses seek out on their own (see "Centers of Competence").[3]

Often the valuable skills that are developed in an organization, such as PepsiCo's consumer marketing know-how, vest in the employees. The easiest way to transfer those skills across the divisions is simply to move people throughout the organization. Indeed, several successful U.S. diversified corporations pursue this approach. General Electric, for example, has created a corporate advantage around the superior managerial skills and knowledge of a cadre of superbly trained people. Although not all firms pursue a corporate strategy based on people as the valuable corporate resource, in those that do the corporate human resources department plays a key role. As such, it exemplifies the modern role of a corporate function

as a center of competence (see "Corporate Human Resources").

Quadrant 2

In contrast, the role of the corporate staff functions has traditionally fallen in Quadrant 2 of the grid. For example, a central staff, such as a manufacturing department, may develop process technologies for divisions to employ and have the authority to interfere in divisional operations to ensure that the manufacturing department's edicts are followed. Staff units in such circumstances have often been viewed as overly interventionist. Bureaucratic and patronizing corporate manufacturing staffs, for example, might establish plant designs that all divisions have to follow, whether or not they are appropriate for their needs.

Operating a staff function in this way is really only necessary for those practices and skills that are absolutely essential to the **integrity of the corporation.** Accounting and control procedures should probably be operated in this fashion, as, for example, should safety, health, and environmental procedures in chemical companies. In these cases, the corporate staff needs to be independent of the business with an oversight and monitoring function that audits compliance. However, policies should be developed by the corporate center and imposed on divisions in this way only for those few activities that, if performed inappropriately, would lead to truly adverse consequences for the company.

[2] R. Eisenstat, "Corporate Staff Work in Divisionalized Corporations," Harvard Business School Working Paper no. 90-056, May 1990.

[3] This sort of activity by a corporate function needs to be distinguished from its role as a central unit that merely performs a scalable overhead function. A central legal department, for example, is not a valuable corporate resource that gives the firm a corporate advantage in a wide range of businesses.

Centers of Competence

To operate effectively as a center of competence and become a real asset to the businesses, corporate staff must be recognized as experts in their field. Thus, staff should not be failed managers who have been shunted aside in the twilight of their career, but those with the most experience and the best exponents of that function in the corporation. One former head of a corporate manufacturing staff of only 16 people, for example, was hired away to be the CEO of America's largest machine tool company because of his outstanding track record. Senior corporate executives also need to validate the expertise of their staff, reiterating how valuable their knowledge can be. The staff need to see their role vis-à-vis the divisions as educational, rather than authoritarian. They are not remote bureaucrats imposing a particular approach but advisers and consultants, coaching and supporting the businesses. Indeed, they need to continually sell their capabilities to the businesses, encouraging them to seek out their experience and know-how. Finally, it appears that successful centers of competence are best charged as a corporate expense, not as a direct cost to the businesses. Operating as an unallocated overhead charge encourages divisions to employ the staff as they are effectively free. It also identifies the staff as what it truly is when operating as a center of competence—a valuable corporate resource.

Corporate Human Resources

The strategic value of the corporate HR function revolves around **the recruitment, training, and career development** of a pool of corporate employees who possess valuable skills that create competitive advantage in the divisions. The brand managers of consumer packaged goods companies, for example, can be thought of in this light. These individuals will be involved in a substantial amount of personnel transfer across divisions and often across functions (perhaps 5 to 15 percent of the critical employees will have interdivisional transfers each year) in order to deploy the employees' skills throughout the corporation.

To facilitate corporatewide acceptance of the practice, the corporate HR function must establish a uniform compensation system and also, ideally, a common culture. It also needs training and career development programs that ensure skills truly are competitively superior and up to a common standard throughout the corporation. This gives divisions the confidence not to obstruct transfers of their best employees because they know that a replacement will be of equally high quality.

Since one of its valuable corporate resource is its people, HR also needs to develop careers that remain within the firm, and promote from within; this also prevents competitors from benefiting from the employees' knowledge. Procter & Gamble, Johnson & Johnson, and Marriott, for example, consider employees as lifetime partners and plan their career paths accordingly.

The synthesis of these organizational requirements is the strategic importance given the HR function by CEOs at companies that develop people as valuable resources. At GE, for example, Jack Welch spent two months a year on personnel evaluations of his top 400 managers and maintained that 70 percent of his time was spent on "people" issues. At PepsiCo, Wayne Calloway personally interviewed proposed candidates for any one of the company's top 600 jobs. These and other executives view the people in their organizations as critical assets and allocate to them, and their HR roles, the amount of time they deserve.

Quadrants 3 and 4

Rather than valuable resources being developed by a central corporate function, they can instead be developed in the divisions. One division, for example, may build a unique logistics capability; another may have a distinctive competence in high-volume data processing.[4] The critical task for the corporate office in creating corporate coherence around these resources then becomes ensuring that those skills are transferred around the organization. Typically, this is achieved by either encouraging (Quadrant 3) or mandating (Quadrant 4) the adoption of **best demonstrated practices** throughout the organization. Between these two extremes exist corporate policies that stimulate self-interested divisions to use a resource or skill available elsewhere in the firm, such as regular cross-divisional meetings of particular functional areas, company newsletters that describe breakthrough best practices, or intracompany yellow pages that list individuals who possess a particular expertise.

In the "bad old days" of bureaucratic corporate headquarters, many staffs saw their functions as formulating and dictating policies to the divisions (Quadrant 2). For example, a corporate manufacturing staff might write lengthy manuals that specified exactly how every plant should be operated, believing that only they had the expertise to optimize production. Divisional managers responsible for the daily functioning of the facilities, appropriately resented the interference by a staff that had no access to the realities of the shop floor. Those days are gone. Today, far-sighted corporate executives view themselves as a center of competence (Quadrant 1)—supporting and guiding the businesses, but in no way dictating how they should operate.

This transition illustrates the importance of understanding which of the four options firms should adopt for transferring skills among businesses.

Many professional service firms, for example, now have knowledge management functions. Although these operate in different ways at different companies, each is designed to make subject matter experts available to anyone in the company. General Electric, again, is a good example of a company that uses the variety of approaches in Quadrants 3 and 4 to transfer skills across its many varied businesses. The annual Florida meeting of the top two hundred executives in the corporation falls in Quadrant 3. The agenda is explicitly arranged to feature business heads talking about their latest management innovation, whether it concerns the best process for offshoring call centers to India, or transferring technology to plants in developing countries. Disseminating information in such a visible way allows all divisions to access the part of the organization that possesses the state of the art on any particular process. Jack Welch's personal role in transferring skills fell in Quadrant 4. On every visit to GE units he was on the lookout for novel best practices, such as having junior staff mentor senior executives on the Internet. When he found such an example, he mandated its adoption throughout GE within 48 hours.[5]

In summary, practices that facilitate the transfer of resources throughout an organization are many and varied in nature. When used appropriately, they can generate substantial value for a firm, often with modest costs to the organization. In contrast, scope economies that call for coordination of activities across business units tend to challenge firms more, and often necessitate fundamental changes in organizational infrastructure.

Coordination of Activities

As discussed in Chapter 6, to achieve the benefits of coordination, a firm should carefully identify the coordination mechanisms that are most appropriate for a given activity. This is done by disaggregating an activity into discrete steps that can be

---

[4] While divisional level resources give the division concerned a competitive advantage, they only create a corporate advantage if they can be deployed in other divisions. A purely divisional-level competence cannot be the justification for a multibusiness corporation. No matter how valuable a resource is to competitive advantage in a particular division, there must still be mechanisms to deploy it throughout the organization if it is to be the basis for a corporate advantage. A corporate strategy of owning only number 1 or number 2 brands, therefore, is unlikely to be successful if the only resource is the market-leading position of each individual brand.

[5] C. Bartlett, "GE: Two Decades of Transformation" Harvard Business School Case no. 9-399-150.

FIGURE C.2
Coordination
Hierarchy

Mode	System	Process
Discrete shared activity	Organization structure	Formalized
Centralized decision maker	Hierarchy	
Prescribed behavior	Manual	
Define responsibilities	Decision grid	
Recommendation/persuasion	Integrator	
Coordination of information flow	Council	
Team consensus	Task force	
Bilateral flow of information	Personal network	Self-interested

Source: Adapted from J. R. Galbraith and R. K. Kazanjian, *Strategy Implementation: Structure, Systems and Process* (St. Paul: West Publishing Company, 1978), p. 72.

treated separately. For each of these steps, management can choose the coordination mechanism which works best.

Coordination mechanisms range from those that are freely elected by the divisions to those that are imposed on the divisions by corporate management. The **hierarchy of coordination** (Figure C.2) illustrates these possibilities.

At the bottom of the hierarchy are **personal networks** that develop among individuals in different divisions and that can lead to the coordinated sharing of activities. Although such networks of interdivisional contacts are established in the ongoing activities of a firm—in corporate training sessions, planning meetings, and so forth—the corporate office can facilitate the process. For example, annual meetings of divisional presidents or heads of purchasing, at which each presents his or her ideas for coordination opportunities, can be valuable forums for developing such networks.

The next step up the hierarchy involves the creation of ad hoc **task forces** to address particular coordination needs that have been identified.[6] At this stage, more detailed analysis might be necessary because the ideal solution is no longer immediately visible or agreeable to all concerned. Instead, a team representing all the affected parties investi-

gates possible options and recommends a solution. At this point, the hierarchy begins to diverge from pure divisional self-interest: instead of allowing the divisions to accept or reject the task force's recommendation, the rule might be that a majority vote of the team is sufficient to implement the recommendation. Thus, coordination begins to supplant divisional autonomy.

More structured than personal networks or task forces are formal **councils** whose specific agenda is to search out opportunities for cooperation. Many corporations have such groups, under different names, for activities that divisions can profitably share with little compromise, such as stationery purchasing. Indeed, the first step of such a council is often to select those activities that fall into this category and can readily be implemented with the approval of all the interested parties.

Moving up the hierarchy, an **integrator** without formal authority to override divisional management may be given responsibility for implementing the sharing of activities across businesses. This is similar to the role of an executive whose job is to coordinate joint purchasing but who has no formal authority over purchasing decisions. Because of the lack of formal power over decision making, the individual has to have the respect of the operating divisions' management. This implies that the integrator has to be an experienced and successful line executive, not a staff functionary. He or she should also have a broad background and a wide network of contacts within the organization and be an effective resolver of conflicts. To balance divisional conflicts, and to provide the appropriate incentives, the reward

---

[6] Many corporations use teams as ad hoc mechanisms for reaching major onetime decisions, such as the choice of location of a new, shared manufacturing facility. They are less useful for managing ongoing coordination issues because of the continual intrusion in divisional autonomy.

FIGURE C.3   **Decision Responsibilities for Worldwide TV Business (U.S. and European Relationships)**

Legend:
D – Decides TC – Technical concurrence
A – Approves C – Concurs
R – Recommends I – Initiate
BC – Business concurrence IP – Inputs
* Joint decision
** For U.S. decisions only

Decision	Business Development Liscomb	Controller Russell	Business Manager TV Galley	Manager Manufacturing Friley	General Manager Dawson	TV Division/Plant Controller Hoflack	TV Production Timbal	TV Sales and Marketing Prestat	Division Manager TV Picol	Technical Director Ayotta	Head of Staff Maurice	President Regis	General Manager CEE McCann	Planning Manager Winkler	Licensing Roederer	Socialist Countries Roederer	Financial Manager Hamer	General Sales Manager Stoff	Deputy Area Manager Wuensch	General Manager Dulude	Staff Marketing and Business Development	Staff Manufacturing and Engineering	Control and Planning	Worldwide Manager Dawson	Treasury	Control	Business and Financial Planning	Manufacturing and Engineering	Technical Staffs	Purchasing	Manufacturing Services	Industrial Relations	Manpower Development	Public Relations	Legal	Government Affairs
Worldwide Resource Allocation																																				
1. Recommend allocation of resources to major new product development programs	R_1	IP	R_1	R_1	R_2	IP	R_1	R_1	R_2	IP	IP	BC			C				IP	BC	R_3	IP	IP	D	TC	IP	R/TC	R/TC				IP/TC			TC	
2. Recommend allocation of resources to major process development programs	IP	IP	IP	R_1	R_2	IP	R_1	IP	R_2	IP	IP	BC			C					BC	IP	R_3	IP	D	TC	IP	R/TC	R/TC				IP/TC			C	
3. Recommend allocation of resources for major cost reduction programs		IP	IP	R_1	R_2	IP	R_1	IP	R_2	R_1	IP	BC			C				C	BC	IP	R_3	IP	D	TC	IP	R/TC	R/TC			C	IP/TC				
4. Determine need, location, and timing for adding or reducing plant capacity	IP	IP	R_1		D*	IP	R_1	IP	R_2	IP	R_2	D*	R	IP	IP					D*	IP	R	IP	D*	TC	IP	R					IP/TC	IP/TC		TC	C**
5. Decide management of production work force (expansion, contraction, assignment)		IP	D	C		R_1		R_2		R_2	D	D					C					C										TC**		IP	TC**	C**
6. Decide on interarea sourcing		IP	IP	R_1	R_2	IP	IP	IP	R_2		R_1	BC	R_2				R_2	IP	IP	BC	IP	IP	R_3	D	TC	TC	IP	IP							C	C
7. Decide who maintains existing technologies (e.g., black-and-white, spinning)		IP	R	R		R	IP	R	IP			BC	R							BC	IP	R	IP	D			R/TC									
8. Assign specialized people resources to temporary assignments (e.g., to implement special three-month project)																																				
a. Assign operating personnel (e.g., marketing, manufacturing) to another area			R	R	D/BC		R	R	D/BC	C	C						R	R		BC	C	C	BC									R				
b. Assign technical staff and M&E personnel				R		R				D	C		R				R	R	IP	BC		R		BC							D	D			R	

Source: Reprinted from "Corning Class Works International (B-1)," by C. Bartlett and M. Y. Yoshino, HBS case number 381-161. Used by permission of Harvard Business School Publishing Corporation; all rights reserved.
Note: McKinsey-prepared form as filled out during a decision grid meeting.

scheme for the integrator has to be based on corporate goals and performance.

The explicit allocation of decision-making authority takes place at the next level in the hierarchy. This is captured in McKinsey's notion of a **decision grid** (see Figure C.3); it specifies which divisions and corporate functions have what degree of say in which decisions. The allocation of decision-making rights within a grid varies on a continuum from absolute control, through veto power, to input, and finally to no influence at all.

The decision grid clarifies where the responsibility for shared decisions lies. It does not, however, specify how to resolve conflict when multiple parties are vested with decision-making authority or when those with approval rights disagree. It is, therefore, most useful for demarcating who has no involvement in certain decisions. It does not by itself solve the most difficult and controversial aspects of achieving coordination.

The existence of a written **manual** marks the level in the hierarchy at which divisional discretion is removed. Manuals may eliminate conflict, a direct cost of coordination, but often do so at the expense both of divisional autonomy and, potentially, of finding the best solution to each situation. An example would be transfer pricing between divisions. Lower down the coordination hierarchy, divisions would be allowed to negotiate transfer prices among themselves. With a manual, the way to calculate the transfer price would be prescribed, with no scope for discretion. Doing so is often appropriate for recurring issues that have little effect on corporate performance. In those situations, a manual prevents repeated conflict. For substantive onetime decisions, however, the loss of discretion is more likely to produce a suboptimal decision.

The final step in the hierarchy involves taking away decision-making authority from the business units. This can be achieved through either of two **formal organizational structures.** The first is to give one individual authority over the divisions that share activities. The second is to split off the shared activity into a separate unit with its own management hierarchy. Both mechanisms eliminate the need for negotiation between divisions.

In many organizations, the first structural solution is captured in the role of **group vice president.** This person is put in charge of several related businesses with the responsibility and authority for maximizing the performance of the group.[7] It is, therefore, in a group vice president's interest to implement any coordination that benefits the corporation, even if it is at the expense of a single business. Although this has historically been the typical corporate solution, it is not without drawbacks, particularly in terms of diminished divisional autonomy and the concentration of decision-making power in the hands of someone who may be removed from the relevant specific knowledge and overloaded with critical decisions.

The second structural solution begins to approach a **functional organization:** discrete functional units perform common activities for multiple businesses. The argument for this solution is that it recreates the benefits of autonomy, since the shared activity is now a separate, self-contained unit, and so provides the correct incentives, particularly if the new unit sells to outsiders and treats its sister divisions as equal customers. It also facilitates the exploitation of scale economies.

However, this solution also creates its own problems. Creating an organizational unit to perform the shared activity shifts the coordination issue from a struggle between divisions to a struggle between the new unit and each division, particularly when it is set up as an internal market.[8] As we observed in the Principles section, no organization structure can completely resolve the tension between differentiation and integration,[9] so the coordination issues may remain problematic under any proposed solution.

Either of these structural approaches may be appropriate when extensive interdependencies exist among divisions. However, they are extreme solutions and should probably only be used after other levels in the coordination hierarchy have been tried.

Because most corporations have been structured with a bias toward the autonomy of discrete business units, moving to achieve a higher degree of coherence is often problematic. Any sudden attempt to impose formal integrative structures will most likely be resisted. Conversely, the partial introduction of some limited coordination mechanisms might founder on a lack of perceived commitment to change. Nevertheless, for those activities for which there are real benefits from sharing, the challenge for many corporations is to introduce the appropriate mechanisms that capture those benefits while minimizing the costs of doing so.

Coordinating Strategies

A special case of coordination involves the coordination of divisional strategies. In this situation, the sharing among divisions involves not an internal company activity, but the external customer base or competitors of the divisions.

COORDINATING MARKET POSITIONS

When considering whether to coordinate strategies toward the same customers, corporations must

---

[7] The group vice president role does not necessarily involve coordination responsibilities. It can also be a device to break spans of control in a purely monitoring function. Conglomerates, for example, are frequent users of group vice presidents, but their role is often confined to monitoring delegated decision making, not coordination.

[8] William E. Halal, A. Geranmayeh, and J. Pourdehnad, *Internal Markets: Bringing the Power of Free Enterprise Inside Your Organization* (New York: John Wiley & Sons, 1993).
[9] Proponents of core competence who argue for the creation of independent units responsible for a corporation's "platform products" are, therefore, advocates of an extreme structural solution that is not universally appropriate.

decide whether divisions should be allowed to freely compete with one another or should have their spheres of activity clearly demarcated to prevent interdivisional competition. The choice is not simple because there are costs and benefits to each approach.

The advantage of free competition is that it maximizes divisional autonomy and fosters entrepreneurialism in the divisions. PepsiCo, for example, pursued this policy in its restaurant businesses, even though its three fast-food chains consequently compete vigorously with one another. The primary disadvantage of interdivisional competition is that it can lead to the duplication of effort and allow opportunities for coordination to be overlooked. It also eliminates the opportunity to earn oligopolistic profits from coordinating strategies and prices. Marriott, for example, would prefer that its various hotel chains, which are often located close to one another, did *not* compete with one another on price.

Resolving the trade-off primarily depends on whether the market can be proactively segmented. When it can, it makes sense to assign one business to each segment and let each optimize its performance within a segment. GM perfected this strategy under Alfred Sloan with "a car for every purse": each of the divisions was assigned a target market, from luxury (Cadillac), to mass market (Chevrolet), to sporty (Pontiac). Historically, this arrangement worked very profitably until it broke down when the brand images of the divisions became blurred (Figure C.4).

However, it can be impossible to segment the market in an economically meaningful way. In the case of fast-food restaurants, customer segmentation varies from day to day, according to how their stomachs feel. In such cases, artificially restricting divisional activities will weaken performance by preventing each from optimizing its own strategy.

The argument for coordination to prevent divisions from cannibalizing each other's sales is also less compelling when competitors are already doing it. The motto here might best be expressed as "do unto yourself what others do unto you." In contrast, preserving discrete market positions is more appropriate when the firm's decision to compete with itself will exacerbate negative externalities, such as increasing the rate of substitution to a lower-profit item. Gillette, for example, was slow to introduce disposable razors because they were less profitable than razor and blade systems.

COORDINATING MULTIMARKET COMPETITION

Multimarket competition occurs whenever a corporation faces the same competitor in more than one market. This raises, at least, the possibility of a coordinated competitive response across markets in order to optimize corporate performance. Examples of multimarket competition abound, from airlines competing with one another on different routes, to consumer packaged goods companies competing with multiple brands across market segments.

There are three fundamental questions raised by multimarket competition. The first is whether such competition stabilizes or intensifies rivalry among the players. The second is how a competitor should allocate its resources across the various markets in which it faces a competitor. The third is how the firm should be organized to capitalize on the opportunities for coordinated response.

Mutual Forbearance

In the heyday of the conglomerates, Corwin Edwards raised a novel concern.[10] His thesis of "mutual forbearance" was that as industry became dominated by conglomerates that competed in a slew of different markets, conglomerates would recognize the futility of competing intensely with one another. Since competition in one market would spill over into all the other markets in which they met, he argued that conglomerates would reach a tacit oligopolistic agreement to maximize profits. This, Edwards believed, represented an important threat to consumer welfare. Conversely, it can be argued that firms that compete in multiple markets are less able to sustain any tacit agreements

---

[10] C.D. Edwards, "Conglomerate Bigness as a Source of Power," in *Business Concentration and Price Policy,* National Bureau of Economic Research (Princeton, NJ: Princeton University Press, 1955).

FIGURE C.4 **Historic GM Brand Positioning**

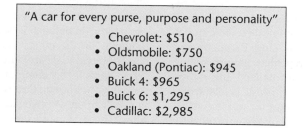

1924 "Touring Car" Price Points

"A car for every purse, purpose and personality"
- Chevrolet: $510
- Oldsmobile: $750
- Oakland (Pontiac): $945
- Buick 4: $965
- Buick 6: $1,295
- Cadillac: $2,985

1984 Brand Image

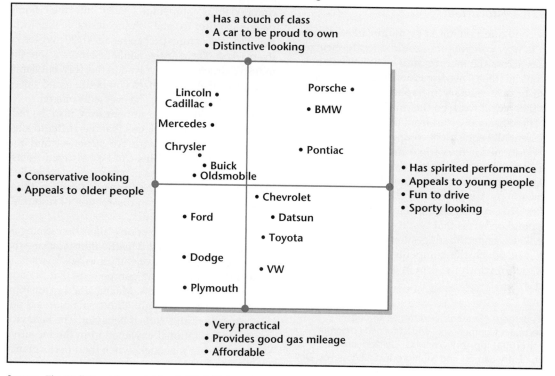

Source: *The Wall Street Journal*, March 22, 1984, p. 33.
Reprinted by permission of *The Wall Street Journal*, © 1984 Dow Jones & Company, Inc. All rights reserved worldwide.

either because a breakdown in any one market can spill over to all markets or because firms have an incentive to subsidize attacks on competitors across markets.

Early empirical evidence was supportive of the competition-reducing impact of multimarket contact.[11] More recent empirical work has confirmed evidence of a competition-reducing effect

[11] J.T. Scott, "Multimarket Contact and Economic Performance," *Review of Economics and Statistics* 64 (1982), pp. 368–75.

from multimarket competition, usually where the markets are different geographies or different product lines with some underlying economic relatedness.[12] In addition, theoretical work, although not conclusive, suggests that mutual forbearance is more likely to occur than spoiling. Bernheim and Whinston's analysis of repeated games among multimarket competitors formalized the notion that the threat of destroying profit levels across many markets raised the stakes for aggressive action in any one market so high that competitors refrained from undertaking such moves.[13]

Resource Allocation

The second question raised by multimarket competition is how competitors should allocate their resources across the markets in which they compete with one another. This discussion has given rise to a whole host of military metaphors and analogies, since theoretical work on this subject has been limited. These generally start from the assumption that two essentially equivalent competitors are differentially positioned in the various markets, so that each has a "home base" where it is the dominant player.

One proposal for managing the competitive interaction is to attack the competitor's home market. This, it is argued, will force the competitor to respond on terms that cost it disproportionately more. Thus, a specific suggestion is to cut price in a market in which the competitor has a dominant share, but in which the firm in question has only a small share.

An extension of this proposal, which has some support from the mutual forbearance theory, and which had a direct analogy to the cold war, is "mutually assured destruction." The idea is that if each competitor maintains a small market share, "a foothold," in the others' home markets, each possesses a threat to destroy the others' profitability—a "cross parry." This common threat should stabilize competition, since no firm wants to launch an attack that will bring overwhelming retribution on both sides. The pragmatic suggestion is, therefore, that competitors should always try to hold some market share in the others' strong markets and should accommodate a competitor's entry into their home market in order to establish the desirable interlocking market structure (perhaps at an 80/20 division of the market). There are certainly instances where the industry structure has evolved in this way, but definitive proof that it stabilizes competition and raises profits for all competitors has yet to be offered.

A very different argument can also be advanced. This position claims that it is better to allocate resources where you are strongest and the competitor weakest. This can be bolstered by asserting that attacks on a competitor's "walled cities" are often the worst strategic moves and that concentration rather than dissipation of resources is the preferable strategy.[14]

Other multimarket resource allocation strategies have also been observed. *Mimetic diversification*—the matching of a competitive entry into new markets is frequently found among competitors that already meet in multiple markets. Matsushita's acquisition of MCA after Sony bought Universal Studios is but one example of this sort of behavior. The behavior has an organizational explanation in the incentive structure facing managers when their performance is evaluated against competitors rather than in absolute terms.[15] In such cases, a manager may blindly copy a competitor's moves for fear that he or she

[12] W.P. Barnett, "Strategic Deterrence among Multiproduct Competitors," *Industrial and Corporate Change* (1993), pp. 249–78; M.D. Gelfand and P.T. Spiller, "Entry Barriers and Multiproduct Oligopolies: Do They Forbear or Spoil?" *International Journal of Industrial Organization* 5 (1987), pp. 101–23; and A. van Witteloostuijn and M. van Wegberg, "Multimarket Competition: Theory and Evidence," *Journal of Economic Behavior and Organization* 18, (1992), pp. 273–82. See also, J. Baum and H. Grieve, *Multiunit Organization and Multimarket Strategy* (Oxford: Elsevier, 2001).

[13] B.D. Bernheim and M.D. Whinston, "Multimarket Contact and Collusive Behavior," *RAND Journal of Economics* 2 (1990), pp. 1–26; A. Karnani and B. Wernerfelt, "Multiple Point Competition," *Strategic Management Journal* 6 (1986), pp. 87–96; and M.E. Porter, *Competitive Advantage* (New York: Free Press, 1986).

[14] This idea has roots in some of the earliest writings on military strategy, notably Sun-Tzu's *The Art of War* (New York: Ballantine Books, 1993). See also D. Yaffic and M. Kwak, *Judo Strategy* (Boston: Harvard Business School Press, 2001).

[15] S.T. Knickerbocker, *Oligopolistic Reaction and Multinational Enterprise* (Boston, MA: Harvard Business School Press, 1973).

might be "punished" for failing to match the competitor's diversification, while knowing that he or she will not look bad if the diversification does fail, provided someone else made the same mistake.

In spite of these varied recommendations, there are some conclusions that can be drawn from these armchair intuitions as to how to coordinate multimarket competition. These hinge on the distinction between whether the markets are economically related or not. If they are related—if there are scale or scope economies linking markets—then markets should be treated as an integrated whole. If, in contrast, the markets are unrelated—as they would be for a conglomerate—linkages have to be behavioral rather than economic, and concern the ability to exercise some form of market power.

More specifically, this suggests that in the case of related markets, a firm should be concerned whenever a multimarket competitor has a strong market share, because that allows the competitor to exploit scale and scope economies. A firm should also be prepared to cross-subsidize an entry into a new market, or into a competitor's strong market, because there is a benefit over and above the return that is earned in the new market alone.

In contrast, if markets are economically unrelated, the firm should, in the first instance, treat each one as independent. Entry into one market, or a competitive move in a market where competitors overlap, will be merited if the returns to investment in that one market alone justify the move. In principle, there should be no cross-subsidization between markets since there are no spillovers between them. Indeed, firms can quite happily let competitors build dominant positions elsewhere since they give the competitor no additional strength in the markets in which the players do meet. However, the interconnection between markets that must be overlaid on this analysis concerns the need to build a set of market positions that induce firms to stabilize competition in all markets where they overlap.

Organizing for Multimarket Competition

The following story (possibly apocryphal) illustrates the difficulty of implementing multimarket competition. A major airline divided its pricing group into East and West Coast rooms. One day, the manager

for one of the airline's major East Coast hubs was disturbed to find a competitor had cut prices out of the hub. He adjusted prices accordingly and raised some prices he had recently cut at the competitor's hub, in order to signal that he did not want a price war. But it was to no avail. The next day, the competitor came back with even more aggressive price cuts. All attempts to restore pricing rationality failed. On the third day, during an unusually tense cigarette break in the lounge between the East and West Coast rooms, a colleague from the West Coast pricing room asked what the problem was. When told, he countered with, "but didn't you know we cut prices into *his* West Coast hub last week?"

The lesson is that unless the organization is set up, both informationally and managerially, for multimarket competition, the coordination of competitive responses cannot happen. Managing multimarket competitive interaction, therefore, requires an individual to have both responsibility for competitive interaction across multiple markets and the necessary information about the relevant markets. Assigning responsibility is relatively straightforward, although few firms are currently structured this way. A category manager who is responsible for a set of related brands at a consumer packaged goods firm is one such example.

The information that is required to coordinate multimarket competition is considerably more complex.[16] In principle, the firm needs to monitor the activities in all the businesses of all the competitors that it meets in at least one market. Even more problematic is structuring the firm to allow for the required cross-subsidization from one business to another. This would involve telling one division manager that it is okay to lose $X million this year by attacking a major competitor in one market "for the good of the firm," while a colleague in another division has his or her profit target raised.

All of this suggests that the theory and the practice of multimarket competition are only just beginning. Theorists have not resolved the way to play the game, and few companies are structured to take advantage of what can, in principle, be the value of exploiting multimarket competition.

[16] M.E. Porter, *Competitive Advantage* (New York: Free Press, 1985).

RESOURCES

BUSINESSES

- VISION

- GOALS & OBJECTIVES

ORGANIZATION

CREATING CORPORATE ADVANTAGE

▲ Introduction

Chapter 1 introduced the Corporate Strategy Triangle. The chapters that followed examined individual elements of the Triangle in detail from a theoretical as well as a practical perspective, identifying their salient characteristics and respective roles in building an effective corporate strategy.

An equally challenging analysis focuses on the Triangle as a whole and how the individual elements relate to one another to create a corporate advantage. We will now consider the Triangle in its entirety and how a well-constructed corporate strategy can create value for a firm.

Principles

▲ A System of Value Creation

Corporate Strategy—The way a company seeks to create value through the configuration and coordination of its multimarket activities.

Effective corporate strategy is not just about having valuable corporate resources, competing in attractive businesses, or having efficient management systems. Outstanding corporate strategies depend not only on the quality of their individual elements, but also, and just as important, on how the elements work together as a whole.

An effective corporate strategy can best be thought of as an **integrated system** in which all elements of the strategy are aligned. Only then will the system as a whole create value and not be pulled apart by internal dissonance. The Corporate

FIGURE 7.1
Critical Linkages in
the Corporate
Strategy Triangle

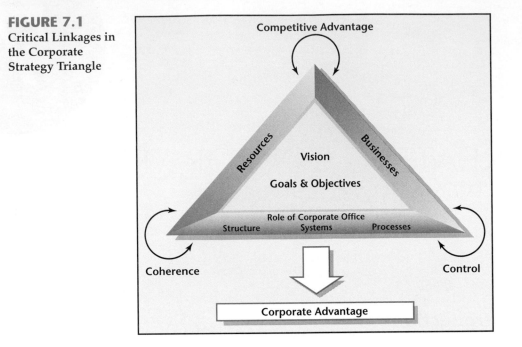

Strategy Triangle captures this logic. Its five elements—vision, goals and objectives, resources, businesses, and organization—form the foundation of the corporate strategy system. For maximum effect, each element should depend upon and support each of the others, working in a way that is mutually reinforcing. When this occurs, the strategy is said to be *internally consistent*.

Consistency originates with a vision that describes how the system will create value. Out of that vision flows not only the qualities the individual elements should take on and more immediate goals and objectives, but also the linkages that will be required across the individual elements. There are three junctures at which achieving consistency is particularly important but very challenging: in the fit between the firm's resources and its businesses; between the businesses and the organization's structure, systems, and processes; and between the organization and the firm's resources (Figure 7.1).

Competitive Advantage

The logic behind the requirement for consistency between a firm's resources and businesses is that the resources should **create a competitive advantage** in the businesses in which a firm competes. To meet this requirement, corporate resources should be evaluated against the key success factors in each business. When doing so, it is important to keep in mind that in order to justify retaining a business, or entering a business, the resources should convey a substantial advantage. Merely having pedestrian resources that could be applied in an industry is rarely sufficient to justify entry or to maintain a presence in an attractive industry.

Moreover, managers must remember that, regardless of the advantage a particular corporate resource appears to yield, the firm must also compete on all the other resources that are required to produce and deliver the product or service in each business. One great resource does not ensure a successful competitive position, particularly if a firm is disadvantaged on other resource dimensions. Overall, the firm must be confident that its resources give it an advantage against competitors, including those pursuing different strategies based on different Corporate Strategy Triangles.

In turn, by competing in the set of businesses in the corporate portfolio, the firm's resources **should be strengthened and upgraded.** In Chapter 4, for example, we suggested how firms could progressively improve their resource bases through a carefully planned sequence of market moves—leveraging existing skills to enter a new market where competing required the development of a new capability that in turn could be used to enter another market. Thus, in Figure 7.1, a bilateral relationship between businesses and resources is illustrated.

Control

The requirement for effective control addresses the fit between the businesses and the organizational structure, systems, and processes. The principal issue here is whether the individual businesses can be effectively **monitored and controlled** under the corporate infrastructure. If the corporate office cannot adequately control its independent businesses, it will never be able to create value.

Consistency between these two sides of the Triangle does not require that all the businesses under a corporate umbrella have identical systems and processes, such as personnel policies, MIS systems, or bonus plans. Good corporate strategies can accommodate some organizational differences among divisions. However, a firm's primary operating principles and systems, as well as the experience and capabilities of corporate executives, should apply across the set of businesses in its portfolio (see Chapter 6).[1]

This is necessary for several reasons. First, running multiple control systems inside a single organization is very difficult to do. It can thwart the development of efficiency and expertise in any given system, which is likely to cost the firm a critical edge in performance, and it can create confusion at headquarters for corporate executives who must work with a number of business units. Multiple systems can also inhibit, if not prevent, the transfer of managers across divisions, or create interdivisional

---

[1] C.K. Prahalad, and R.A. Bettis, "The Dominant Logic: A New Linkage between Diversity and Performance," *Strategic Management Journal,* November–December 1986, pp. 485–502.

Negative Synergy at Saatchi & Saatchi

In the late 1980s, Saatchi & Saatchi, the world's largest advertising agency and consulting firm, overestimated the generalizability of some of its business systems. Of particular note was the firm's effort to use a budgeting system from its consulting business in its advertising business. The system's inappropriate fit with the latter business contributed to Saatchi & Saatchi's eventual downfall.

In consulting, yearly budgeting typically begins with the number of personnel the company wants to employ, because consultants, by and large, generate their own business. In contrast, in advertising, budgeting typically starts with estimates of anticipated future revenues from existing clients. This revenue number is then used to determine the number of personnel the agency needs to employ, the floor space required, and so forth to remain profitable.

When Saatchi & Saatchi placed the consulting budgeting system in the notoriously optimistic advertising business, disaster ensued. The advertising agencies predicted their personnel needs would grow dramatically as they gained share in the fast-growing industry. To house this planned growth, they signed long-term leases for additional office space, and fixed costs escalated. Unfortunately, a recession hit the advertising industry, and the expected demand never materialized. Before the damage was over, Saatchi & Saatchi had written off over 350 million pounds to cover losses on unnecessary floor space.

problems if managers in one unit resent the systems or level of autonomy afforded managers in other divisions.

The obvious solution to this problem may appear to be the separation of businesses that require different modes of control. However, if the separation was as complete as it would need to be, it is unlikely that there would be any value in having the businesses under the same corporate umbrella. Warner-Lambert, for example, realized this in 1993, having for many years operated its chewing gum and pharmaceutical businesses completely separately, even down to having different colored carpets for their offices at headquarters. Not surprisingly, it finally sold off the chewing gum and candy business.

When companies enter businesses that are not compatible with their control systems, it is rare to find value being created, even if some of their resources could, in principle, contribute to competitive advantage (see "Negative Synergy at Saatchi & Saatchi"). Indeed, such businesses have appropriately been referred to as *value traps*, where the allure of value creation turns into an illusion as the corporate office loses operating control of the businesses.[2]

Coherence

The previous consistency requirement concerned the role of organization in ensuring adequate control over a firm's individual businesses. A firm's infrastructure must also be designed to enable it to achieve **coherence**

[2] A. Campbell, M. Goold, and M. Alexander, "Corporate Strategy: The Quest for Parenting Advantage," *Harvard Business Review*, March–April 1995, pp. 120–32.

across those businesses. This is done through the design of structures, systems, and processes that enable a firm to effectively deploy its resources in its businesses.

As we saw in Chapter 3, scope economies are not vague notions, but realized economic benefits that can occur across functions or units that share value-chain activities or directly benefit from the transfer of corporate capabilities. These cost savings rarely happen spontaneously; instead, they are the result of specific organizational mechanisms that make them a reality. It is for want of such systems and structures that many potential synergies never materialize.

A firm's infrastructure, therefore, must be designed to leverage each of its valuable resources with a minimum of corporate intervention. Carefully choosing systems and processes to transfer skills and resources, and coordinate relevant activities, is a requirement for the achievement of coherence. (See Chapter 6 and, particularly, Appendix C.)

In Figure 7.1, the arrow back to resources shows the role of the corporate office in fostering the development and upgrading of valuable resources. Whether or not those resources actually reside at the corporate or divisional level, it is the role of the corporate office as resource guardian to ensure that the desirable type and level of investment in resources is occurring.

▲ A Continuum of Effective Corporate Strategies

The consistency requirements outlined above suggest that effective corporate strategies are not random collections of individual elements but carefully constructed systems of interdependent parts. Despite the attention specific strategies, such as "stick to the knitting," have received in the business press, this implies that there is not one best type of corporate strategy that fits all firms. Fads and flavors of the month that work for some companies or in some situations pass in time. What endures is the **logic of internally consistent corporate strategies** that are tailored to a given firm's resources and opportunities.

In principle, this suggests there are limitless varieties of successful corporate strategies and that every corporate strategy will have its own unique system. It is important to recognize, however, that there will be patterns among successful strategies since those built around similar types of resources will tend to do things in similar ways. This contingency view suggests that corporate strategies can be usefully arrayed along a continuum that is defined by the *specificity of their underlying resources*, for it is from these that a firm's corporate advantage is derived (Figure 7.2). Usually, the corporate strategies of firms sharing similar positions along the continuum will be more similar than those at greater distances.

Due to fungibility of their resources, corporations pursuing strategies near the general end of the continuum will tend to operate in a wide range of businesses, whereas those near the specialized end will tend to operate

FIGURE 7.2
The Corporate
Strategy
Continuum

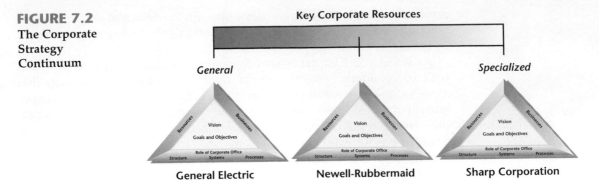

in a much narrower set. As we saw in Chapter 6, organizational structures and systems should vary accordingly: firms leveraging specific resources into tightly connected businesses will generally be designed to foster cross-linkages and synergies among units, whereas the infrastructure of firms leveraging general resources into a wide set of businesses will be far simpler and focused on maintaining financial control of independent units (see Table 7.1).

Sharp Corporation's resources and strategy place it near the specialized end of the continuum. Its strategy is built around its world-class optoelectronics technology, particularly LCDs, that serves as a nucleus for its growth and steers, and is steered by, its presence in numerous related product markets. The firm's organization structure is built around key

TABLE 7.1   Corporate Strategies

		Resources	Businesses	Role of Corporate Office	Structure, Systems, and Procedures
Resources (Related ↓ Unrelated)	Sharp	• Product development • LCD technology	• Consumer electronics	• Coordination	• Functional organization • Formal integrative devices
	Newell-Rubbermaid	• Merchandising • Operating excellence • Reputation	• Staple products for volume merchandisers	• Transfer skills • Shared activities	• Variable budgeting • Uniform compensation • Cross-divisional meetings
	General Electric	• Corporate reputation • World-class management • "Learning organization"	• Market leaders • Attractive industries	• Outcome control • Resource allocation	• Top-down financial control • Pay for performance • Decentralized business responsibility

functional activities, the heads of which report to a small group of top managers. Sharp's success depends critically on its ability to share information and integrate activities throughout the firm; this is achieved through extensive formal and informal coordination mechanisms, including standing committees, task forces, job rotations, and a corporate culture that emphasizes teamwork and shared responsibility. The firm employs approximately 1,500 people in its corporate headquarters, which bolsters the firm's coordination efforts and provides administrative support.

General Electric is at the other end of the continuum. Its critical resources are its corporate reputation, and its cadre of world-class managers that have built a "learning organization." Under Jack Welch's 20-year reign, GE became a conglomerate that outperformed the S&P 500 by a factor of four while operating in 14 business segments and 350 units as disparate as dishwashers, jet engines, a television network, and consumer credit. Each business unit was structured with a discrete P&L statement, and coordination among businesses was so limited that it was said to be easier to work with any other company than another GE unit. Value was created by training managers, notably in GE's famed Crotonville center, and by regularly moving them between businesses. In addition, Welch's periodic strategic initiatives, such as six sigma, were driven across the entire corporation. GE's control system is based on outcome measures with compensation and promotion driven by the annual review process. Notoriously, managers ranked on a forced curve in the bottom 10 percent of their cohort were asked to leave. To manage this set of businesses, GE had a limited corporate staff. At LBO firms, which have some similarities to conglomerates, the head office can be as small as 40 people to run a $15 billion operation.

Consistent with its position at the middle of the continuum, Newell's (now Newell-Rubbermaid) strategy is built around its merchandising and supply chain management skills—resources that are more specific than GE's, yet considerably more fungible than Sharp's. Newell's structure is built around divisions that are organized into groups to promote opportunities for coordination. The firm's senior managers have extensive operation experience that enables them to give credible, specific advice to the business-unit managers and to employ an evaluation system (behavior control) that makes exceptions for unusual circumstances or events. Newell's corporate IT group provides critical data links for all the businesses to the 20 or so power retailers that make up Newell's target customers—both capitalizing on scale economies and ensuring that every unit optimizes its supply chain links. In 1998, Newell maintained a corporate staff of 375, mostly in the IT area.

The corporate strategies of these firms reflect their very different positions along the resource continuum. The strategies themselves differ dramatically, with few, if any, similar elements within their respective Triangles. This is as it should be: the tasks these firms are trying to accomplish are very different, as are the resource bases they are leveraging.

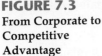
FIGURE 7.3
From Corporate to
Competitive
Advantage

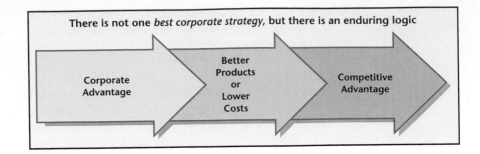

Nevertheless, each strategy in itself is a finely tuned system and adds value to the businesses within its fold (Figure 7.3).

Despite the fact that no two strategies will ever look exactly alike, much can be learned by observing a range of strategies along the continuum. Firms can identify other firms with effective strategies and similar types of resources to serve as role models, while firms at greater distances along the continuum can provide meaningful contrasts. Each in its way can be instructional—one by highlighting similarities, the other by reinforcing differences. Such comparisons compel a firm to clarify its own vision and assess its relative ability to create value in a given way. On close examination, for example, many related diversifiers discover that they are in effect behaving as conglomerates but with larger and more expensive corporate staffs. On the other hand, traditional conglomerates may find themselves at a disadvantage relative to leveraged-buyout firms, whose costs may be lower and whose benefits may be more compelling. Like competitive advantage, corporate advantage is relative and should be assessed as such.

Practice

▲ Evaluating Corporate Strategy

The fact that there are potentially an unlimited variety of effective corporate strategies does not mean that most corporate strategies are effective. In fact, as we discussed in Chapter 1, an observation of practice suggests just the opposite—that many corporate strategies have serious flaws and do not serve to enhance firm value.

Some corporate strategies fail because of weaknesses in **individual elements** of the strategy. For example, a firm may lack valuable resources, its portfolio of businesses may be in industries that are fundamentally unattractive, or its organizational design may be too interventionist and bureaucratic, given the tasks that need to be accomplished.

A company may also fail because the elements of its corporate strategy are not in **alignment,** that is, they do not form a coherent whole. For example, a firm's resources may not make an important contribution to competitive advantage in its businesses, its organizational design may prevent the sharing of valuable resources across businesses, or its goals and objectives may not lead to the fulfillment of the company's vision.

Finally, corporate strategies may fail because they do not adapt to the changing **external environment.** Shifts in consumer demand, technology, or channels of distribution, for example, may invalidate previously secure strategies and require dramatic alterations in corporate scope or organization.

Regardless of a firm's place on the resource continuum, the viability of its corporate strategy, and the likelihood that it will yield a corporate advantage, can be systematically appraised by examining its Corporate Strategy Triangle. We turn now to the question of evaluating corporate strategy in practice. In doing so, we examine the question of how, in the midst of implementation or in advance of implementation, a firm can assess the potential effectiveness of its corporate strategy. Five criteria are particularly helpful in that evaluation: vision, internal consistency, external consistency, feasibility, and corporate advantage.

Vision

• Is there a clear and well-articulated corporate vision?

Many firms lack a clear corporate vision, a well-articulated idea about how the company as a whole intends to create value. To provide meaningful direction for a firm, this statement must be more than a platitude. It must convey a sense of the corporate advantage the firm will exploit and be specific enough to guide a firm's actions. Although few firms are without vision statements, far fewer have ones that are truly serviceable.

Firms often confuse what they want to *achieve* with what they want to *become.*[3] In such cases, goals and objectives do not emanate *from* a vision, they drive it. The Walt Disney Company, for example, has pursued an annual growth target of 20 percent since 1984. Growth that is mandated in this way often proves not to be tenable in the long haul; near-term targets may be met, but they often do not translate into a consistent long-term development path. Being able to suitably describe a firm's vision, and determine that the firm's goals and objectives match it, is a very good test of whether managers have a clear understanding of where the company is heading.

> *"The installation of purpose in place of improvisation and the substitution of planned progress in place of drifting are probably the most demanding functions of the president."*[4]

---

[3] This insight is due to Seymour Tilles, "How to Evaluate Corporate Strategy," *Harvard Business Review,* July–August 1963, p. 112.

[4] C. Roland Christensen, Kenneth R. Andrews, and Joseph L. Bower, *Business Policy, Text and Cases* (Burr Ridge, IL: Richard D. Irwin, 1973), p. 17.

Internal Consistency

- Are the elements of the firm's corporate strategy aligned with one another?

- Do they form a coherent whole?

The need for internal consistency in corporate strategy was stressed in the Principles section. Firms that work at cross-purposes with themselves not only are inefficient, they often fail to develop or leverage the kind of system that yields important advantages.

Problems in internal consistency are commonplace and reflect the lack of a clear sense of how the firm intends to add value to its businesses. Despite profound differences in resources and business portfolios, for example, most multibusiness firms operate with highly decentralized structures and systems. These infrastructures may be simple to administer and may solve the control problem, but they are not effective in fostering scope economies or deploying resources to create corporate coherence.

To test for consistency, it is prudent to begin with the three critical junctures discussed earlier—competitive advantage; control; and coherence. It is also important to assess the alignment between these elements of strategy and the firm's vision and goals and objectives.

External Consistency

- Does the strategy fit with the external environment?

- Is the strategy sustainable against changing environmental and competitor strategies?

External consistency requires that a strategy fit with the external environment. Corporations do not act in isolation, but against specific competitors in specific markets. Thus, a strategy must stand up to competitive challenges and be robust to predicted changes in the environment.

These challenges may come at the business-unit level where an analysis of a firm's resource base and relative competitive position are particularly useful. In this regard, it is important to consider whether the key success factors of an industry are changing and whether the strategy anticipates these changes by repositioning the business or investing in resources that will be critical in the future. Moreover, firms should never forget to assess the underlying attractiveness of the industries in which they compete (see Chapter 4). No matter how effective the corporate strategy, if the firm's businesses are tough to make money in, the financial results from the strategy are likely to be poor.

Multibusiness firms also face competition at the corporate level from other Corporate Strategy Triangles. These assaults can directly challenge the logic holding the businesses together and, in doing so, threaten the means by which value is created. For example, a popular premise in the sixties was that firms were better allocators of capital than were banks. As this assumption was challenged by the emergence of new financial instruments and markets, many multibusiness firms functioning primarily as banks scrambled to find new identities. Similarly, as industries mature, many large vertically integrated firms find that they cannot produce the efficiency or rapid response of smaller, focused competitors, and are compelled to "demerge" as many companies, like Du Pont, have done in the chemical industry. Thus, external analyses must be dynamic and consider the continued viability of the overall strategy.

Feasibility

- Is the organization being asked to do too much in too short a time?

- Is the strategy too risky?

Striking the right balance between setting a challenging strategy and overextending an organization is a difficult task. While "stretch" strategies and targets are popular, in advance of implementation, the line between *stretch* and *infeasible* is often unclear.

To evaluate the feasibility of any strategy, it is important to ask whether the firm will have the requisite resources to implement the strategy when it needs them; whether the time frame for the changes is realistic; and whether the firm is capable of implementing changes on multiple fronts simultaneously. These questions can be captured by asking whether the firm's goals and objectives plot a feasible expansion path.

When implementing a strategy, for example, it may first be necessary to uncouple an old strategy.[5] If that strategy has been followed for a number of years, its impact on the organization will be deep and broad, affecting not only the formal systems and structure, but the informal ones as well. The challenges and ramifications of dismantling that system, and the time it will take to do so, must therefore be carefully assessed and planned for.

Firms have different preferences for risk. Nevertheless, every firm must evaluate whether its intended path is predicated on the favorable resolution of too many uncertainties. Ultimately, the level of risk intrinsic in the implementation of a strategy must be seen to be realistic.

Strategies that call for fundamental corporate transformation can be particularly difficult to implement because there are rarely blueprints to follow. Bringing the strategy to fruition is likely to involve many unknowns and substantial amounts of time. In such cases, aggressive implementation efforts may not only be costly, they may be ineffective. Gauging the time line for implementing these strategies and finding the appropriate

[5] See John M. Hobbs and Donald F. Heany, "Coupling Strategy to Operating Plans," *Harvard Business Review,* May–June 1977, pp. 119–24.

mix of urgency and patience are some of the most challenging tasks managements will face (see Chapter 8).

Corporate Advantage

- Does the strategy truly produce a corporate advantage?

- Is value creation from that advantage ongoing?

Ultimately, the acid test for any corporate strategy is its ability to yield a corporate advantage—to create value through multimarket activity. This advantage is usually realized in the businesses themselves where the benefits of corporate affiliation translate into competitive advantage. In Chapter 1, we suggested three tests of corporate advantage that can be applied to each business. We repeat them here to establish the hurdle that corporate advantage must overcome:

- Does ownership of the business create benefits somewhere in the corporation?

- Are these benefits greater than the cost of corporate overhead?

- Does it create more value than any other possible corporate parent or alternative governance structure?[6]

When evaluating a corporate strategy, it is important to assess not only the *amount* of value it may create, but also the *timing* of when that value creation occurs (see Figure 7.4). In some companies, the majority of value is added to a business unit in a relatively short time period. This is common, for example, in firms that specialize in business turnarounds, where companies are restructured, plants are rationalized, and product lines are pruned. Once these activities are completed, the corporate resources may generate little additional value. In such cases, the rationale for continued ownership of a business may be difficult to justify. Indeed, Hanson, once the archetypal British restructurer, split itself apart while Textron, once the archetypal U.S. conglomerate, now stresses relationships and synergies across its businesses. In contrast, in other firms, such as Sharp, corporate value added may increase over time as critical resources are shared and scope economies develop, ever deepening the connections among businesses.

As these examples suggest, for many businesses the benefits and costs of corporate membership change over time. In some cases, these changes may be unexpected and occur as a result of changes in the external environment. In others, the pattern of value creation is simply the result of the nature of the corporate resources and the systems through which they

---

[6] M.C. Goold, A. Campbell, and M. Alexander, *Corporate-Level Strategy* (New York: John Wiley & Sons, 1995).

FIGURE 7.4
Timing of Value Creation

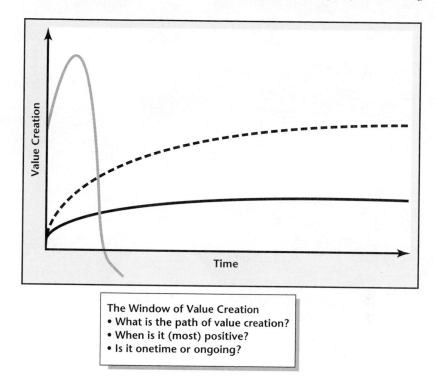

Value Creation

Time

The Window of Value Creation
• **What is the path of value creation?**
• **When is it (most) positive?**
• **Is it onetime or ongoing?**

are deployed. In all cases, however, it is important to assess a strategy's *ongoing* potential for value creation and to make decisions accordingly.

Summary

Although no set of analytical questions can predict with perfect accuracy whether a corporate strategy will be a success, the above criteria provide a powerful means for assessing the viability of a particular strategy, regardless of its location on the resource continuum. When the elements of the Corporate Strategy Triangle are internally and externally consistent, when they are guided by a powerful vision and support a feasible expansion path, the strategy as a whole should create a corporate advantage and truly generate value.

It should be emphasized that developing a corporate strategy is one of the most challenging tasks of management. It requires not only good analytical skills and data but in-depth knowledge of managerial behavior and systems, as well as intuition and creativity. Without real inspiration and insight, it is rare that any corporate strategy would be remarkable. The challenge for all corporate strategists, therefore, is to develop such an insight and to translate it into a unique and viable corporate advantage.

RESOURCES

BUSINESSES

• VISION

• GOALS & OBJECTIVES

ORGANIZATION

8

CORPORATE GOVERNANCE

▲ Introduction

The development and implementation of corporate strategy has long been understood to be the responsibility of senior executives. In fulfilling that role, managers have not only been expected to have the appropriate skills and vision to lead a corporation; it has also been presumed that they would be stalwart corporate citizens who would discharge those responsibilities with due attention to all stakeholders. Consistent with this view, managers were expected to be above the need for discipline in their conduct, and to act in ways that would require few outside controls.

Despite this optimism, a number of problems in corporate governance emerged over time. In the 1970s, corporate leadership was broadly criticized for not discharging its "social responsibilities"—for polluting the air and waterways, for perpetuating unfair employment practices, and for participating in illegal transactions abroad, among other transgressions. As a result, the U.S. government initiated a series of controls, such as those enacted by the Environmental Protection Agency and the Foreign Corrupt Practices Act.

In the mid- to late 1980s, the charge against management was a different one: a lack of attention to its fiduciary responsibilities toward shareholders. On the one hand, it was charged that some senior managers have been **inept.** This harkens back to an insightful distinction Peter Drucker made between organizational efficiency (doing things right) and organizational effectiveness (doing the right things). Many of these managers presided over firms that did things right—executed deals correctly, performed sound due diligence, and the like—but did the wrong things by, for example, entering the wrong businesses or failing to adapt to new technologies or global competitive threats. Yet despite their having implemented fundamentally flawed strategies, a significant number of these senior managers were so well entrenched in their positions that they stayed on and continued the same strategies, even as they destroyed shareholder value.

In the 1990s and 2000s, senior executives were increasingly accused of acting in their own **self-interest** at the expense of the company's shareholders and outside stakeholders. Egregious examples of self-interested behavior at well-known corporations such as Enron, Worldcom, Adelphia, and Tyco went undisciplined by any external constituency. Once again, managers appeared to have total control of corporate governance, and some abused the privilege.

This chapter examines these failures of corporate governance and the context in which they have occurred.[1] Specifically, the focus is on the mechanisms that determine the allocation of decision-making authority in a firm and, in particular, on whether those mechanisms are sufficiently strong to protect the interests of shareholders. A number of theoretical arguments are introduced, along with a discussion of the checks and balances that are used (with varying degrees of success) to monitor and discipline managerial behavior.

Principles

▲ Why Governance Fails

Agency Problems and Self-Interest

In 1932, Adolph Berle and Gardiner Means noted the consequences of the **separation of ownership and control** when they cautioned against separating the owners (principals) and the managers (agents) of firms.[2] They established the basis for what became known as *agency theory*, a key factor in debates about corporate governance. Chapters 5 and 6 addressed agency problems within a firm and the importance of aligning the interests of managers with the demands of a strategy. Here we examine another set of agency issues: the conflicts that arise between the interests of a firm's owners and its managers. As Morck, Shleifer, and Vishny explained, "When managers hold little equity in the firm and shareholders are too dispersed to enforce value maximization, corporate assets may be deployed to benefit managers rather than shareholders."[3]

---

[1] This chapter primarily reflects corporate governance in the Anglo-Saxon context. Governance structures in other countries, particularly Germany and Japan, are noticeably different.

[2] Adolf A. Berle and Gardiner C. Means, *The Modern Corporation and Private Property,* New York: Macmillan (1932).

[3] Randall Mork, A. Shleifer, and R.W. Vishny, "Management Ownership and Market Valuation: An Empirical Analysis," *Journal of Financial Economics,* January–March 1988, pp. 293–315.

These conflicts can lead not only to earnings adjustments (such as managers paying themselves too much), but to fundamentally wrong strategic choices. How might this occur, and why would managers behave in ways that are not in the interest of the firm's owners? To begin, many economists argue, the interests of managers often diverge from those of the owners.

Maximizing Growth, Not Earnings　In response to a question about why his firm had not divested more units, one CEO we interviewed quoted Winston Churchill: "I did not become prime minister of the British Empire to preside over its demise!"

Whereas shareholders (owners) typically want to maximize earnings, managers often want to maximize **firm size.**[4] Ironically, in many cases, this in part has been due to the structure of managers' compensation packages, which historically placed a heavy emphasis on firm size.[5] In addition, rewarding employees with job promotions rather than just pay increases necessarily creates a need for more jobs within the organization, further compelling managers to push for growth. Finally, managers receive purely social benefits from heading larger firms: in the eyes of their community and peers, they gain power and prominence as the size of their firms increase. Thus, they may have an incentive to grow their firms regardless of the long-term profit potential associated with the expansion. Size for the sake of size alone can become the corporate mantra.

Diversifying Risk　Shareholders want to own a *portfolio of stocks* that together have a desirable risk/return profile. Managers, however, often interpret this objective as applying to their company alone. As a result, they diversify into a number of businesses to reduce total firm risk. The nature of the mistake that arises from this partial view of shareholders' interests can be explained by a closer look at financial economics.

According to the capital asset pricing model, the total risk of any stock can be broken down into two components:

$$\text{Total risk} = \text{Systematic risk (nondiversifiable)}$$
$$+ \text{Unsystematic risk (diversifiable)}$$

Systematic risk, called *beta,* describes the variability of a security's return relative to the returns of all other securities in the market; it cannot be diversified away either by a firm or by an individual investor. Unsystematic, or firm-specific, risk relates to idiosyncratic firm events. It can be reduced, even eliminated, by spreading one's holdings across a variety of firms. The critical question is, How should this diversification be achieved?

---

[4] Robin Marris, *The Economic Theory of Managerial Capitalism* (New York: Free Press, 1964).
[5] M.C. Jensen and K. Murphy, "Performance Pay and Top Management Incentives," *Journal of Political Economy,* April 1990, pp. 225–64.

Should firms provide this service for their shareholders by buying other firms, or should it just be left to shareholders to do for themselves?

When firms attempt to reduce unsystematic risk by buying companies with different risk profiles, they often pay a large premium and incur substantial transaction costs at the time of acquisition. Further, these transactions usually involve all of the acquired firm's stock: buying and selling fractions of the whole is rarely done. Consequently, unless a firm can substantially improve the operations of the acquired business, this is likely to be an expensive and clumsy route to risk reduction.

The inverse is true in the stock market where there are many buyers and sellers, fractions of firms can be bought and sold, and transaction costs are relatively low. Individual investors, therefore, can achieve the benefits of diversification by acquiring a portfolio of stocks or through buying mutual funds run by professional portfolio managers. Consequently, the public markets provide investors with their best opportunity to mitigate risk. Diversification, for the purpose of reducing risk, is not a service that corporations should provide for their shareholders.

Managerial Risk Aversion　Even though shareholders can efficiently diversify their own portfolios, managers cannot efficiently diversify their own **employment risk.** As a result, they may pursue diversified expansion as a means of reducing total firm risk and increasing their own job security. For example, U.S. Steel's acquisition of Marathon Oil might be explained by management's feelings of job insecurity as the U.S. steel industry underwent massive downsizing. Diversification for this purpose may improve the lot of managers, but it could prove to be a detriment to shareholders. According to Amihud and Lev, such mergers may be viewed as a form of managerial perquisite intended to decrease the risk associated with managerial human capital. Accordingly, their consequences may be interpreted as an agency cost.[6]

Managerial Self-Preservation　Shleifer and Vishny have suggested another form of managerial perquisite: **management entrenchment.**[7] Entrenchment occurs when managers direct firm expansion in ways that are consistent with their own skills, but not necessarily in the best interests of the firm. For example, this could be done by investing in businesses that require specific knowledge current managers possess, thus increasing their importance to the firm and reducing the likelihood that they would be replaced. When Jim Ketelsen was CEO of the broadly diversified Tenneco, he poured money into the agricultural equipment business

---

[6] Yakov Amihud and B. Lev, "Risk Reduction as a Managerial Motive for Conglomerate Mergers," *Bell Journal of Economics,* Autumn 1981, p. 605–6.
[7] A. Shleifer and R.W. Vishny, "Management Entrenchment: The Case of Manager-Specific Investments," *Financial Economics* 25, November 1989, pp. 123–39.

where he had spent much of his career. He even spun off the company's oil business to support the cash drain from these marginal investments before he was finally replaced.

Although one might think that instances of managerial entrenchment are rare, bringing the point a little closer to home may illustrate its prevalence. Imagine being the chief information officer in a company that is considering outsourcing all of its information processing. Would you argue to close the unit that you run, or would you appeal to continue to operate it—perhaps even take in business from outside customers? This drama is repeated daily in every corporation and illustrates the conflicts that can arise when decision makers have private stakes in strategic outcomes.

Managerial Enrichment   Due to the separation of ownership and control, managers may also prefer to unduly enrich themselves rather that maximize shareholders' returns. Because managers may benefit personally from stately headquarters, generous compensation, or extensive retirement packages, while bearing a disproportionately small part of the costs, their incentives to spend corporate funds in these ways often diverge from those of the owners.

Contextual Factors That Exacerbate Agency Problems

The issues discussed above are persistent and tend to split the interests of owners and managers. These divergences may explain a fair amount of the diversified expansion undertaken by firms. However, it is also important to note specific contextual factors, inside and outside of firms, that may accentuate or dampen this behavior.

Antitrust Enforcement   Many corporations in the United States diversified significantly during the 1960s and 1970s, when antitrust enforcement was particularly severe.[8] Government authorities disallowed a number of related mergers and aggressively challenged a host of others. This climate had a profound impact on the number and type of opportunities that were available to firms. Related diversification that might have been attractive earlier, and would become so again, was simply made difficult during this time, narrowing the range of options from which firms could choose. Consequently, a large amount of unrelated diversification took place during the period.

---

[8] For a discussion of the role of antitrust in diversified expansion, see Andrei Shleifer and Robert Vishny, "Takeovers in the '60s and the '80s: Evidence and Implications," *Strategic Management Journal* 12, 1991, pp. 51–59; and S. Bhagat, A. Shleifer, and R. Vishny, "Hostile Takeovers in the 1980s: The Return to Corporate Specialization," *Brookings Papers on Economic Activity: Microeconomics 1990,* special issue, pp. 1–84; and Andrei Shleifer and Robert Vishny, "Stock Market Driven Acquisitions," June 2001. http://ssrn.com/abstract=278563.

Even though most firms at that time had little experience in managing unrelated diversification, there was an optimistic sense that it could be handled with ease, and made profitable for the firm. Conglomerates were emerging as a new organizational form, and many managers believed that a well-disciplined team with professional management systems could add value to any business. Richard Roll has referred to this kind of unbounded optimism as management "hubris."[9]

Life Cycles and Free Cash Flow   It has been suggested that diversified expansion may be tied to the life cycle of a firm. Young and growing businesses often have abundant opportunities to reinvest earnings profitably. As businesses mature, however, these opportunities may become scarce. In such settings managers may be tempted to use cash flows generated by earlier innovative efforts to pursue increasingly far-flung opportunities that are not in the shareholders' interests.[10]

Michael Jensen extended this argument and articulated a definition of **free cash flow:** "cash flow in excess of that required to fund all projects that have positive net present values when discounted at the relevant cost of capital."[11] He maintained that conflicts of interest between shareholders and managers are particularly acute over the payout of free cash flow: "The problem is how to motivate managers to disgorge the cash rather than investing it at below the cost of capital or wasting it on organizational inefficiencies."[12]

Jensen noted that internally funded acquisitions are one way managers spend cash, rather than redistributing it to shareholders:

> [The free cash flow] theory implies managers of firms with unused borrowing power and large free cash flows are more likely to undertake low-benefit or even value-destroying mergers. Diversification programs generally fit this category, and the theory predicts that they will generate lower total gains.[13]

To combat this problem, Jensen suggested that debt could play a powerful role in motivating organizational efficiency, particularly in firms that generate large cash flows but have unattractive growth prospects. By paying out cash and taking on debt, a firm effectively bonds its promise to pay out future cash flows. This reduces the resources that are at the discretion of top managers and decreases the likelihood that they will invest in uneconomic projects that satisfy only their self-interest. (See "Eclipse of the Public Corporation.")

---

[9] Richard Roll, "The Hubris Hypothesis of Corporate Takeovers," *Journal of Business* 59, no. 2, April 1986, pp. 197–216.

[10] Dennis C. Mueller, "A Life Cycle Theory of the Firm," *Journal of Industrial Economics,* July 1972, pp. 199–219.

[11] Michael C. Jensen, "Agency Costs of Free Cash Flow, Corporate Finance and Takeovers," *American Economic Review,* May 1986, p. 328.

[12] Ibid., p. 323.

[13] Ibid., p. 328.

Eclipse of the Public Corporation

Michael C. Jensen published a provocative article titled "Eclipse of the Public Corporation" in which he argued that in certain sectors of the economy, the historical model of the publicly held corporation had become obsolete. In place of the old model, a new kind of organizational form was emerging to correct the pathologies that had enabled corporations to waste resources and destroy value. By relying on private debt rather than public equity as the major source of capital, the new form eliminated the basic conflict between owners and managers and fostered greater efficiency in operations, productivity, and shareholder value.

The rise of the LBO association was one of the most prominent manifestations of the trend toward eliminating the separation of owners and managers. By gaining substantial equity stakes in their firms, managers became owners. Moreover, the terms associated with the LBO form of organization worked to impose a tighter discipline on managers. In particular, debt covenants forced managers to distribute cash and to utilize corporate resources wisely to optimize cash flow. Moreover, Jensen argued, high levels of debt forced companies into "crisis mode"—making difficult choices to sell assets that were more highly valued elsewhere and

taking necessary, painful steps toward restructuring to promote efficiency sooner than in a corporation with a more traditional capital structure. The idea was to ensure that cash could flow freely to the market, which in turn would allocate the resources to their highest valued use. Only in this way, he argued, would the long-term interests of corporations, shareholders, and society in general be best served.

Importantly, Jensen argued that these new organizations were only appropriate to a specific type of company, or to companies in industries with certain characteristics: slow long-term growth, mature or declining markets, and excess cash. Where this argument did not apply was in the context of rapid-growth, high-investment industries such as computer software and biotechnology which consumed cash to fuel growth and R&D. These companies generally were not cushioned by excess cash and were more easily disciplined by external capital markets and competitive forces in their industries.

Source: Michael C. Jensen, "Eclipse of the Public Corporation," *Harvard Business Review,* September–October 1989, pp. 61–74.

Market Pressures   Over time the U.S. stock market began to focus strongly on corporations' quarterly earnings figures, to the point that a penny up or down from the expected earnings per share could cause the stock to fluctuate. This created a number of potential problems. First, a short-term focus by the market could dictate a short-term focus by management and the board of directors, at the expense of long-term shareholder value. For example, management might decide not to invest money in research and development on projects that would only pay off five years down the road. Second, the pressure from the market could tempt managers to cheat, or "manage earnings" to meet investor expectations. This could potentially lead to aggressive or improper revenue recognition, as occurred with companies like HealthSouth, MCI, and many of the Internet companies. Third, companies might hold onto underperforming business units to avoid the short-term costs of disposal.

FIGURE 8.1

The Level and Composition of Median CEO Pay in the United States from 1980 to 2001* (in 2001 dollars)

Source: ExecuComp and data derived and spliced together from Hall and Liebman (1998) and Hall and Murphy (2002). The data from 1992 to 2000 are from S&P500 Industrial companies while the data from the earlier years are from a sample of Forbes 500 companies.

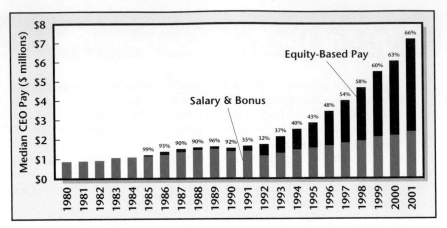

*Chart taken directly from Brian J. Hall, "Six Challenges in Designing Equity-Based Pay," NBER Working Paper No. 9887, July 2003.

Executive Compensation Michael Jensen and Kevin Murphy published a study in 1990 that showed that for every $1,000 change in a company's market value in one year, CEOs' compensation changed by only $3.[14] The study was widely interpreted as evidence that managers were not being rewarded for increasing firm value. In an effort to better align management's interests with those of shareholders, corporations began to award stock option grants to senior management. By the year 2000, the link between CEO pay and performance had increased almost tenfold.[15]

While beneficial in some ways, this new form of compensation also created problems. The overall level of executive compensation jumped from a median of $1 million in 1980 to $7 million in 2001,[16] with stock-based compensation accounting for two-thirds of the median CEO's compensation. (See Figure 8.1.) This generated considerable resentment among the average "rank and file" workers, who saw their pay increase by 20 percent over that period, versus the CEOs' increase of 600 percent.[17]

There were other unexpected consequences as well. The incentive for management to "manage earnings" or to artificially inflate profits became so strong that between January 1, 1997, and June 30, 2002, the U.S. General Accounting Office (GAO) reported 919 separate instances where 845

[14] Michael C. Jensen and Kevin J. Murphy, "Performance Pay and Top Management Incentives," *Journal of Political Economy,* April 1990, pp. 225–65.

[15] Brian J. Hall and Jeffrey B. Liebman, "Are CEOs Really Paid Like Bureaucrats?" *Quarterly Journal of Economics,* August 1998, pp. 653–91; and Brian J. Hall, "What You Need to Know about Stock Options," *Harvard Business Review,* March–April 2000, pp. 121–29.

[16] Both figures are in 2001 dollars.

[17] Brian J. Hall, "Six Challenges in Designing Equity-Based Pay," National Bureau of Economic Research, July 2003.

companies restated their earnings or balance sheet to correct previously filed "questionable" or fraudulent financial statements.[18]

Disengaged Shareholders   When shareholders are uninvolved and exert weak board oversight, corporate governance tends to deteriorate and agency problems rise. Throughout the 1990s, large institutional investors typically stayed out of governance issues and avoided weighing in on issues. Often, their lever was not "voice" but "exit." They voted with their feet by buying or selling shares, rather than attempting to influence management practice. Research has shown that companies with a higher percentage of institutional investor ownership were more likely to restate earnings or to engage in accounting "improprieties."[19] The existence of an outside blockholder, a shareholder owning 5 percent or more, made the firm less likely to engage in such conduct.[20]

Corporate governance practices are shaped by many forces both inside and outside the firm. One can understand a great deal about how a company is run by examining its broad business environment alongside its more idiosyncratic firm practices. Although significant progress has been made over the past several decades, the foibles of human nature suggest that there will always be a place for checks and balances and a well-tuned mechanism of governance that anticipates problems that are likely to occur.

Practice

▲ Corporate *Mis*management

The arguments and contextual factors laid out above explain aspects of managerial actions that could result from a separation of ownership and control. To be a real concern for corporate governance, it must be demonstrated that such behavior is more than a theoretical possibility and of material significance.

Although the theories explaining mismanagement are credible, do they really account for a significant amount of corporate activity, or only a few notable outliers? Unfortunately, the empirical evidence suggests that the excesses they describe are neither infrequent nor small.

---

[18] "Financial Statement Restatements: Trends, Market Impacts, Regulatory Responses, and Remaining Challenges," United States General Accounting Office (GAO), October 2003, GAO-13-038.
[19] Patricia M. Dechow, Richard G. Sloan, and Amy P. Hutton, "Causes and Consequences of Earnings Manipulation: An Analysis of Firms Subject to Enforcement Actions by the SEC," *Contemporary Accounting Research* 13, no. 2, Spring 1996.
[20] Ibid.

Managerial Indulgences

Over the last several decades, a pattern of the abuse of corporate resources has emerged. In the 1980s, entrenched CEOs reacted to the growing threat of takeovers. The so-called **golden parachute**—a takeover-activated severance pay contract—was a creation of this period. Golden parachutes were defended on the grounds that they supposedly aligned the incumbent managers' incentives with those of the shareholders. In the event of a hostile bid that would maximize the return to shareholders, the CEO and other top executives would not be motivated to block the acquisition. Critics pointed out that the same terms amounted to a financial incentive to cultivate the likelihood of a takeover. By the late 1990s, shareholders were submitting resolutions to stop such oversized payouts, and eventually companies such as Delta Airlines began adopting measures requiring shareholder approval for golden parachutes.[21]

Also during this period, corporations were adopting self-defense mechanisms such as **poison pills.** These too were activated in the event of a hostile takeover attempt and, for example, authorized issuance of preferred stock that existing shareholders could redeem at a premium after the takeover. The intended effect was to make the company's stock less attractive to potential acquirers—an objective that became increasingly frowned upon in the 1990s and beyond. Again some companies, such as Hewlett-Packard and Raytheon, began adopting resolutions requiring shareholder approval before such a scheme could be implemented.[22]

In the late 1990s, the spectacle of CEOs enjoying a wealth of expensive perquisites, from country club memberships to the personal use of corporate jets, came to be viewed as evidence that managers were lining their own pockets at the shareholders' expense. For example, when Robin Lay, stepdaughter of then-Enron chairman Kenneth Lay, wanted to come home from a vacation in Nice, France, he sent an empty Enron corporate jet.[23] Frank Biondi, president and CEO of Seagram's entertainment division in the mid-1990s, received a custom-built movie theater in his home, courtesy of the company.[24] Examples also came to light of personal expenses being placed on the corporate tab, such as Tyco CEO Dennis Kozlowski expensing his wife's $2 million 40th birthday party in Sardinia.[25]

[21] Amy Borrus and Michael Arndt, "Executive Pay: Labor Strikes Back," *BusinessWeek,* May 26, 2003.
[22] "Hewlett-Packard Shareholders Adopt 'Poison Pill' Resolution," *Silicon Valley/San Jose BusinessJournal,* April 2, 2003.
[23] Robert Bryce, "High Fliers: The Enron Jet Set," *The Guardian,* November 4, 2002.
[24] Gary Strauss, "Firms Supersize Executive Perks," *USA Today,* March 17, 1999.
[25] John W. Schoen, "Financial Scandals Alive and Well in 2003. Mutual Fund, Corporate Scandals Continue to Pile Up," MSNBC, December 23, 2003.

Disillusioned by unimpressive earnings, shareholders became further incensed when they found out how much money CEOs were paying themselves. Dick Grasso, chairman of the New York Stock Exchange, came to symbolize that excess when it was revealed in 2003 that he had been paid $139.5 million and was owed $48 million more.[26] There was such outrage that on September 17, 2003, Grasso resigned from the exchange. **CEO compensation** continues to be a lightning rod, calling attention to suboptimal governance practices, and in the early 2000s shareholders filed resolutions trying to rein in CEO compensation in record numbers.[27]

Empire Building

An indication that managers have in fact pursued strategies that are at odds with the interests of their shareholders comes from an analysis of acquisitions and divestitures. A substantial number of business units acquired in the late 1960s and early 1970s were later divested.[28] One study of 424 companies found that 29 percent of the firms' unrelated acquisitions were later divested, compared to 21 percent of the related acquisitions.[29] A separate study of 33 large U.S. corporations found that 74 percent of the unrelated acquisitions were eventually divested.[30]

Another clue can be taken from the stock market's response to the announcements of the acquisitions, discussed in Chapter 4. Many studies across a wide variety of time frames have shown that, on average, at the time of announcement, the stock price of target firms increased significantly while that of bidder firms experienced neutral or negative returns.[31] Later analyses refined these results in terms of the types of

---

[26] Joann S. Lublin, "Where Was the NYSE Board?" *The Wall Street Journal,* September 11, 2003.

[27] Ali Velshi, Pat Kiernan, and Myron Kandel, "Myron's Call: Escalation of CEO Compensation," *CNNfn: The Money Gang,* April 22, 2003.

[28] David J. Ravenscraft and F.M. Scherer, *Mergers, Sell-Offs, and Economic Efficiency* (Washington DC: The Brookings Institution, 1987); and Steve Kaplan and M.S. Weisbach, "The Success of Acquisitions; Evidence from Divestitures," *Journal of Finance,* March 1992, pp. 107–38.

[29] Cynthia A. Montgomery and Vicki A. Wilson, "Mergers That Last: A Predictable Pattern?" *Strategic Management Journal 7,* 1986, pp. 91–96.

[30] Porter: this is in contrast with 60 percent of the acquisitions in "entirely new fields" and approximately 50 percent of those in "new industries." Data taken from Michael E. Porter, "From Competitive Advantage to Corporate Strategy," *Harvard Business Review,* May–June 1987.

[31] For example, see M. Bradley, A. Desai, and E.H. Kim, "Synergistics Gains from Corporate Acquisitions and Their Division between Stockholders of Target and Acquiring Firms," *Journal of Financial Economics,* May 1988, pp. 3–40; M.C. Jensen and R.S. Ruback, "The Market for Corporate Control: Scientific Evidence," *Journal of Financial Economics,* April 1983, pp. 5–50; and Roll, "The Hubris Hypothesis."

companies acquired, the firm's track record of previous mergers, the size of the acquirer, whether the target was private or public, and the type of payment.[32]

A 1997 study by Loughran and Vijh examined postacquisition returns for acquirer and target firms. In the quartile containing the largest acquisitions they found that if the target shareholders had used their proceeds to buy stock in the acquiring firm, their returns five years later, on average, would have turned negative, suggesting that these combinations destroyed a substantial amount of value.[33]

Jensen's notion of free cash flow is difficult to operationalize, but some reasonable attempts have been made to do so. Defining free cash flow as operating income before depreciation, less interest expenses, taxes, and preferred and common dividends, one study found returns to the acquirer in tender offers were negatively related to the acquirer's free cash flow.[34] Consistent with Jensen's characterization of firms pursuing ill-founded diversification programs, this result was stronger for firms whose assets were valued lower by the stock market. Another study found evidence corroborating this effect.[35] In its sample, acquirers who were considered successful after the fact had lower free cash flows at the time of acquisition than those who were later considered unsuccessful. This evidence is consistent with the agency view of corporate diversification.

Rather than looking through the prism of free cash flow, other researchers have tackled these questions by comparing manager-controlled firms with those that are owner controlled. One study found that manager-controlled firms engaged in more conglomerate acquisitions than owner-controlled firms and in general were more diversified.[36] Two other studies showed that low levels of managerial ownership in bidding

[32] Boyan Jovanic and Serguey Braguinsky, "Bidder Discounts and Target Premia in Takeovers," NBER Working Paper No. W9009, June 2002; Richard J. Rosen, "Merger Momentum and Investor Sentiment: The Stock Market Reaction to Merger Announcements," SSRN Working Paper, November 2003; Sara B. Moeller, Frederick Paul Schlingemann, and Rene M. Stultz, "Do Shareholders of Acquiring Firms Gain from Acquisitions?" Dice Center Working Paper No. 2003-4; Saeyoung Change, "Takeovers of Privately Held Targets, Methods of Payment, and Bidder Returns," *The Journal of Finance* 53, Iss. 2, April 1998, pp. 773–85; Mehmet E. Akbulut and John G. Matsusaka, "Fifty Years of Diversification Announcements," November 1, 2003.

[33] Tim Loughran and Anand M. Vijh, "Do Long-Term Shareholders Benefit from Corporate Acquisitions?" *The Journal of Finance* LII, no. 5, December 1997.

[34] Larry Lang, R.M. Stulz, and R.A. Walkling, "A Test of the Free Cash Flow Hypothesis: The Case of Bidder Returns," *Journal of Financial Economics* 29, Iss. 2, Amsterdam, October 1991, pp. 315–36.

[35] Steven N. Kaplan and Michael S. Weisbach, "The Success of Acquisitions: Evidence from Divestitures," *The Journal of Finance* 47, iss. 1, Cambridge, March 1992, p. 107.

[36] Y. Amihud and B. Lev, "Risk Reduction as a Managerial Motive for Conglomerate Mergers," *Bell Journal of Economics,* Autumn 1981, pp. 605–17.

firms correlated with lower returns to the acquiring firm.[37] Consistent with the view that managers want to reduce total firm risk, rather than allowing shareholders to do so for themselves, another study found that firms pursue mergers with negatively correlated cash flows.[38]

In light of this evidence, it would seem unwise to conclude that managerial motives or hubris have not played an important role in major corporate decisions. There are simply too many results that are consistent with those explanations.

▲ Changes in the Governance Environment

Historically, senior corporate executives were often able to act with few checks on their behavior. Since the mid-1980s, however, a host of changes have dramatically altered the face of corporate governance and limited managers' freedom of action. Among the most important of these have been changes in the market for corporate control, and new requirements for corporate governance.

The Market for Corporate Control

Historically, the market for corporate control was not a threat to managers. Seemingly unfettered growth and diversification were possible, since corporations were not subject to discipline from the capital markets. In particular, takeovers were not an imminent threat for the largest of corporations. Analysis has shown that successful takeover bids typically involved at least a 29 percent premium over the original market price, which rose over time, sometimes reaching as high as 75 percent.[39] Thus, theoretically, it was possible for a company to operate at 71 percent efficiency and still not be vulnerable to takeover.

With the stock market boom of the 1980s came the end to the immunity of even the largest firms. Rapidly increasing stock prices appeared to reduce the cost of acquiring with stock, while the availability of debt gave rise to the onslaught of the leveraged buyout (LBO) phenomenon (see Figure 8.2). Over the course of the decade, LBOs not only became increasingly common, they also grew to represent a disproportionately large percentage of the value of all merger and acquisition activity. Although LBOs

[37] W.G. Lewellen, C. Loderer, and A. Rosenfeld, "Merger Decisions and Executive Stock Ownership in Acquiring Firms," *Journal of Accounting and Economics,* April 1985, pp. 209–31; and V.L. You et al., "Mergers and Bidders' Wealth: Managerial and Strategic Actors," in *The Economics of Strategic Planning,* ed. L.G. Thomas (Boston: Lexington Books, 1986), pp. 201–20.

[38] W.J. Marshall, J.B. Yawitz, and E. Greenberg, "Incentives for Diversification and the Structure of the Conglomerage Firm," *Southern Economic Journal,* July 1984, pp. 1–23.

[39] Kevin S. Nathan and Terrence B. O'Keefe, "The Rise in Takeover Premiums: An Exploratory Study," *Journal of Financial Economics* 23, iss. 1, Amsterdam, June 1989, pp. 101–20.

FIGURE 8.2   The Leveraged Buyout Market, 1981–2003 ($ billions)

Source for chart and table on the right: SDC

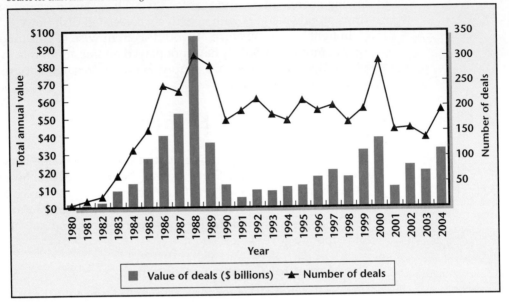

accounted for less than 10 percent of the total number of mergers and acquisitions in 1989, they represented more than 25 percent of their total value.[40]

Because they utilized debt to finance acquisitions, LBOs were free from the size restrictions that had limited takeovers in the past. By the end of the decade, investment banks and LBO partnerships had more than 50 funds, each of which contained at least $100 million in equity capital. On the basis of a 10-to-1 leverage ratio, these funds could make more than a billion dollars' worth of deals each. Suddenly, virtually no company in America was free from the threat of takeover.

In *Barbarians at the Gate*, Bryan Burrough and John Helyar provided a provocative account of the corporate control contest for RJR Nabisco that took place in October and November of 1988. Several well-known Wall Street financiers took part in the hotly contested struggle around Ross Johnson, RJR's flamboyant president. Burrough and Helyar described the events as a "huge power struggle," characterized by "brazen displays of ego not seen in American business for decades."[41] Though the contest for RJR Nabisco may have been extreme in certain of its aspects, it was by no means alone. The opportunity to restructure huge American companies was both highly sought after and, potentially, highly rewarding.

[40] *Mergers and Acquisitions,* May–June 1990.
[41] Bryan Burrough and John Helyar, *Barbarians at the Gate* (New York: Harper & Row, 1990).

Hostile Takeovers: Of Villains and Victims

Sociologist Paul Hirsch applied his discipline's perspective to an analysis of the struggle for corporate control between 1965 and 1985. His conceptualizations convey the drama inherent in these passionately fought, if bloodless, battles. Most important, Hirsch's analysis documents the strong social forces that served to protect the status quo, and the nature of change that was required to overcome them.

As Hirsch shows, the earliest hostile takeovers were not initiated by the corporate mainstream, but by renegades who appeared from outside and used unorthodox means to shake up the old order.* Those who brought the change were like foxes— predators who operated on the periphery, like Carl Icahn and T. Boone Pickens—not the corporate lions who defined and operated at the center of the business community.

The language used to describe these events mirrored their timing and the players' status. Initially, when the bidding party was outside the corporate community, accounts of the transactions incorporated violent, "one-way stigmatizations" of bidders, condemning the deviant outsiders as pirates, pariahs, proxy artists, and raiders. Target firms, on the other hand, were portrayed as unfortunate victims, "upstanding citizens placed in the role of 'defenders of the faith.' " Language of this nature was not only used by corporate insiders, but was also widely adopted in the business press.

In time, however, these corporate lions themselves became involved in the whole spectrum of takeover activity, first as "white knights" to save their beleaguered fellows, and later as hostile bidders themselves. As this happened, takeovers were increasingly viewed as legitimate business activities. Roles and rules were defined, and the language used to describe the events became more balanced; scenarios of violent conflict gave way to spectator sport analogies and references to corporate soap operas.

As Hirsch explains, the framing of takeovers expanded "from a simple shootout between the forces of good and evil to a less clear-cut morality play." In some cases, criticism shifted from the acquirer to the target firms themselves. If managers were seen as resisting attractive offers, accusations were made that they were "feathering their own nests," or seeking side payments to soften their own landing.

In summary, after 20 years, both hostile and friendly takeovers were viewed as normal events rather than deviant innovations. Many came to see the activity as serving the best interests of institutions, shareholders, and society in general.

* As Hirsch notes, Menzel suggested that early adopters include those cut off from positions of status and centrality and not well integrated into their peer community.

Source: Paul M. Hirsch, "From Ambushes to Golden Parachutes: Corporate Takeovers as an Instance of Cultural Framing and Institutional Integration," *American Journal of Sociology,* January 1986, pp. 800–37.

Takeovers can be full of color and zest. If one looks closer, however, it is clear that they chronicle an important transition in the history of corporate control. This change was documented by Paul Hirsch, an organizational sociologist.[42] Most notably, Hirsch showed the remarkable degree of resistance to change that the corporate establishment displayed during this period and the extreme pressure that those outside the corporate mainstream had to apply to overcome that resistance. (See "Hostile Takeovers: Of Villains and Victims.")

[42] Paul M. Hirsch, "From Ambushes to Golden Parachutes: Corporate Takeovers as an Instance of Cultural Framing and Institutional Integration," *American Journal of Sociology,* January 1986, pp. 800–37.

LBOs retreated during the early part of the 1990s and surged again at the end of the decade. By 2000, the transactions again accounted for 10 percent of all merger activity.[43] However, this time things were different. LBO firms were less ostracized than they had been before. Large lay-offs and dramatic restructurings had become increasingly accepted as common business practice. Many pension funds, for example, were openly disclosing their investments in LBO funds and other private equity investment vehicles.[44]

By the close of the century, hostile takeovers—even if resisted—were an accepted tool in the business arsenal. As a consequence, the threat to poorly performing companies from the capital market increased considerably. One more lever in an elaborate system of checks and balances was in place. But, like other levers, the market for corporate control often didn't function perfectly. Several egregious examples of botched restructuring efforts came to the fore, including Macy's, which filed for bankruptcy a year after its LBO by Goldman, Sachs;[45] and Revco DS, Inc., which was forced to file for bankruptcy protection after it was taken private in a $1.23 billion LBO by Salomon Brothers.[46]

Institutional Investors

Challenges to corporate control coincided with a profound shift in the patterns of stock ownership. For decades, ownership of public stock had been migrating from fragmented holdings by millions of individuals, to indirect beneficial ownership through large pools of capital, including **mutual funds** and corporate and governmental **pension funds.** In 1988, the combined value of these funds exceeded $1.5 trillion.[47] By the end of November 2003 mutual funds alone held $7.2354 trillion[48] and owned over 15 percent of all publicly traded companies.[49]

Over time, many institutional investors came to believe it was difficult to consistently outperform the market. As a result, they placed a significant proportion of their capital in index funds, matching, for example, the S&P 500. When confronting lackluster performance by one of their

---

[43] Emily Thornton and Stephanie Anderson Forest, "Embracing Barbarians at the Gate," *BusinessWeek,* November 18, 2002.
[44] Ibid.
[45] Sidney Rutberg, "LBO Parade Rained on Macy's. (Macy's Leveraged Buyout Deals of 1980's Prove Disastrous, Bringing on Bankruptcy Proceedings In 1990's)," *Daily News Record,* February 6, 1992.
[46] "Salomon Settles with Failed Firm It Leveraged," *The Seattle Times,* October 31, 1991.
[47] Jay O. Light, "The Privatization of Equity," *Harvard Business Review,* September–October 1989, pp. 62–63.
[48] According to the Investment Company Institute, www.ici.org.
[49] Burton Rothberg and Ned Regan, "A Seat at the Corporate Governance Table," *The Wall Street Journal,* December 17, 2003.

portfolio companies, they had to retain stock ownership to maintain the market basket of stocks. Moreover, even in their actively traded portfolio, they sometimes had trouble selling stock in an underperforming company if their holdings were large enough to send shock waves through the market.

Facing these circumstances, some institutional investors such as CalPERS were no longer content to loyally follow management's lead in voting their shares. They became more activist, pressuring underperforming companies to change their strategies.[50] They also made specific policy recommendations, lobbied for the dismissal of CEOs, and engaged in proxy fights with management to prevent the introduction of self-serving corporate policies.[51]

CalPERS, America's largest state pension fund (over $80 billion in assets), began fighting proxy battles in 1985. Over the next 15 years, CalPERS successfully passed shareholder proposals at Texaco, Gillette, W.R. Grace, Sears, Scott Paper, ITT, General Motors, American Express, Reebok, and Lone Star Steakhouse & Saloon, Inc.[52] CalPERS also successfully called for the ouster of NYSE chairman Richard Grasso, after it was revealed that he had received almost $140 million in pay.

CalPERS is not the only pension fund to force corporate changes. In 2002, the Teachers' Retirement System of Louisiana sued Siebel Systems charging that Chairman and CEO Thomas Siebel had been awarded more stock options than was allowed by the corporate charter, allowing him to cash in options worth over $1 billion, and that Siebel Systems had also failed to disclose grants to directors. Siebel returned 26 million options in January of 2003 and the company settled the suit, agreeing to elect an independent director that would represent the pension funds' interests, limit the number of stock options awarded to directors, and increase compensation disclosure for top officers and the board.[53]

This process was aided in part by the emergence of **shareholder activists,** who analyze company performance and provide information to institutional investors for use in voting. Because their findings are observed by shareholders, directors, CEOs and their peers, some of these individuals and advisory groups can wield considerable influence (see "Corporate Gadfly").

---

[50] Albert O. Hirschmann, *Exit, Voice, and Loyalty* (Cambridge, MA: Harvard University Press, 1970).

[51] Shareholder activism also has been stimulated by the perceived trend toward erosion of shareholder rights. As an example, critics point to the Delaware court's support of Time's decision to refuse a takeover bid from Paramount in order to pursue its long-time strategy. Similarly, a number of states have enacted antitakeover laws that shield management from hostile bids.

[52] See CalPERS Web site, http://www.calpers-governance.org.

[53] Mark Schwanhausser, "Pension Fund Settles with Siebel Systems over Executive Pay," *San Jose Mercury News,* August 27, 2003.

Corporate Gadfly

Who owns your company, anyway? With that simple question, Robert A.G. Monks has embarked on his latest crusade, one with an agenda even more ambitious than fixing corporate governance: He wants to align corporate interests with the goals of society as a whole.

That may sound quixotic, but to Monks it is entirely logical, once company managers think clearly about who's the boss. He says, "It isn't the arbitrageur. It isn't the program trader. It is the beneficiary of the defined-benefit pension funds and 401(k)s who are the largest shareholders by far, and who on average are going to live 17 more years until retirement. They have a long-term viewpoint. And they have a spacious viewpoint. They want to retire into a clean, civil, and safe world."

Given that, managers should run their companies to build shareholder value for the long term, and not worry about today's stock price, he says. Monks also argues that they should factor in the social and environmental concerns of their long-term shareholders.

This year Monks gave money and advice to a coalition of church groups and environmentalists who ran a shareholder campaign against Exxon Mobil. They put forward resolutions asking the company to study renewable energy sources, link executive pay to social criteria, adopt a policy of nondiscrimination against gays, and protect human rights abroad—making the argument that those goals are good for the bottom line. Monks helped underwrite a report by a former Chase Investment Bank analyst assessing the "reputational damage" and litigation risks that Exxon Mobil could face if it did not make changes.

The resolutions lost but did much better than in past years. Significantly, Institutional Shareholder Services, the research firm founded by Monks, which has traditionally avoided social issues, this year recommended voting for the resolutions on renewable energy and gay rights.

Source: Excerpt from Mark Gunther's "Investors of the World, Unite! It's Up to Institutional Owners to Fix Corporate America, Says the Dean of Shareholder Activists," *Fortune Magazine,* June 24, 2002.

Beginning in 1990, a series of rulings by the Securities and Exchange Commission (SEC) also contributed to the shift in the balance of power between managers and shareholders. The government made it easier for shareholders to initiate and fight proxy battles, and gave them the right to challenge golden parachutes, request detailed information regarding executive compensation, and pursue the formation of a shareholders' independent advisory committee to work with directors on key issues. Shareholders took advantage of their new power, filing 1,084 shareholder proposals in 2003, an increase of 35 percent from the year before.[54]

Mutual Funds   Despite their significant share holdings, many mutual funds maintained a low profile in affairs of corporate governance. Most often portfolio managers voted proxies reflexively, in line with management, and demonstrated a great reluctance to get involved in the intricacies of

[54] Avrum Lank, "Shareholders and Their Mood," *Milwaukee Journal Sentinel,* February 7, 2004. Data originally compiled by Investor Responsibility Research Center and AFL-CIO.

firm management. In the wake of the corporate accounting scandals, the SEC challenged this lack of oversight. Starting in 2003, mutual funds were required to disclose the principles that guided their proxy votes and beginning in 2004 they were obliged to disclose the actual votes.

Legislation

Beginning in late 2001, several large American companies—Enron, Global Crossing, Worldcom, and Adelphia, to name a few—experienced spectacular bankruptcies because of fraud on the part of their executives and less than optimal corporate governance practices on the part of their boards. Enron became the largest bankruptcy in history until Worldcom declared bankruptcy in July of 2002, breaking the record. Many retirees lost their life savings and the boards of these companies came under considerable fire for not detecting the frauds. From the front pages of the business press to the halls of Congress, the nation began to carefully scrutinize corporate governance practices.

Sarbanes-Oxley Congress held hearings and quickly passed reform legislation with far-reaching consequences. Going forward, the CEOs and CFOs of the approximately 1,000 largest companies in the United States would be required to personally sign off on their company's financial statements, certifying that they were true and accurate. The penalty for violating could be as long as a 20-year prison sentence. The legislation also spelled out a new definition of "independent director," changed the rules as to how audit firms were hired and what type of work they were allowed to perform, added a board hotline to report fraud, and required that the majority of a board's directors be independent.

While many praised the new rules as much-needed reform, others questioned their efficacy and believed they only added to the already onerous requirements for board members.

Shareholder Service Organizations and Corporate Governance Rating Firms

The turmoil in corporate governance created opportunities for a number of entrepreneurial service organizations. A new corporate governance ratings industry sprang up almost overnight. GovernanceMetrics International offered a 10-point scale and Moody's and Standard & Poor's also offered their own corporate governance ratings systems.

Institutional Shareholder Services, Inc. (ISS), created a Corporate Governance Quotient (CGQ), a numerical score based on 61 board characteristics that supposedly represented the quality of a company's governance practices. ISS offered its scores for sale to both the companies themselves and institutional investors. In addition, ISS was willing to work with companies to help them improve their corporate governance practices. Some observers alleged that this created a conflict of interest, compromising ISS's position as an independent evaluator. Other organizations such as the Corporate Library and GovernanceMetrics that offered governance assessments eschewed selling or consulting to the corporations they rated.

Despite this flurry of activity, there is still widespread disagreement about what defines best practice, and whether mechanical indexes can capture the essence of good governance. It is for this reason that another organization, The Corporate Library, offers an in-depth analysis of a company's governance practices rather than a numerical score. Even so, they are rating the strength and viability of a board without ever attending its meetings. That's not to say that these efforts are without merit, but to underscore the difficulties of the undertaking.

▲ The Role of the Corporate Board

The business and affairs of every corporation organized under this chapter shall be managed by or under the direction of a board of directors.

The General Corporation Law of the State of Delaware

Disengaged Directors

In theory and in law, boards of directors exist to represent shareholders and provide a critical check and balance on the management of corporations. Historically, however, when company performance languished and value-destroying strategies were sustained, these august groups rarely rose to the occasion. In 1971, a major study of corporate governance described directors as "ornaments on a corporate Christmas tree."[55] The positions were often filled by current and retired management, business acquaintances and friends of the CEO, and representatives of banks and law firms that had a financial interest in the continuity of management. Despite their legal obligations, most directors did not see their role as one of protecting shareholders' interests or evaluating the performance of management. Instead, most boards functioned largely as supportive audiences, listening to the plans of CEOs and, on occasion, offering advice and counsel.

Not surprisingly, the impetus to change this comfortable state of affairs did not come from the boards themselves; it came from a number of external sources. Beginning in the 1970s, a series of lawsuits were filed charging firms with corrupt foreign practices (including bribery) and questionable political contributions at home. These suits raised serious questions about the controls that were in place within firms.

Boards also had to confront the realities of the burgeoning market for corporate control. As these contests gained legitimacy, directors were held

---

[55] M. Mace, *Directors: Myth and Reality* (Boston: Harvard Business School Press, 1971).

accountable for maximizing shareholder returns. An example is the public campaign waged against Hewlett-Packard's merger with Compaq Computer. The board was deeply divided on the issue, with CEO Carly Fiorina leading the movement to merge and company founder Bill Hewlett's son Walter Hewlett waging the battle against the merger. With board members and institutional investors taking sides, shareholders finally voted for the $18 billion merger by a 2.8 percent margin,[56] after strong board and shareholder activism on both sides of the issue. Hewlett actually took his case on the road to over 20 large institutional investors, but ultimately lost.[57]

Shareholder Lawsuits

Because so much money was lost in the Enron era, and so many people's lives were affected by the mismanagement of some large corporations, investors as well as the public began to fight back. Not only were corporations being sued, but increasingly the suits were naming individual board members, placing both their reputations and fortunes at risk. When Enron's fraud was announced, board members across America must have watched with alarm as the reputation of Robert K. Jaedicke, a highly regarded professor emeritus of accounting at Stanford Business School and chair of Enron's audit committee, was battered. This shift in climate has driven up both the stress level and the insurance rates for directors, and forced some companies to increase directors' compensation.

The Structure of Good Governance

If you had asked me 10 years ago where the next wave of reform would come from, I would never have guessed it would be the boardroom. But, it's happening.

*A member of the board of directors of Scott Paper Co.,
on the occasion of the board's dismissal of the CEO*

Board Composition   Structural shifts on corporate boards, such as changing the **ratio of insiders to outsiders,** have made the job of governance easier. Examples of boards stacked with insiders and friends of the CEO are dwindling in number. In 2003, the Investor Responsibility Research Center (IRRC) found that 83 percent of the boards of the S&P 500, the S&P MidCap, and S&P SmallCap indexes were composed of a majority of independent directors, compared with 72 percent five years earlier.[58] (See

---

[56] Michael Davis, "Official Tally of HP-Compaq Merger Vote Confirms Approval," *The Houston Chronicle,* May 2, 2002.
[57] Pui-Wing Tam and Molly William, "HP Deal Opponent Begins Road Show," *The Wall Street Journal,* January 7, 2002.
[58] Mohammed Hadi, "IRRC Study Shows Boards Are Becoming More Independent," *Dow Jones Newswires,* December 4, 2003.

Trends in Governance

Public companies have increased the autonomy of their corporate governance structures by choosing a larger **number of independent directors** and lowering directors' stock options grants, according to a study conducted by Investor Responsibility Research Center.

Of the 1,275 companies that the Washington, DC, center surveyed, 83 percent have a majority of independent directors on the board, up from 78 percent last year and 72 percent five years ago.

An independent director typically is not employed in any other way by the company and has no additional involvement with the management of the company in question.

The study also found that 30 percent of companies have a different person in the chairman and chief executive officer positions, up from 26 percent in 2001. Further, nearly a fifth of the surveyed companies now have a lead or presiding director, up from 3 percent a year earlier.

In addition, the average board size has decreased to 9 from 10, the first decline since the IRRC began tracking the data in 1997.

The average director was paid about $102,000 in 2003, about 4 percent lower than a year ago. That decline was largely driven by a 22 percent drop in the average value of stock option grants, IRRC said.

Directors' annual retainers, however, have increased about 10 percent to a value of $32,000 in cash and unrestricted shares.

The changes have been prompted by more stringent stock exchange listing rules, increased scrutiny and criticism of stock options, and investor outcry following several public cases of alleged corporate fraud and mismanagement.

The companies surveyed by IRRC are in the S&P 500, S&P MidCap, and S&P SmallCap indexes.

Source: Mohammed Hadi, "IRRC Study Shows Boards Are Becoming More Independent," *Dow Jones Newswires,* December 4, 2003.

"Trends in Governance.") Academic studies indicate, however, that having a majority of independent directors on the board doesn't necessarily increase firm performance.[59]

Board Committees   Having recognized the need for more control over management, most U.S. boards have several outstanding committees to assist directors with their work. Two of the most powerful of these are the audit and compensation committees. Both of these came under considerable fire for not detecting the accounting scandals earlier and for the widespread escalation of CEO compensation. The Sarbanes-Oxley bill required that all members of audit and compensation committees be independent. It also gave audit committees (not management) the exclusive power to hire and fire the auditors, who would now report directly to that group. In addition, the new law mandated that a hotline be set up for employees and other individuals to report fraud anonymously. Finally, the audit committee would be required to have a "financial expert" in the group.

[59] Sanjai Bhagat and Bernard S. Black, "The Non-Correlation between Board Independence and Long-Term Firm Performance," *Journal of Corporation Law* 27, 2002, pp. 231–73.

Many boards have also formed governance/nominating committees. An important aspect of this committee's work is to constrain the previously accepted practice of having CEOs select their own directors and successors. Nonetheless, the influence of such a committee may be limited when compared to that of a dominant chairman/CEO.

Board Actions In the last decade, more and more boards have taken the lead in initiating corporate change. The most celebrated of these have been in prominent industrial firms, where bitter stand-offs between directors and CEOs have ended with the unceremonious departures of the latter. These actions were often taken after years of poor firm performance and increasing pressure from shareholders. CEO turnover reached an all-time high in 2000, when 13 percent of North American public companies lost a CEO.[60]

Many corporate boards have generated guidelines to clarify their organizational roles and responsibilities. At General Motors, for example, the board produced a 28-point plan outlining its functions, which included selecting the chairman/CEO, establishing agenda items for board meetings, defining what constitutes independence for outside directors, and controling succession planning.

Limitations on the Board's Ability to Govern

Despite these prominent changes, there are still a number of forces that limit the effectiveness of boards. Jay Lorsch, author of *Pawns or Potentates: The Reality of America's Corporate Boards*, identifies three of these constraints:

> While [board members] don't see themselves as pawns of management, as did their predecessors of a decade ago, they acknowledge a number of constraints on their ability to govern in a timely and effective manner. Such constraints include their own *available time and knowledge, a lack of consensus* about their goals, and the *superior power of management*, particularly the CEO-chairman.[61] (emphasis added)

In the United States, 70 percent of public companies still have one person fill the roles of chief executive officer and chairman of the board.[62] In such a situation, the person at the helm controls both the agenda and the flow of the discussion. Further, most directors have full-time responsibilities in other organizations, and many hold positions on other boards. The net effect of these conditions is a limit on the boards' ability to govern.

Cynthia Montgomery and Rhonda Kaufman highlight another impediment to good corporate governance. In an article entitled "The Board's Missing Link" they underscore a rarely acknowledged fact: directors have

[60] Phyllis Plitch, "CEO Turnover Declines in U.S. Amid Global Rise," *The Wall Street Journal*, May 21, 2003.

[61] Jay Lorsch and Elizabeth MacIver, *Pawns or Potentates: The Reality of America's Corporate Boards* (Boston: Harvard Business School Press, 1989).

[62] Mohammed Hadi, "IRRC Study Shows Boards Are Becoming More Independent," *Dow Jones Newswires*, December 4, 2003.

Board Cultures Work against Shareholders

Many reformers believe that a critical mass of independent directors will create a boardroom climate that will right this [shareholder/board] imbalance. However, board cultures have a lot of inertia; the likelihood that directors will be conditioned by the existing climate on a board, rather than create a new one, is high.

Consider the forces at play when an individual joins a board. Typically, new members are added one or two at a time. This means that each new director is joining a group with already established norms. As astute observers of human behavior, directors soon learn the unwritten rules and elaborate dances that are part of a company's board culture. Not surprisingly, directors often learn to be reticent about raising objections in the face of expert opinions, CEO preferences, and apparent majority views. Directors may ask thoughtful, probing questions, but there is a big difference between making a polite inquiry and mounting an adversarial challenge to the prevailing mind-set.

Admittedly, this level of passivity is not what one might expect from a group of highly accomplished people in leadership roles. What accounts for it?

Quite simply, internal board dynamics take on primary importance when shareholders are remote. Lacking an external counterweight, directors—even those with all the chevrons of independence—often find it difficult to move boldly against the tide, especially in the absence of crisis conditions.

When directors receive neither kudos nor censures from shareholders, their risk equation lies squarely in the boardroom. In this context, the determined pursuit of an issue on behalf of the shareholders requires the expenditure of political capital and emotional energy—potentially big costs to a director. When time pressures and the lack of adequate information are added to the mix, the path of least resistance can become very tempting.

Does this mean that without rewards or fear of negative consequences, directors—even very good ones—will do bad things? Not necessarily. The much greater likelihood is that they just won't be as vigorous in doing good things. In a job where vigilance is of primary importance, this is a major concern.

Source: Excerpt from "The Board's Missing Link," by Cynthia A. Montgomery and Rhonda Kaufman, *Harvard Business Review,* March–April 2003.

little individual accountability to shareholders. Though the relationship between the two is much talked about, in fact the tendon tying them together is far more tenuous than most people realize. For example, shareholders historically have had little influence on the slate of director nominees. Like in the Soviet Politburo, if the board has two openings, typically two candidates are nominated—and not by shareholders, but by the board. Once they are elected, the performance of individual directors becomes opaque to the very shareholders who elected them. Although votes on board resolutions are dutifully taken and recorded, shareholders have no legal access to that information, and no way to know how individual directors voted. In other words, the principals (the shareholders) who elect directors to serve as their agents have no way of knowing whether those individuals are in fact acting in their interests. The authors argued that this lack of individual accountability and the perceived distance between directors and shareholders could have profound effects on boardroom behavior. (See "Board Cultures Work against Shareholders.")

As remedies, Montgomery and Kaufman recommended that individual director's votes on key corporate resolutions be recorded in proxy statements, and that shareholders be encouraged to play a more active role in firm governance. While both steps would be rather radical departures from past practice, more recent proposals by the SEC and others have echoed these sentiments.

▲ Role of the CEO

The CEO may be on a shorter leash, but he's a more valuable dog.

Thomas A. Stewart

The clearest casualty in the battle over corporate governance is the old-model CEO, characterized by virtually imperial prerogative. An oft-cited example of the old ways, a former CEO of Sears at one time filled a multitude of executive positions, including one that made him directly accountable only to himself.

As noted earlier, some corporations have begun to separate the positions of CEO and chairman of the board, and to increase the autonomy of the board as a check on the CEO's power. Although many herald this shift as a sign of good governance, the solution is not without controversy. Critics claim that the move may compromise the authority of CEOs, or dampen the entrepreneurial spirit of firms. Management by committee, they might argue, is rarely inspired. Similarly, arousing drowsy shareholders and inviting them to play a more active role in the process will not be without controversy.

Corporate governance is a delicate system of checks and balances. Unless all three parties—management, boards of directors, and shareholders—play their parts well, the integrity of the whole is threatened. Forging stronger links across these parties will help rebalance the corporate governance system, and help pave the way for lasting change.

Creating Corporate Advantage

In spite of all these improvements in corporate governance, CEOs continue to bear ultimate responsibility for the performance of their companies. Although this requires them to fulfill a broad range of leadership functions, from maintaining ethical standards to creating a challenging work environment, the CEO's primary task is the establishment or maintenance of corporate purpose, which is codified and implemented through the vehicle of corporate strategy.

Even though boards in particular, and stakeholders more generally, are playing a greater role in strategic decisions, the CEO remains the only person with the knowledge, time, and authority to truly understand the firm's position and develop the appropriate corporate strategy. Others may critique or suggest amendments, but the CEO and his or her team of corporate executives are the ones in a position to initiate and deliver on a strategy.

CEOs need to remember that there is not one ideal corporate strategy for all companies. Rather, as this book has described, there is a compelling logic behind all effective strategies that overrides their inherent differences. When CEOs understand the resources of their corporations, the limit to the scope of those resources, and the organizational mechanisms that will release the value therein, they are in the position to develop a strategy that truly builds corporate advantage.

Recommended Readings

Akbulut, Mehmet E., and John G. Matsusaka. "Fifty Years of Diversification Announcements," November 1, 2003. http://ssrn.com/abstract=469781.

Bhagat, Sanjai, and Bernard S. Black. "The Non-Correlation between Board Independence and Long-Term Firm Performance." *Journal of Corporation Law*, Vol. 27, 2002, pp. 231–73.

Bhagat, S., A. Schleifer, and R.W. Vishny. "Hostile Takeovers in the 1980s: The Return to Corporate Specialization." *Brookings Papers on Economic Activity: Microeconomics*, 1990, Special Issue, pp. 1–84.

Dechow, Patricia M., and Richard G. Sloan, and Amy P. Hutton. "Causes and Consequences of Earnings Manipulation: An Analysis of Firms Subject to Enforcement Actions by the SEC." *Contemporary Accounting Research*, Vol. 13, No. 2, Spring 1996.

"Financial Statement Restatements Trends, Market Impacts, Regulatory Responses, and Remaining Challenges." United States General Accounting Office (GAO), October 2003, GAO-13-038.

Finkelstein, S., and D.C. Hambrick, "Chief Executive Compensation: A Study of the Intersection of Markets and Political Processes." *Strategic Management Journal*, March–April 1989, pp. 121–34.

Hall, Brian J. "What You Need to Know about Stock Options." *Harvard Business Review*, March–April 2000, pp. 121–29.

Hall, Brian J. "Six Challenges in Designing Equity-Based Pay." National Bureau of Economic Research, July 2003.

Hall, Brian J., and Jeffrey B. Liebman. "Are CEOs Really Paid Like Bureaucrats?" *Quarterly Journal of Economics*, August 1998, pp. 653–91.

Hall, Brian J., and Kevin J. Murphy. "Stock Options for Undiversified Executives." Journal of Accounting and Economics, Vol. 33, April 2002, pp. 3–42.

Hirsch, P. "From Ambushes to Golden Parachutes: Corporate Takeovers as an Instance of Cultural Framing and Institutional Integration." *American Journal of Sociology*, January 1986, pp. 800–37.

Jensen, M.C. "Eclipse of the Public Corporation." *Harvard Business Review*, September–October 1989, pp. 61–74.

Jensen, M.C., and R.S. Ruback. "The Market for Corporate Control: Scientific Evidence." *Journal of Financial Economics,* April 1983, pp. 5–50.

Jovanic, Boyan, and Serguey Braguinsky. "Bidder Discounts and Target Premia in Takeovers." NBER Working Paper No. W9009, June 2002.

Kaplan, S., and M.S. Weisbach. "The Success of Acquisitions: Evidence from Divestitures." *Journal of Finance,* March 1992, pp. 107–38.

Lorsch, J., with E. MacIver. *Pawns or Potentates: The Reality of America's Corporate Boards.* Boston: Harvard Business School Press, 1989.

Loughran, Tim, and Anand M. Vijh. "Do Long-Term Shareholders Benefit from Corporate Acquisitions?" *The Journal of Finance,* Vol. LII, No. 5, December 1997.

Mace, M. *Directors: Myth and Reality.* Boston: Harvard Business School Press, 1971.

Moeller, Sara B., Frederick Paul Schlingemann, and Rene M. Stultz. "Do Shareholders of Acquiring Firms Gain from Acquisitions?" Dice Center Working Paper No. 2003-4.

Monks, R.A.G., and N. Minow. *Corporate Governance.* Cambridge, MA: Blackwell, 1995.

Montgomery, Cynthia A., and Rhonda Kaufman. "The Board's Missing Link." *Harvard Business Review,* March–April 2003.

Ravenscraft, D.J., and F.M. Scherer. *Mergers, Sell-Offs, and Economic Efficiency.* Washington, DC: The Brookings Institution, 1987.

Roll, R., "The Hubris Hypothesis of Corporate Takeovers." *Journal of Business,* Vol. 59, April 1986, pp. 197–216.

Rosen, Richard J. "Merger Momentum and Investor Sentiment: The Stock Market Reaction to Merger Announcements." SSRN Working Paper, November 2003.

Shleifer, A., and R.W. Vishny. "Management Ownership and Market Valuation: An Empirical Analysis." *Journal of Financial Economics,* January–March 1988, pp. 293–315.

Shleifer, A., and R.W. Vishny. "Takeovers in the 60s and the 80s: Evidence and Implications." *Strategic Management Journal,* Winter 1991, pp. 51–59.

Shleifer, Andrei, and Robert Vishny. "Stock Market Driven Acquisitions," June 2001. http://ssrn.com/abstract=278563.

RESOURCES

BUSINESSES

- VISION

- GOALS & OBJECTIVES

ORGANIZATION

9

CORPORATE TRANSFORMATION: THE DYNAMICS OF CORPORATE STRATEGY

▲ Introduction

A new CEO taking charge of a corporation inherits an entity that possesses both momentum and inertia. The former ensures that even without intervention, the corporation can coast for several years with little change to economic performance or organizational climate. The latter makes the task of wrestling the corporation from its current path extraordinarily difficult. And yet that is the challenge for many corporate leaders. Unhappy with the current corporate strategy, concerned that performance is poor, or aware that continuing the same strategy will not create adequate long-term shareholder value, how do they radically transform the corporation? How do they get from a place they are uneasy or uncomfortable with, to a more desirable location along the corporate strategy continuum?

Earlier chapters outlined the need to align the elements of corporate strategy in accordance with the chosen logic of corporate advantage. Many corporate strategies fail or perform poorly because some elements of organizational design, portfolio composition, or resource configuration are inconsistent or incompatible with each other. Amending individual components of a strategy to achieve static fit and consistency can be difficult, but the task does not approach the challenge of fundamentally transforming an entire corporate strategy over a period of years. Yet for many CEOs this is the primary task—to craft a new corporate strategy and migrate the company to this strategy.

Principles

▲ Problem: Causes of Failure

Although many firms, even within a single business, may simply never have possessed any resources on which to base an advantage and so must develop a strategy to identify and then invest in a set of valuable resources (see Chapter 2), we are concerned here with those that previously had a viable corporate strategy which no longer works or are trying to design a corporate strategy for the first time.

The triggering event that brings about the need for transformation can be found in any one of the three elements of corporate strategy, but their underlying causes will come either from **outside** or **inside the firm.**

External Change

External changes that cause a company to alter its corporate strategy affect primarily the attractiveness of the businesses in which it competes or the value of a company's resources.

Changes within the **businesses** in a company portfolio can lead to the need to fundamentally transform a corporate strategy, because the **attractiveness and growth rate of industries** alter over time. If a corporation's success has been based on exploiting a single industry's rapid growth and structural attractiveness, when those conditions end, the strategy may require fundamental change. Fidelity Investments rode the growth of the 401(k) business and the reputation it had built for investment performance with the Magellan mutual fund, and diversified into a number of financial services businesses. When the 401(k) business matured, Fidelity had to reexamine its strategy.

Indeed, the combination of slowing growth and increased competition that defines industry maturity is often the trigger for a fundamental strategic reevaluation.[1] Southwest Airlines, after two decades of growth flying only a short-haul point-to-point network, has come close to saturating the market for such routes and now faces equivalent low-cost competition from airlines such as JetBlue and ATA.[2] In response, the company has begun to fly long-haul routes where its cost advantage from fast turnround times is minimal.

The trigger of deteriorating industry structure can have a silver lining. Forced to diversify into new industries, companies can use that experience

---

[1] C. Baden Fuller and J.M. Stopford, *Rejuvenating the Mature Business* (Boston: Harvard Business School Press, 1994).

[2] U.S. Department of Transportation data reported in the *Boston Globe,* September 12, 2004, p. B1.

to build new capabilities or acquire additional resources. Traditionally only a discount retailer, Wal-Mart, which like Southwest suffered from saturation in its core market, has since developed new skills as a grocer as it diversified into superstores that combine discount and supermarket formats. The result of this expansion can resemble the successful stepping-stone approach to diversification described in Chapter 4.

As we stated in Chapter 2, the value of a firm's **resources** can also vary over time. The zone of value creation expands and contracts as external circumstances alter the demand for, and the scarcity and appropriability of, those resources. The two most common external forces that threaten the value of a company's resources are substitution and imitation.

History is replete with examples of how technology has ruined companies and corporate strategies by **substituting** alternative resources for those on which a sustainable corporate advantage had been built. Railroads dominated the industrial landscape in the early 20th century. Then the internal combustion engine and the long-haul trucking industry brought an end to their leadership, as ownership of thousands of miles of track became a liability rather than an asset.

More recently, there are a number of dramatic examples of the Internet substituting firms' resources. The value of the bricks-and-mortar stores that book retailers—Barnes & Noble, Borders, etc.—had constructed by the mid-1990s and which had allowed them to diversify into on-site coffee shops, was substantially eroded by the online retailing model that Amazon implemented over the Internet. Microsoft's great concern is that open source software, such as Linux, will be so widely adopted that it finally erodes the value of the Windows operating system.

It is not just technology that leads to the substitution of valuable resources on which a successful corporate strategy has been based. Sears leveraged its valuable resources in brand reputation, which at one time saw half the U.S. population visit a Sears store in any given month, into real estate (Coldwell Banker) and financial services (Dean Witter) businesses. Unfortunately, the value of Sears' resources was substituted by Wal-Mart and the discount retailers, which forced it to undo those diversifications in order to (unsuccessfully) protect the core retailing business. Many high-end fashion brands, like Gucci and Coach, are temporarily able to leverage their brand reputation into a wide range of businesses from perfume and scarves to sunglasses and watches. Unfortunately, the fickle consumer quickly shifts loyalty to another, newer "exclusive" image, destroying the empire created on the basis of a brand.

Competitive **imitation** also reduces the value of a corporation's resources and so threatens its corporate strategy. After a decade of shareholder value creation under Michael Eisner, Disney's performance has recently suffered. Part of the explanation is that Disney's most valuable resource—its animated cartoon characters—has seen substantial imitation. After Jeffrey Katzenberg left Disney to cofound DreamWorks, and when several of the entertainment conglomerates, like Warner and Sony Pictures, realized the potential profit from leveraging cartoon characters across multiple media, there was a proliferation of animated movies. Instead of Disney having the summer audience to itself, numerous characters vied for children's attention, seriously eroding the value of each new Disney character. Indeed, no Disney animated movie has been able to match the success of *The Lion King*. Imitation of a valuable resource typically leads to oversaturation of the market and a consequent loss in the value of the resource.

External threats to the viability of a corporate strategy are less likely to be found in the **organization** element of the Corporate Strategy Triangle. Indeed, the more common cause of failure on this dimension is internal, resulting from the adoption of a trendy but inappropriate organizational form that fails to deliver the appropriate forms of control and coordination and so disrupts the entire corporation. Many corporations have been through the "organizational merry-go-round"[3] as they struggle to find the appropriate structure with which to manage a diversified firm. Rapidly going from a functional to a divisional and then a matrix structure was certainly the fate of many diversified U.S. multinationals in the seventies and eighties.

Organizational changes that are truly required by external changes are likely to be caused by a shift in the **relative governance costs** of market transactions and internal hierarchies. Many pundits have argued that the Internet fundamentally transforms the scope and structure of the modern corporation. Their arguments are derived from the reduced costs of managing market and contractual relationships. They will, for example, observe that minimal communication costs and synchronous multimedia interaction allow independent contractors, even those that are geographically distant, to function as effectively as employees physically located in a firm's offices.

Although it is true that the cost of market transactions has decreased substantially, pundits ignore the equally rapid reduction in internal governance costs. The Internet makes it possible for firms to operate seamlessly in many countries, to monitor individual performance in novel (and potentially intrusive) ways, and to easily foster coordination between different businesses in different locations. The result, it could be argued, is the expansion of the scope of the firm. The Thomson Corporation, for example, which used to be involved only in the provision of financial data via printed material, has capitalized on the information revolution to become much more broadly involved in customers' businesses. Rather than just sending them a daily newspaper with stock

[3] C. Bartlett, "MNCs: Get Off the Reorganization Merry-Go-Round," *Harvard Business Review,* March–April 1983, pp. 138–45.

FIGURE 9.1
The Effect of
Reduced Costs on
Firm Scope

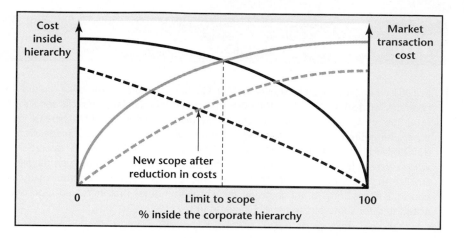

listings, Thomson now controls screens on traders' desks that provide real-time data and analysis.

How these two forces play out cannot be unambiguously resolved. The determinant of the scope of the firm is the *relative* cost of the market and the hierarchy (see Chapter 6). If new technologies reduce both internal and external governance costs, whether the firm should expand or contract cannot be decided *ex ante,* but will depend on particular circumstances (see Figure 9.1).

Indeed, corporations are now facing a **paradox of scope.**[4] Are corporations today larger or smaller than they were 20 years ago? The answer is unclear since on some measures they are larger, while on other dimensions they are smaller. (See "The Paradox of Scope at GE.") What has in fact been happening at large corporations is the consequence of two simultaneous but offsetting forces—a shrinking core and an expanding periphery.

The traditional core of the corporation has been shrinking as companies outsource a broad range of activities and substitute part-time or contract employees for their permanent staff.[5] Most PC companies, such as Dell, actually do no manufacturing themselves—they outsource everything to contract manufacturers, such as Flextronics. Many corporations no longer administer their own HR programs, but rely on companies, such as

---

[4] D. Collis, "The Paradox of Scope: A Challenge for University Governance," in *Competing Conceptions of Academic Governance: Negotiating the Perfect Storm,* ed. W. Tierney (Baltimore: Johns Hopkins University Press, 2004), pp. 33–76.
[5] The phenomenon of outsourcing has to be distinguished from the related but more contentious phenomenon of offshoring. The former refers to the shedding of noncore activities. The latter refers to the movement of white-collar jobs overseas, typically to India and other developing countries. While the two may go together, as when a company's internal U.S. call center is replaced by a contract with an Indian call center, outsourcing is much more common than offshoring.

The Paradox of Scope at GE

In 1981 when Jack Welch took over as CEO, GE had revenues of $30 billion and 400,000 employees (300,000 of whom were in the United States). When he retired in 2000, GE had revenues of $300 billion, and 300,000 employees (170,000 of whom were in the United States). Was GE bigger or smaller in 2000 than in 1981? The answer, of course, is it was both. Although productivity growth accounted for some of the tenfold increase in revenue per employee (as did a mix shift to services, particularly financial services, from manufacturing), a large part of the increase came from the operation of the paradox of scope. General Electric outsourced large parts of its operations, reducing the head count of full-time employees. At the same time, it was putting together many alliances and joint ventures that increased reported corporate revenues.[8]

Fidelity, to manage many aspects of their employees' salary and benefit programs. Outsourcing is now a $1 trillion industry (according to Dun and Bradstreet). Even if not outsourcing the work entirely, companies have been reducing their core of full-time lifelong employees in search of workforce flexibility. Indeed, the share of part-time and contract employees in the United States is now up to 31 percent of the workforce.[6]

In contrast, the periphery of the corporation has been expanding through a series of alliances, joint ventures, and partial ownership stakes. It is estimated that 15 percent of the U.S. economy is now generated by alliances or other corporate forms involving partial or shared ownership stakes.[7] Many corporations, for example, such as Philips and GE, have divested businesses through spin-offs that enable them to retain a partial ownership of the now independent entity.

The net result is that although firms today are active in a much broader range of businesses and geographies than ever before, they do not necessarily have authority over those activities. Such corporations may find the administrative task of running the company easier because day-to-day operations are managed by others, but the strategic challenge will be more difficult because they do not fully control those activities.

Internal Failure

The internal sources of corporate strategy failures are ultimately attributable to a failure either in the vision and logic of the strategy itself or in its implementation.

[6] Bureau of Labor Statistics, 1997.
[7] Gary Hamel, and Yves L. Doz, *Alliance Advantage: The Act of Creating Value through Partnering* (Boston: Harvard Business School Press, 1998).
[8] C. Bartlett and M. Wozay, "GE's Two-Decade Transformation. Jack Welch's Leadership," Harvard Business School Case no. 9.399–150, February 2004.

There are no guarantees that every strategy a firm pursues will be successful. Indeed, many companies have had to fundamentally reconfigure their corporate strategy (usually under new management) because an original corporate strategy was flawed.[8] Unfortunately, we have myriad recent examples of ambitious corporate strategies that were never going to succeed, however grandiose the **vision** espoused by a messianic CEO. Jean-Marie Messier's attempt to transform a French sewer and water utility, Minerales des Eaux, into a global entertainment conglomerate, Vivendi, was doomed to failure. In the absence of any of the resources necessary to succeed in media businesses, acquisition was his only vehicle to create the conglomerate. Yet every potential seller of a business knew the value to be gained from cross-media synergy and sold to Messier at prices that only exceeded this value. Assembling the pieces, without regard to acquisition prices, was easy. Creating real value from the resulting potpourri was more difficult, as Messier found to his cost when he was fired in 2002.[9]

Jeff Skilling's failure at Enron, even before the adoption of fraudulent accounting practices by CFO Andrew Fastow, was in believing that the absence of markets represented an economic opportunity, rather than an economically rational equilibrium. Operating on an assumption that deregulation and falling transaction costs allowed markets to replace the corporate hierarchy in a range of businesses from energy and water to telecommunications and newsprint, Enron attempted to become the dominant intermediary in new markets it created. Unfortunately, such markets did not exist for many reasons—illiquid assets, thin markets, hard to specify contracts—dooming the attempt to failure.

More mundane and less catastrophic failures of corporate strategy vision abound. Masco Corporation believed that its success in good, better, best product differentiation in faucets could be replicated in furniture. After many acquisitions, Masco dropped the diversification strategy and sold off its furniture companies at a loss. Unlike the faucet business, the key success factors in the various segments of the furniture business were so different that a single company could not quickly develop the requisite set of resources.[10]

Ultimately, all such disasters (other than the fraudulent behaviors) can be attributed to the failure to understand or think through the underlying logic of the chosen corporate strategy. Strategic visions that are not backed up by careful analysis and the rigorous application of the ideas described in the earlier chapters are doomed to disaster, regardless of the execution abilities of the organization.

---

[9] Robert A. Burgelman, and Philip Meza, *Vivendi Universal Case Study* (Boston: Harvard Business School Press, 2001).
[10] Cynthia A. Montgomery, Charles W. Moorman, and Michael E. Porter, *Masco Corp. (A) Case Study* (Boston: Harvard Business School Press, 1989).

Other corporate strategy debacles are more failures of **implementation** than of conception. Gerald Levin gave away more than half of Time Warner to AOL in its 2000 merger, believing that AOL's "bubble" valuation fairly represented its potential contribution as a channel of distribution for Time Warner's media content.[11] The failure to realize almost any of the promised synergies is symptomatic of many grandiose corporate strategies that never pay attention to the details of exactly how sharing activities or transferring skills will be achieved after a merger has been finalized.[12]

SCI, originally a Canadian company, embarked on a global strategy to consolidate the funeral home industry. While the original vision involved transferring best demonstrated practices in merchandising and sales practices among acquired homes, and the centralization of certain activities in order to consolidate scale in purchasing, neither of these ideas was effectively implemented. After a multiyear acquisition binge, the company's share price fell dramatically, acquisitions ceased, and SCI, under the threat of bankruptcy, finally took on the hard challenge of integrating funeral homes to realize the original promised vision.

Similarly, however masterful the corporate strategy plan, ineffectively implementing the entire strategy by not **aligning all elements** in support of the chosen corporate advantage will cause failure. SCI's implementation failure can be attributed to the inability to put in place the organizational processes necessary to achieve the appropriate level of coordination. Chrysler never built the resources required to justify its ownership of a range of transportation companies, including airplanes and military vehicles. An example of failure to align the last element of corporate strategy—organization—in support of the chosen vision was Saatchi and Saatchi's adoption of the budgeting system from the consulting business in its advertising agencies.

These failures to align the elements of the corporate strategy can be interpreted as concerning the **fit** of two sides of the Corporate Strategy Triangle, either resources and businesses (Chrysler), resources and organization (SCI), or organization and businesses (Saatchi and Saatchi). If CEOs do not take the time and care to shape the administrative context in ways that align the three elements of corporate strategy to provide competitive advantage, control, and coherence, that strategy will be doomed to failure.

Finally, failure of the corporate strategy can occur because of **failures in individual businesses.** Ultimately, corporate performance is the sum of individual business performance. If those begin to deteriorate, the overall

---

[11] Stephen Bradley, *AOL Time Warner, Inc., Case Study* (Boston: Harvard Business School Press, 2002).

[12] Philip C. Haspeslagh and David B. Jemison, *Managing Acquisitions: Creating Value through Corporate Renewal* (New York: Free Press. 1991), and M. Sirower, *The Synergy Trap* (New York: Free Press, 1997).

corporate strategy will also collapse, however much value the corporate parent claims to add to the businesses.

In many companies, particularly those implementing an acquisition strategy, the cause of business-unit underperformance is simply that they **overpay** for businesses added to the portfolio. Although the corporate strategy itself might not be flawed, and the firm's resources may actually add value to its businesses, overpaying to implement the strategy is an easy way to destroy shareholder value. In Chapter 4 we observed that, on average, acquirers capture none of the value in an acquisition, so the odds are always stacked against the acquirer. However, it is easy to get caught up in the thrill of the chase, or to be seduced by the easy money offered by investment bankers into believing that any price is justified by the strategy (see " P/E Chain Letter Game").

Similar to overpaying for an acquisition is **overinvesting to hurdle the entry barriers** of a new business. If a business is saddled with an initial investment that can never be recovered, its long-term performance will always be a drain on the corporation. Many of the consumer electronics companies that entered the liquid crystal display business invested hundreds of millions dollars to develop the technology and master the difficult manufacturing process, never to recover those start-up costs, in spite of the fact that the market grew rapidly. Only huge write-downs of past investments or the goodwill incurred on acquisition can solve the problem of overpaying to expand the scope of the corporation, even if there was an initial corporate advantage in the new business.

More mundane implementation failures also occur when corporate management simply do not sustain the performance of the individual businesses. If executives take their eyes off the ball, or give too little attention to their monitoring and control function and so tolerate **inferior business unit performance,** the corporate strategy can slowly unravel. Unfortunately, the inherent momentum of large corporations tends to breed this sort of behavior. Too many CEOs avoid the challenge and personal confrontation required to sustain pressure on business-unit heads, in order to take the easy life and prestige and high pay of an incumbent atop the corporate hierarchy.

Unfortunately, the excesses of the nineties also caused corporate strategy failures through outright **fraud,** rather than flawed vision or inadequate implementation. Dennis Kozlowski had successfully grown the conglomerate Tyco for nearly a decade, before succumbing to personal greed and hubris. Even though the basic Tyco strategy remains unchanged, his successor, Ed Breen, has a challenge to rejuvenate the organization. Unfortunately, the recent cult of personality seduced too many CEOs, who naively misinterpreted a rising market for a signal of their own abilities, believing that they were beyond fault and above the law. The hope is that changes to corporate governance can remedy the worst of these excesses (see Chapter 8).

P/E Chain Letter Game

A surprisingly large number of companies over the years have, consciously or unconsciously, adopted a corporate strategy that contains the seeds of its own destruction. The Greek tragedy that follows has as its ingredients acquisition with stock and an inordinate focus on earnings per share growth. It is known as the P/E (price/earnings) chain letter game.

Consider two firms A and B. A has been growing earnings per share (EPS) at 20 percent per annum and so trades at a P/E of 20. B, in contrast, has been a zero-growth company and so trades at a P/E of only 10. If both have earnings of 1 and shares outstanding of 1, their share prices and market capitalization are as shown in the following table, with A worth twice as much as B. This is entirely correct and appropriate. What happens next however is pure financial magic.

	A	B	A&B	A&B Year 2
Profit	1	1	2	2
Shares outstanding	1	1	1.5	1.5
Earnings per share	1	1	1.33	1.33
Growth in EPS	20%	0%	33%	0%
P/E ratio	20	10	33	10
Share price	20	10	40	13.3
Market capitalization	20	10	60	20

A now acquires B for stock and issues one-half a share (valued at 10) to do so. The combined company, even if it does absolutely nothing to integrate the two firms or in any way create synergies, will show an earnings per share increase of 33 percent in the year of acquisition. This rapid growth justifies a 33 P/E ratio, and with earnings per share of the combined entity now at 1.33, this increases the stock price to 40. "POOF"—magic. Merely acquiring another company has doubled the stock price!

What is the fallacy in this accounting? Nothing, except for what happens the next year when the fact that 33 percent earnings per share growth was only a one-time event is exposed. In that year, if A makes no more acquisitions (and setting aside the combined entity's organic growth which would only complicate the numbers without changing the logic), the growth in EPS is 0, the P/E ratio drops to 10, the stock price falls to 13, and the market cap is 20. To avoid this disaster, companies pursuing the strategy have to make ever larger acquisitions each year or else the whole edifice falls apart!

That was why we saw companies like Worldcom seemingly unsatisfied with huge acquisitions, like MCI, but intent on even larger purchases of Sprint or European companies. Similarly, the advertising agency Saatchi and Saatchi, which pursued this strategy in the late seventies, ended up bidding for banks in a desperate attempt to keep boosting its earnings per share.

Notice one thing that helps the acquirer sustain the strategy. The arithmetic works provided that the P/E ratio of the acquired company is lower than that of the acquirer's. But if that is the case, the P/E of the acquirer will rise, which opens up a new set of firms whose P/E ratio is now lower that can be acquired in order to keep the strategy going.

The hallmarks of the P/E chain letter, which the savvy investor should be on the lookout for, are acquisitions and an inordinate emphasis on communications with investors on earnings per share growth. The CFO will never talk about return on equity or other such operating measures of performance since these do not move in the required upward direction—in fact they typically decline even while rapid earnings per share growth continues. The CEO is also likely to have some strategic story to tell that will promise all sorts of synergy as a cover for the underlying financial engineering, but operationally the company will do little or nothing to integrate acquisitions, or even to sustain the performance of the individual businesses.

Types of Transformation

Whatever the reason, many corporate strategies gradually unravel over time or require periodic rejuvenation. To remedy this, CEOs have to recognize that they have one of three slightly different types of corporate transformation to consider:

Create: When a company initially moves from operating in a single business to multiple businesses, and so confronts the need for an explicit corporate strategy for the first time. Unfortunately, at many companies the development of a corporate strategy is often deferred until long after the firm has already become a multibusiness entity.

Renew: When an effective corporate strategy needs to be rejuvenated because the firm has become complacent or accepted mediocrity, but when the strategy itself does not necessarily need to be redefined.

Transform: The subject of this chapter, when all elements of the strategy need to be changed in order to relocate along the corporate strategy continuum and exploit an entirely new corporate advantage.

Creation

All diversified firms have at some stage in their lives undergone the transition from a single business, or migrated from an ad hoc portfolio of independently operated businesses into a more coherent corporate strategy. Other firms may simply never have possessed any resources on which to base a corporate advantage even if they operated in multiple businesses. The advantage that such companies possess is that they lack a legacy and, therefore, are in no way restricted or constrained in their actions. At the moment of decision they have a **free choice of what to become and where to locate** along the corporate strategy continuum. In many cases, this choice can simplistically be characterized as locating between one of three places—as a conglomerate with independent businesses monitored by a tiny corporate office; with autonomous businesses sharing some activities and services and adopting conscious policies to transfer skills between those businesses; or as a single functional organization with discrete markets under the control of different product managers.

American Brands (now renamed Fortune Brands) had the legacy collection of businesses remaining when the former American Tobacco Company disposed of its cigarette assets and faced such a decision. Owning the brands Titleist and Footjoy in golf, Jim Beam in spirits, and a number of stationery and hardware products like Masterlock and Waterloo, American Brands had a range of alternative corporate strategies it could choose from in the mid-nineties. It could retain all these unrelated businesses, in which case the corporate headquarters would have to act like a conglomerate and create value through tight financial controls and an unremitting attention to short-term performance. It could manage a portfolio of consumer brands, perhaps selling off those like Waterloo for whom branding was not critical to success, while building a distinctive competence and a small corporate staff in consumer marketing and sharing media purchasing in order to exploit scale economies. Or it could have defined itself more tightly, in a number of possible ways—as a golf company, a spirits company, or a supplier to mass merchants of stationery and hardware. Any one of these choices would create something close to a single business entity in which the corporate headquarters would become heavily involved in operations.

Renewal

Many companies gradually allow the vigor and enthusiasm that have driven a successful corporate strategy to diminish. Complacency and routine replace initiative and risk taking, allowing competitors to usurp or threaten their leadership positions. The fundamentals of the strategy might not have failed, but the energy with which it is implemented can lag. In these situations, as Xerox, for example, faced in the eighties, or Kodak faced in the nineties, the challenge is to revitalize and rejuvenate the organization rather than radically alter the strategy. The task, therefore, is primarily concerned with leaders reviving a culture of excitement and innovation and an expectation of superior individual and business performance.

While many of the techniques of transformation described below apply to this challenge, the CEO primarily operates within the **organizational** element of strategy. There is less need to change the resources (although they might well need upgrading), or rearrange the portfolio. Instead, the emphasis must be on reenergizing behavior. Particularly important in this context is the use of **symbolic actions** which of themselves have little impact but which send a visible and powerful message to the organization that what passes for acceptable behavior and attitudes will now be different.

In many ways this is what Michael Eisner achieved in his first 10 years at Disney. The company already knew about synergy—pictures that described the phenomenon of Disney "teamwork" were first drawn in the mid-seventies—and had in place most of the building blocks of an effective corporate strategy when he arrived in 1984. Disney World, for example, opened in 1971, and the cable network Disney Channel began in 1983. Eisner, for the first time, brought in outside executives, such as Jeffrey Katzenbach and Frank Wells, and raised the bar by demanding the company deliver 20 percent per annum EPS growth. Most of all, his hyperactive appearances and interventions shook up the firm and drove individuals to greater energy and heights. Whether the same executive can repeat the performance after a 20-year tenure is perhaps the biggest question facing Disney's board and shareholders today.

Transformation

In contrast, true transformation requires selecting and then implementing a new strategy that metamorphoses the company into a different entity. Michael Jordan did exactly this when after a six-year tenure as chairman, he left Westinghouse in 1998 an unrecognizably different company than it had been before. Instead of an industrial giant that for years had been a poor sister of GE, he created an entertainment company that dominated the radio station business. Although corporate transformation need not be that radical—the Westinghouse name was ultimately sold to British Nuclear Fuels—the notion behind transformation is that the entire Corporate Strategy Triangle is altered in pursuit of an entirely different corporate advantage.

The challenge of achieving this is that there is neither a clean slate on which to write nor an underutilized set of resources already in place. True transformation involves a **dramatic change process that affects all elements of corporate strategy,** which is why many of the techniques described in the following discussion are the same that drive any major change process in an organization.

▲ Remedies: Levers of Change

Identify the Problem

The first step in any corporate transformation is to recognize that there is a **need for change.** As suggested above, even if there is an underlying malaise with their corporate strategy, many CEOs either don't see, or refuse to confront, underperformance. Historically the minimum 20 percent takeover premium required in a hostile takeover provided a cushion of inefficiency for a lazy or weak CEO to hide behind. Today that premium might still be present but pressure from shareholders and active boards has weakened the authority of an entrenched CEO who is not delivering against his corporate strategy.

Continual close monitoring by the CEO of financial performance—both external shareholder value measures and internal growth and profitability measures—is, therefore, necessary to provide advanced warning of strategic concerns. However, it is not necessarily sufficient. It can be years before the stock market catches up to the inadequacy of a corporate strategy, while internal financial measures can often be a lagging indicator of underlying strategic position. What is required is for the CEO to be managing a dashboard, or a balanced scorecard of measures that are customized to the corporate strategy (see "The Balanced Scorecard"). Only close attention to a myriad of details can provide the CEO with the early warning necessary to identify a flaw in the corporate strategy.

The Balanced Scorecard

Bob Kaplan and Dick Cooper have introduced the notion of a balanced scorecard as a way to monitor and control the implementation of a strategy.[13] While they focus on single-business strategy, their ideas are also relevant to the multibusiness corporation.

They argue that a single measure of performance inadequately captures the overall health of an organization. It is easy to deliver results against a narrow definition of success at the expense of other aspects of the business. Achieving rapid growth is easy. Doing so profitably can be more difficult. But doing so without placing so much pressure on the workforce that the growth becomes unsustainable is almost impossible.

To prevent such an occurrence, Kaplan and Cooper suggest that firms monitor performance on four dimensions—financial, customer, employee, and internal processes. Rather than advocating that every firm monitor the same set of variables in these categories, they argue that each firm should choose the specific measures that address the key success factors of their own strategy.

This is an approach which is consistent with our view of corporate strategy. Companies that have different locations on the corporate strategy continuum should be monitoring different sets of variables. Thus a conglomerate will have more detailed financial measures and will monitor more aggregate employee performance measures than a functional organization, for whom the ability to work across functions might be the single most important leading measure of success.

Once the warning flag has been raised, the next step is to determine the cause of the problem. Many times weak performance can be attributed to a specific and identifiable failure, and that failure can then be addressed. Only when, like leaks in the dike, it becomes impossible to plug all the holes that are dragging down performance, is it necessary for a firm to consider a fundamental transformation. Thus it could take several years to reach the conclusion that such a transformation is required. Many attempts will be made to fix individual aspects of the strategy—executives might be replaced, some businesses bought and sold, organizational redesign pursued—before the realization dawns that something profound is wrong with the strategy.

At this stage a fundamental **audit** of the company is required. Analyzing all aspects of the Corporate Strategy Triangle, and critically assessing each element of the triangle becomes vital. Only then is it possible to determine that, indeed, the firm now requires a corporate transformation.

Vision

Once change has been determined to be necessary, any corporate transformation has to begin with, and be driven by, a coherent vision of "Where we want to go." As the saying suggests, "If you don't know where you are going, any road will take you there." The basic thesis of this book is that it is the internal fit and alignment of the elements of corporate strategy that determine success, yet without a sense of where on the continuum a company wants to be, it is impossible to know how to align those elements.

[13] Robert S. Kaplan and David P. Norton, *Strategy Maps: Converging Intangible into Tangible Outcomes* (Boston: Harvard Business School Press, 2004); and Robert S. Kaplan and David P. Norton, *The Balanced Score Card: Translating Strategy into Action* (Boston: Harvard Business School Press, 1996).

It is important to remember that the **choice** of which new corporate strategy to pursue is exactly that—a choice. There is no sense in which a particular location on the corporate strategy continuum is in any way "better" than other locations. Companies at every location can be successful and have durable corporate advantages provided they build the appropriate valuable resources and align other elements of the strategy around those resources. Choosing which strategy to pursue, therefore, is as much about discovering what corporate executives are comfortable with as it is about searching for the "optimal" strategy. It will be easier to implement a strategy that theoretically will earn a little less for shareholders but which executives believe in and want to achieve, than try to pursue the ideal strategy that no one is truly committed to.

This does suggest that the sensible place to start when envisaging the new strategy is with the audit of the firm's existing resources and businesses because managers will have some comfort and experience with those. When Michael Jordan took over at Westinghouse, he spent a considerable time trying to discover whether the firm had any nuggets that could be transformed into something substantial before realizing that the deregulation of radio broadcasting created a golden opportunity to leverage Westinghouse's previously moribund ownership of radio station licenses.

Often there will be a variety of strategic options that the firm could seriously consider. The ideal process, therefore, applies the ideas in this book to generate a set of alternative corporate strategies that can be tested under alternative scenarios. Typically this process compels managers to confront a choice among very different futures for the firm in a way that can be effective in driving consensus among executives and the board.

The most important task in crafting a new vision is to develop and articulate the **logic** that underpins the corporate advantage. Such a logic should be simple and, once described, readily apparent to all. There is nothing complicated about the relationship between resources and competitive advantage in a business, which is the essence of value creation through corporate strategy. This is what should be captured in a statement of logic that supports such simple, catchy, and motivational tag lines as "value-added transaction services" that encapsulate in memorable fashion the new corporate strategy (see Table 9.1).

With identification of the vision and logic for the new corporate strategy, the task becomes moving the organization from where it is today to where it needs to be in the future. We will examine this challenge in two parts—what changes can be made, which we will address below, and how to make those changes, which will be the subject of the Practice section.

There are four **levers of change** that a CEO has to work with when embarking on a corporate transformation. Three of those are the elements of corporate strategy that we have already identified—resources, business portfolio, and organization structure and processes. The fourth—culture—has

TABLE 9.1
Total Newell
Strategy, 1992

Source: Newell Company.

Definition
Newell manufactures and markets staple volume lines to the volume purchaser.
Mission
To increase shareholder value by continuing to build a company with superior EPS growth and ROI, and to earn a reputation for excellence in performance and management.
Basic Strategy
To merchandise to the customer goods market a multiproduct offering with superior customer service performance for maximum market leverage.
Financial Goals
Return on investment (ROI): 20% plus Debt: 1/2 of equity Earnings per share growth: 15% plus annually

been tacitly embedded within the organization dimension of corporate strategy, but has to be highlighted at this stage. When the issue of organizational change is confronted, softer aspects of organizational design and climate become more salient.

We will discuss these four levers in a particular order—portfolio, resources, organization, and culture—because it mirrors their ease of change, the length of time required to make a change, and, therefore, probably also the sequence in which they should be altered during the transformation process.

Portfolio

Many corporate transformations begin with a rearrangement of the corporate portfolio of businesses. A Rubik's Cube–like reshuffling of the set of businesses in which the company competes, trading out one business and bringing in another, can quickly and visibly alter the appearance of the corporation. This is particularly the case when the activity is conducted through mergers and acquisitions. Disposing of unwanted units and using the funds to replace them with the purchase of a preferred entity rapidly transforms the entity. In some cases, the result can be so radical that the firm is even reclassified from one industrial category to another.

Reassembling the parts of the new corporation is easy to do. Underperforming businesses that are dragging down corporate results can be eliminated. Units that never fit easily in a group with other businesses can be spun off. And if substantial write-offs necessarily accompany these disposals, they can be blamed on past strategy. Choosing which new businesses to acquire is also superficially easy because a few simple criteria can guide the process (see Chapter 4). Acquiring companies with **strong market positions in attractive industries** is a good first principle. Applying the logic of the new strategy to confirm a **fit with corporate resources** is obviously also appropriate.

The results of this aspect of transformation can be dramatic. In his first years at GE, under a mandate to retain only divisions with a number 1,2, or 3 market share, Jack Welch sold off 370 businesses to bring in $21 billion, and bought 200 units at a cost of $11 billion. Among those businesses sold was the cyclical and unattractive semiconductor business in which GE was perhaps the number 11 manufacturer. Among those bought were the medical electronics business that is now a key driver of the firm's performance. Indeed, a large part of Welch's success as "Manager of the Century" was his reshaping of GE's portfolio—moving it into attractive and fast-growth service and financial businesses and away from the mature industrial businesses.

As GE illustrates, this aspect of transformation is easiest to do in a conglomerate. When each business unit is organizationally separate with few, if any, linkages to other parts of the corporation, trading them like playing cards is simple. It is more problematic to implement in a corporation that has been pursuing a corporate strategy at the opposite end of the continuum. It is difficult, if not impossible, to surgically carve out a discrete entity from an organization that has been intertwined with every other part of the corporation. In these cases the portfolio will have to be reshaped more carefully and over a longer period of time. Indeed, such companies will probably slough off businesses by closing down product lines and exiting manufacturing and internal supply activities, and will expand through internal development and greenfield market entry rather than with a blaze of M&A activity.

Unfortunately, the advantage of this aspect of transformation is also its major drawback—it is easy to do. Too many CEOs see this activity as a quick way to build a legacy and get seduced by the thrill of the action. Jean-Marie Messier was only the most notable of a list of CEOs who got carried away by the process itself and so ruined their companies. The glamour of big sums of money, front page stories in *The Wall Street Journal*, the attention of sycophantic investment bankers, all make it easy to get caught up in one's own sense of self-importance without questioning the premium paid for an acquisition or whether it ultimately fits the logic of the new corporate strategy.

Careful reconstruction of the corporate portfolio according to the dictates of the new strategy is, therefore, the first step in any corporate transformation.

Resources

All reshuffling of the portfolio must be done with an awareness of the corporate resources that will underpin future corporate advantage. In parallel to any restructuring, therefore, the CEO has to be performing his role as the guardian of those resources—**identifying, investing, and upgrading** their quality (see Chapter 2). Michael Eisner's great strategic insight, which led to 10 years of superb performance, was that an annual summer animated cartoon blockbuster was the most valuable asset Disney could have. As soon as he arrived at the company, therefore, he committed to invest whatever it took to develop such a resource. Under the direction of Jeffrey Katzenberg, this led to the stream of hit movies from *The Little Mermaid* and *Beauty and the Beast,* to *The Lion King.*

The requirement for implementing this lever of change is to know what resource or resources lie at the core of the corporate strategy, and then to invest in them. Again, Jack Welch at GE is a model for this step in the process. He identified people as his critical resource and invested heavily in their recruitment and career development. Perhaps the best illustration of his commitment to develop a cadre of superb managers was his decision to rebuild the corporate training center at Crotonville in the 1980s at a cost of several tens of millions of dollars, at a time when he was widely rebuked as "Neutron Jack" for firing thousands of workers. His justification for the investment was that the "return is infinite."[14]

Understanding in which resources to invest is never easy and yet is obviously critical to developing the new corporate strategy. Part of that understanding comes from an analysis of why the old strategy failed. If, for example, as with Disney, the failure was lack of investment in the core resource, the solution is simply to make the required investment. If the cause is substitution by an alternative resource, one obvious solution is to invest in that new resource. Barnes & Noble, for example, ultimately chose to enter the business and compete with Amazon.com when its bookstores were threatened by online book retailing. If the cause was competitive imitation of the resource so that its scarcity decreases, the challenge is to upgrade the quality of that resource beyond the capabilities of the imitators, or to add an additional resource that they cannot match.

Even though regenerating the resource base of the firm is a long-term process, it can be made interactive with reshaping the business portfolio by adopting the "stepping-stone" approach (see Chapter 4). Entering a new business to acquire a new resource, leverage that resource to get into a second business, add a new capability from that industry to upgrade the suite of corporate resources, and so on, can produce a symbiotic relationship between resources and businesses like that at Nucor (see Chapter 4).

Organization

Any change in corporate strategy will almost certainly require a change in both organization structure and organizational processes. These two can be thought of as separate but related aspects of the transformation process.

---

[14] J. Welch, *Straight from the Gut* (New York: Warner Business Books, 2001).

Altering the **organization structure** requires redefining unit boundaries. As discussed in Chapter 6, this clarifies the allocation of decision rights within the corporation. The obvious place to begin is with the **operational divisions.** In some instances this can involve a truly dramatic reorganization in which the basic structure of the company is changed. As Thomson went from a traditional print media company to an electronic provider of information, the firm reorganized from nearly 100 discrete business units into four integrated groups. In each of these groups, the separate businesses became more like product management teams supported by a single functional organization.

Such wholesale change is rare. It is even more uncommon for the initial direction of change to be toward more integration among units. Dick Rumelt and others have suggested that the preferred way to transform an underperforming multibusiness organization is to begin by breaking apart the businesses before attempting to promote synergy among those businesses (see the Practice section).

The presumption behind this prescription is that flawed strategies are more typically found at the integrated end of the corporate strategy continuum. For companies in that position, a policy to initially fragment the organization structure is probably appropriate. As the example of Thomson illustrates, however, it is only appropriate if the corporation is located at that end of the continuum. Organization structure, like the other levers of transformation, need to be altered in a manner determined by the new vision and logic of the strategy.

The first organizational move by many CEOs announcing a new corporate strategy is often to cut their **corporate staff.** While this can demonstrate a break with the past and a symbolic commitment to a new frugality, it is often effected as a naive percentage reduction. What is required is a more surgical approach based on an understanding of how the corporate staff adds value in the new strategy.

Such an analysis begins with clarifying the three roles that the corporate headquarters will perform in the new strategy—public company functions, shared services, value adding.[15] Those functions, like treasury and taxation, that are part of the minimal corporate parenting role need to be benchmarked against other firms so that they are staffed to operate as efficiently as possible. Shared services, such as payroll processing and benefits administration, that are believed to be more efficiently provided in a single place than independently by each business unit can be established as central service units. These need to be market-based entities from whom business units are free to buy or not, as they choose. Finally, the value-adding functions, which will vary between companies according to their strategy, should be created as centers of competence (see Chapter 6).

---

[15] D. Young et al., *Corporate Headquarters: An International Analysis of Their Roles and Staffing* (London: Financial Times/Prentice Hall, 2000).

In this modern role as a staff function they become recognized experts at their task and disseminate that knowledge throughout the company as consultants. Only in those activities that are essential to the integrity of the corporation, like financial accounting and legal compliance, should corporate staffs be granted the more traditional authority to mandate business-unit procedures.

It is inevitable that in every organization structure there will be decisions that cut across boundaries or involve participants from ostensibly discrete units. No structure can, of itself, cleanly allocate all decision rights to a single point in a hierarchy. All structures, therefore, need to layer on the appropriate **processes that cut across organizational boundaries.** Often these become critical mechanisms for creating value in the corporate strategy by facilitating the sharing of activities or transferring skills between businesses in the portfolio.

These processes are usually best introduced slowly, working up the coordination hierarchy (see Chapter 6), even if the desired end state is known. Mandating how to work across boundaries can alienate executives and raise resistance. It is better to allow managers themselves to gradually demand more coordination so that they willingly devolve their authority to the joint teams and task forces or executive vice presidents who coordinate decisions. In putting in place these sorts of processes, it has been found that "the journey matters." Managers have to experience the pains and gains of working together across unit boundaries if they are to abdicate some of their authority to others, to have the empathy to know what it is like to be in others' shoes, to have learned for themselves what works and what doesn't, and, above all, to have established personal relationships that complement and facilitate working around the formal organization structure.

This prescription confirms that transformation is a long-term process of organizational change—a work in progress—that perhaps is never in equilibrium, but is continually undergoing change.

Culture

Embedded in the broader administrative context is perhaps the hardest thing of all to change—corporate culture. Because it ultimately requires change in people and attitudes, addressing this can be the most long-term and difficult aspect of corporate transformation.

Culture is the set of norms and behaviors that emerges from the shared experiences and expectations of its members. In turn, it becomes as effective in shaping future organizational behavior as other more overt and extrinsic aspects of organizational design, like compensation and reward schemes. To attempt to formally design such an inanimate object is, however, difficult since culture itself is not directly accessible. As a result, it is better to allow the culture to emerge from the set of design choices and behaviors that can be made more explicit, even if crafting the desirable culture this way is complex and time consuming.

Some contributors to the corporate culture can be managed directly. Most companies today have a statement of values (as distinct from the corporate strategy or vision) that articulates how employees are expected to behave. Terms like "respect the community in which we operate" or "value and empower employees" provide some guidance as to desirable managerial behavior. Other important contributors to the shape of the culture that can be proactively managed include HR policies, particularly hiring and career paths, and compensation and reward systems. Ultimately the objective of these policies is to create such a clear impression of what it is like to work in the company—what the culture is—that the ideal employee self-selects into the organization. At Lincoln Electric, for example, the highly geared compensation system attracts only those types who respond to extreme individual motivation. Although there might be only a small fraction of the population who fall into this category, it is sufficient for Lincoln Electric's purposes.

Culture is, however, the consequence and cumulative interaction of so many different aspects of the organization that it cannot be directly managed. Rather executives have to be aware that every one of their actions can be interpreted symbolically and may leave an enduring legacy. This reinforces the importance of understanding the corporate strategy since it demands that every single action is consistent with that strategy.

Practice

Although recognizing the need for change and committing to a new corporate strategy is a difficult task for many CEOs, it is usually more of a challenge to actually effect a corporate transformation. Rather than focusing on "why" change might be necessary and "what" must be changed, this section, therefore, addresses the process of change itself—the "how to" of corporate transformation.

We begin by noting that a substantial literature exists on the topic of "change management," of which corporate transformation is merely the most dramatic case. Indeed, there is a vast amount of research on the fundamental issue of how to change a bureaucratic organization.[16] While drawing on this work, we will focus on the particular requirements of changing the entire corporation.

---

[16] See Michael Beer, *Cracking the Code of Change* (Boston: Harvard Business School Press, 2000); and Rosabeth Moss Kanter, *Change Masters: Innovation for Productivity in the American Corporation* (New York: Simon and Schuster, 1983); John P. Kotter, *Leading Change* (Boston: Harvard Business School Press, 1996); David Nadler, *Champion of Change: How CEOs and Their Companies Are Mastering Skills of Radical Change* (San Francisco: Jossey-Bass, 1998); and Charles O'Reilly and Mike Tushman, *Winning through Innovation: A Practical Guide to Leading Organization Change and Renewal* (Boston: Harvard Business School Press, 1997).

FIGURE 9.2
Changing a Way of
Life

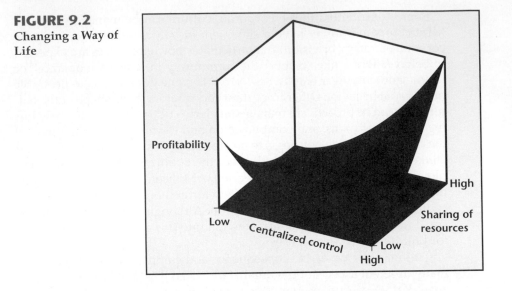

Impediments to Change

Organizational behavior research begins its analysis by asking why change is difficult. What prevents change from being the natural state for a collective body? At the corporate level, perhaps the best articulation of the impediments to change was provided by Dick Rumelt.[17] He identified what he termed **Five Frictions** (with more than just a nod to Mike Porter's "Five Forces"). These barriers operate at the individual, subunit, and organizational levels and so prevent a corporation adapting to an evolving environment.

The first three of these frictions prevent an organization either from recognizing that it has a problem or from developing an effective plan of action. The other two frictions explain why a reasonable transformation plan is not implemented.

First among these frictions is "distorted perception." While Rumelt attributes this to myopia, hubris, or groupthink, the essence is that the firm simply fails to perceive that it has a problem. The second friction arises from the "dulled motivation" that the inevitable costs of change promote. The benefits of corporate transformation are always deferred, while the costs are incurred immediately and are visible to all. The result is that a corporation has to travel through "the shadow of the valley of death" before it begins to see a net benefit from the transformation process (see Figure 9.2). If, for example, the transformation involves more coordinated purchasing,

[17] R. Rumelt, "Inertia and Transformation," in *Resources in an Evolutionary Perspective: Towards a Synthesis of Evolutionary and Resource-Based Approaches to Strategy,* ed. Cynthia A. Montgomery (Norwell, MA: Kluwer Academic Publishers, 1995), pp. 101–32.

the benefits of reduced purchased prices only appear after divisions have had to deal with the aggravation of switching suppliers, changing delivery schedules, and so on. The result is that the incentive to undertake change is reduced, or even that the process is reversed as the initial costs pile up and appear to outweigh the as-yet-undelivered benefits.

The third friction Rumelt identifies is the failure to come up with a "creative response." Even when the problem is clearly identified and the benefit of a response is recognized, an organization might not be able to conceive of an appropriate plan for change. The complexity of the problem, or the speed and magnitude of change required, might simply overwhelm the analytic capabilities of executives who get frozen in the headlights of the oncoming crisis.

The fourth friction has less to do with observing and developing a response to the problem itself, and more to do with internal impediments to acting on a solution. "Political deadlocks" can prevent a company from mobilizing in support of any action. Provided that there is more than one possible course of action, aligning the entire organization around any one solution might be impossible. Such coordination can be difficult not only because subunits with differing vested interests favor different outcomes, but also because honest differences of opinion cannot necessarily be reconciled in any consistent way. Unless a single leader dictates the outcome, therefore, a firm can bog down in political jockeying for position, or endless and circular arguments over the merits of alternative remedies.

Finally, the corporation might simply be unable to galvanize itself into motion because of "action disconnects" or failures to translate plans into reality. These involve the difficulty of changing the routines that are a feature of every organization, and which ensure the efficient repetition of regular behaviors but which impede innovation in those very same routines.

Motivation for Change

Even if the first three frictions can be overcome so that it is recognized by senior executives that transformation is necessary, companies still need some event or process to overcome the resistance generated by the ubiquitous presence of the other frictions. It has been found that the best way to achieve this is to create a sense of **crisis** or urgency that confronts the entire organization with the need for change.[18] Appeals for incremental moves or minor adaptations cannot provide the impetus necessary to overcome organizational inertia. Instead, there has to be a compelling motivation that is obvious to all.

In some cases this crisis is engendered by external factors. Obvious examples include the announcement of very poor financial results, or the

---

[18] J.P. Kotter, *Leading Change* (Boston: Harvard Business School Press, 1996).

loss of market leadership in a key product. Fighting off a hostile takeover or responding to intervention by a disgruntled board or activist shareholder also appears to create the necessary sense of crisis that allows management to galvanize an organization into action. Yet few firms can afford, or want to wait for, such an exogenous shock before they begin to change. Instead, they create their own sense of crisis in order to unfreeze the organization and make it amenable to change.

Proactive ways to achieve this involve a significant and readily observable move that "breaks the ice," such as replacing a senior manager or more radically the entire top management team. Such moves not only illustrate the penalty for refusing to adapt, but also directly bring new blood and the expectation of change into the organization. Indeed, any major corporate action, such as a merger or spin-off, that staff know will inevitably break the status quo seems to unfreeze every aspect of the organization. When, for example, Coopers & Lybrand found resistance to creating a more global partnership from its separate country organizations, a merger with Price Waterhouse provided the shock that forced change (or exit) on its members. Similarly, a feeling at Ciba-Geigy that its internal attempt at transformation in the early nineties had not gone far enough led to the merger with Sandoz that created Novartis. In an entirely new organization, the acceptance that new ways are inevitable can finally break old organizational routines.

While major shocks do trigger change, the real challenge for CEOs is to create that same sense of urgency before performance has deteriorated or radical steps are required. Unfortunately, the cases of an incumbent management team responding effectively and presciently to the need for change are the rarest, but also the most valuable, type of transformation. The Thomson Corporation was able to do this over a 15-year period when it migrated from a print media conglomerate (owning newspapers in Canada, the United Kingdom, and the United States) into an electronic information company in finance, education, legal, and scientific fields. However, it was, perhaps, only able to do so because it was privately held through much of the period, allowing the owners to support a move that would only pay off in the very long term.

Direction of Change

Even though corporate executives should have a broad vision for the new corporate strategy, they never know the complete details of that strategy in advance. As a consequence, transformation has to be achieved through a process of **guided experimentation.** This can be thought of as encouraging the firm to freely evolve within a constrained path. Like an amoeba spreading over a petri dish, the strategy's growth path should be decentralized to front-line managers provided that they operate within parameters set from above (see Figure 9.3). The critical task for senior management in this

FIGURE 9.3
Guided
Experimentation

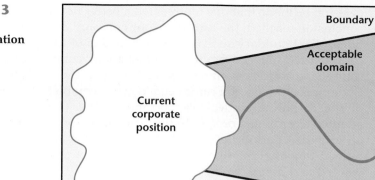

process, therefore, is to define the boundaries beyond which the firm must not go. Rather than specifying exactly what the firm should do in the new corporate strategy, the emphasis is on clearly defining **what not to do.** As a result, managers at every level in the organization do not waste time and effort pursuing opportunities that will later be rejected, but are encouraged to pursue their own ideas within the scope laid down by corporate executives. Such an approach combines the benefits of unconstrained trial and error with the discipline of defined limits, and so allows "a thousand flowers to bloom"[19] within a garden that has been clearly identified.

Such decentralized idea generation has to be complemented by a process that quickly truncates failures, while identifying successes and rapidly replicating them throughout the corporation. This can be achieved by viewing each initiative as an experiment that is carefully monitored and reviewed. Indeed, having initially defined the boundaries, top management spends most of its time in the transformation process understanding which of the initiatives work and don't work, and why they do and do not work. Understanding the underlying causes and patterns then allows them to refine the boundary definition and gradually converge on a complete description of the ultimate strategy.

This process is easiest to see at work in the transformation of the corporate portfolio. It might initially be possible for a CEO to decide to exit certain businesses and to encourage growth within a broadly defined domain such as "industrial products and services." But it would be impossible to know exactly which avenue within that domain presented the best opportunity. Only after lower-level managers choose to test the waters for linear motors and constant velocity joints, could a reasoned

[19] R.M. Kanter, *Change Masters: Innovation for Productivity in the American Corporation* (New York: Simon and Schuster, 1983).

decision be made that one represented a better fit for the firm. With that conclusion reached, the learning would be captured in a tighter definition of the boundary so that future expansion of the portfolio might be confined to "finished products" rather than "components." Finally, at some point, sufficient clarity is reached about the strategy that the period of experimentation can be ended and a complete refined statement of the corporate strategy can be made. The Thomson Corporation adopted exactly this process in the transformation of its portfolio. Over an extended period the firm made acquisitions and dispositions as it refined its definition of where within the electronic media business it wanted to compete.

The same approach can be adopted for the other elements of the corporate strategy. It might, for example, be clear that the new organization structure should involve the establishment of central units to provide shared services to the businesses. Exactly which activities should be dealt with that way, rather than outsourced to third parties, could be left to a process of guided experimentation, after which clearer guidelines could be defined.

Similarly, the specific resources that underpin the new corporate advantage could be identified more precisely after a period of learning. It might, for example, turn out that the corporation develops a set of capabilities in postmerger integration as a result of the moves it made to transform the business portfolio. If that was the case, the future growth of the firm could pursue a slightly different course than was initially envisaged.

Organizing for Change

As mentioned in the Principles section, it has been found that successful corporate transformations typically involve splitting apart the organization before adopting more integrated organizational designs. Simplification and transparency support the accountability that is necessary to drive individual business performance. Only when that has been achieved should entities be recombined to exploit underlying synergies.[20] (See "Organizational Transformation.")

As mentioned in the Principles section, such a mandate is probably appropriate when the transformation involves a strategy that has been to relocate along the continuum. Executives trying to transform corporations that have been acting more like holding companies need to consider an alternative process for organizational change that probably works its way slowly up the coordination hierarchy.

---

[20] R. Rumelt, "Inertia and Transformation," in *Resources in an Evolutionary Perspective: Towards a Synthesis of Evolutionary and Resource-Based Approaches to Strategy*, ed. Cynthia A. Montgomery (Norwell, MA: Kluwer Academic Publishers, 1995), pp. 101–32; and C.A. Bartlett and S. Ghosgal, *Managing across Borders: The Transnational Solution*, 2nd ed. (Boston: Harvard Business School Press, 1998).

Organizational Transformation

Rumelt and others argue that flawed corporate strategies are usually found in the top-left quadrant. Here each individual unit is underperforming, while still being organized in a way that seeks synergy with other units. Clearly, the objective is to move to the top-right quadrant where synergy is achieved among highly performing business units. The appropriate way to achieve this goal, they argue, is not to move directly between quadrants, but first to break apart the organization and concentrate on driving individual business-unit performance. Separating out self-contained units, giving them authority over all aspects of their business, minimizing overlap with other units, and then holding them accountable provide the appropriate incentive structure to drive divisional performance. Only when responsibilities have been clarified, and individual unit performance made transparent, can overall corporate performance be enhanced. It is at this stage, when units are in quadrant 3, that they can recombined in order to capture the synergies that have consciously been ignored. This finally brings the corporation into the desirable quadrant 4 where each individual business is firing on all cylinders, and all are working together to leverage resources throughout the firm (see Figure 9.4).

FIGURE 9.4   Organizational Transformation

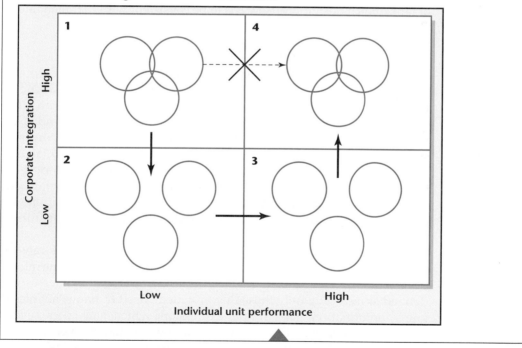

More important, perhaps, is the order of organizational change. In the Principles section we talked about a possible ordering for the levers of change—portfolio and resources, then organization and culture. Here we are concerned with the ordering within the organizational design element itself. In discussing how to introduce more coordination to a strategy in Appendix C, for example, we suggested that the preferred approach would involve a gradual migration up the coordination hierarchy. This suggests that processes and behaviors are best altered before a company's formal organization structure is changed. In a more radical corporate transformation, however, the reverse is probably true. To truly break the old routines, incrementalism might not be sufficient. At P&G, for example, under Organization 2005 a new global business-unit structure was imposed, even before the processes for managing relations between country managers and product line heads had been defined. Although the blunt move led to the removal of the CEO who initiated it, the new structure forced managers to learn behaviors that made it work. A more gradual approach might have impeded the ultimate structural redesign.

By intent, corporate transformation is radical, and so the approach to organizational design probably has to be consistent with that mandate.

Top Management Role in Change

Perhaps the best advice to offer senior executives in charge of corporate transformation is that which propelled Bill Clinton to the presidency—**KISS** (keep it simple, stupid!). Adhering to a simple vision with a few supporting themes that are persistently repeated over an extended period seems to be the key to effective implementation of a new corporate strategy. Indeed, both Jack Welch at GE and Percy Barnevik at ABB viewed their primary role as communicators. Barnevik was notorious for traveling everywhere with a briefcase of overheads which he would present at every opportunity. A stubborn insistence on, and repetition of, a clear and concise message seems to be critical to corporate transformation success.

The precise form of the words used to capture the elements of transformation also matters. At Thomson the new corporate strategy came into focus for the entire organization when the scope of media businesses was defined as including only those that provided "need to know, not nice to know" information. That simple expression, which had taken several years to jell, provided all the direction that the organization needed to rearrange the portfolio. Spending the time to arrive at a sparse insight, and then to wordsmith **a crisp slogan,** such as the Pepsi Bottling Group's "We Sell Soda," might seem to be unnecessary, but has proven to be worth the effort every time. Even if the result is the all too common alliteration, such as the four Es of one of Welch's transformations—Energy, Energize, Edge, Execution—their memorableness and simplicity have enormous impact in galvanizing the organization in support of the new strategy.[21]

Communication alone is clearly not sufficient to implement a transformation, but has to be combined with symbolic actions that reinforce the message, and with executive behavior that stubbornly **walks the talk.** At GE, for example, Jack Welch supported his introduction of the importance of values as a criterion for evaluating personnel by explaining to the top three hundred managers gathered for the famous annual CEC meeting in Boca Raton that the reason 3 of his 14 direct reports were no longer with the firm was that they had not acted in accordance with those values.

A critical part of living the new corporate strategy is consistency in everything that the CEO does. Jack Welch not only repeated the same message hundreds of times over many years to drive it home but, as suggested above, he **aligned all aspects of organizational design** to reinforce that message. The corporation's reward and incentive system, its recruiting and training programs, the formal structure, and so on, all need to be aligned with the new strategy.

Culture for Change

A corporate transformation cannot be achieved without the appropriate culture or attitude within the organization. In the first instance, this requires that employees approach the process from the perspective of finding the **best outcome for the company as a whole,** not for the particular part of the organization that they happen to represent. There can be no room for defensiveness or the protection of individuals or organizational territories in an effective process. Second, the organizational climate has to be one of honesty and openness. Participants cannot delude themselves by relying on inherited dogma or anecdotes to support a position, but should force themselves to acquire the data and perform the analyses necessary to confirm the logic of their arguments. As Jack Welch and others have argued, harshly **confronting the facts** is the most vital aspect of a culture that successfully adapts to an ever-changing external environment.[22]

The process of choosing among alternative new strategies, or more generally for making decisions, should also reflect a culture of **constructive conflict** or confrontation management. Many successful corporations, like Intel and IBM, have formalized this approach into their meetings and decision-making routines. Its essence is that anyone can and should

---

[21] James D. Berkley, Robert G. Eccles, and Nitin Nohria, *Beyond the Hype: Rediscovering the Essence of Management* (Boston: Harvard Business School Press, 1994).
[22] M. Beer, *Cracking the Code of Change* (Boston: Harvard Business School Press, 2000).

challenge any argument with which he or she disagrees. Rank has no privileges in an open process that is designed to fully utilize the firm's capabilities.

Last, while the culture must encourage open and honest debate, once a decision has been made, it must be **embraced and implemented collectively.** Like the British Cabinet, once a policy has been agreed to, members should commit to it or resign. Halfhearted support or backsliding is not a feature of management teams that successfully undertake a corporate transformation. In many cases this implies that some executives should leave the organization. When the new direction is clear, if they cannot wholeheartedly endorse the new strategy with all its ramifications, they should consider moving elsewhere.

Time to Effect Change

One of the more difficult questions concerning corporate transformation is **the length of time the process requires.** Jack Welch was vehement that he never moved fast enough. In a talk at the Harvard Business School looking back over his early years as CEO of GE he stated, "I didn't move fast enough. I wasn't dramatic enough. I relied on too many incremental nudges here and there. I was trying too hard to bring too many constituencies on board." In contrast, he argued for more radical and rapid change—"you should try something, if it works go on and soar. If it fails, give up and try something else."[23]

But how much time should the board give a CEO to change the corporate strategy? Michael Eisner had an outstanding first 10 years at the Walt Disney Company, but has struggled to create shareholder value in his second 10-year stint. Jack Welch's successor, Jeff Immelt, has been in charge for over three years, during which time GE has underperformed the market. Should he be replaced? Or should he be given more time to implement his vision for GE, recognizing that changing a massive corporation takes time. Should he be given five years to effect the transformation? Or 10 years? Roger Smith, CEO of General Motors during the eighties was given 10 years to be in charge, and yet that is now seen as a lost decade for the corporation.

In many ways, this decision is the toughest of all decisions made by a board of directors. Ultimately, it has to be their judgment call. To help in that decision they should insist on the CEO laying out **milestones** along the transformation path by which his progress can be assessed. This would require a balanced scorecard of items including not just the firm's capital market value (which is typically uninformed by the reality of progress toward deep long-term changes) and other external

---

[23] Christopher Bartlett, *GE's Two-Decade Transformation: Jack Welch Leadership (Mulitimedia Case)*, November 1999, Video (Boston: Harvard Business School Press, 2002).

measures—market share, customer satisfaction scores, quality assessments, and so on—but also internal measures of employee satisfaction, turnover, and loyalty.

The problem is that in most cases the company will hit about half its goals and miss the other half! While milestones can therefore inform the decision, they often do not prevent it from ultimately being a judgment call.

Details of the Change Process

Having identified some of the characteristics of corporations that have been able to successfully effect corporate transformation, we have to acknowledge that there are still numerous details that have not been specified. When these provoke debate and require deep thought, it is usually because, in one way or another, they confront an underlying trade-off. Indeed, it is possible to identify a partial list of such trade-offs that organizations face, in various and nuanced ways, during any change process. The list of such trade-offs is long and is never complete, but includes:

- A top-down versus a bottom-up process

- A fully specified road map for change versus an adaptable and flexible evolution

- Keeping existing managers and promoting from within or looking outside for external hires

- Whether change should be fast or slow

- Whether to alter structure first and expect behaviors to adapt, or wait until behaviors have altered before formalizing them in a new structure

Suggestions as to how to answer some of these choices have been given, but it is has to recognized that every transformation process is unique and the one rule that cannot be broken is that the process must be customized to the idiosyncratic heritage and situation of the particular company.

▲ Summary

Developing a vision for the new corporate strategy is often not the most difficult part of the transformation process. Instead, implementing the necessary change inside a large multibusiness entity is the real issue. It is a challenge and an opportunity that many corporations, which continue to fail to create shareholder value through their corporate strategies, still have to address. It is also one that is waiting to be solved by the next generation of corporate executives and academic researchers.

Recommended Readings

Baden Fuller, Charles, and John M. Stopford. *Rejuvenating the Mature Business: A Competitive Challenge.* Boston: Harvard Business School Press, 1994.

Beer, Michael. *Cracking the Code of Change.* Boston: Harvard Business School Press, 2000.

Christensen, Clayton M. *The Innovator's Dilemma.* New York: Harper Business, 2003.

Kanter, Rosabeth Moss. *Change Masters: Innovation for Productivity in the American Corporation.* New York: Simon and Schuster, 1983.

Kotter, John P. *Leading Change.* Boston: Harvard Business School Press, 1996.

Nadler, David. *Champion of Change: How CEOs and Their Companies Are Mastering Skills of Radical Change.* San Francisco: Jossey-Bass, 1998.

O'Reilly, Charles, and Mike Tushman. *Winning through Innovation: A Practical Guide to Leading Organization Change and Renewal.* Boston: Harvard Business School Press, 1997.

Rumelt, R. "Inertia and Transformation." In *Resources in an Evolutionary Perspective: Towards a Synthesis of Evolutionary and Resource-Based Approaches to Strategy,* ed. Cynthia A. Montgomery. Norwell, MA: Kluwer Academic Publishers, 1995, pp. 101–32.

Welch, Jack. *Straight from the Gut.* New York: Warner Business Books, 2001.

Index